open

open

an uncensored memoir of love, liberation, and non-monogamy

rachel krantz

HARMONY
BOOKS · NEW YORK

Published in the United States by Harmony Books,
an imprint of Random House, a division of Penguin Random House LLC, New York.
harmonybooks.com

Harmony Books is a registered trademark,
and the Circle colophon is a trademark of Penguin Random House LLC.

Library of Congress Cataloging-in-Publication Data
Names: Krantz, Rachel, author.
Title: Open : an uncensored memoir of love, liberation, and non-monogamy /
Rachel Krantz.
Description: First edition. | New York : Harmony Books, [2022] |
Includes bibliographical references.
Identifiers: LCCN 2021012528 (print) | LCCN 2021012529 (ebook) |
ISBN 9780593139554 (hardcover) | ISBN 9780593139561 (ebook)
Subjects: LCSH: Krantz, Rachel—Sexual behavior. |
Non-monogamous relationships—United States.
Classification: LCC HQ980.5.U5 K73 2022 (print) | LCC HQ980.5.U5 (ebook) |
DDC 306.84—dc23
LC record available at https://lccn.loc.gov/2021012528
LC ebook record available at https://lccn.loc.gov/2021012529

ISBN 978-0-593-13955-4

Ebook ISBN 978-0-593-13956-1

Printed in the United States of America

Editor: Donna Loffredo
Designer: Mia Johnson
Production Editor: Serena Wang
Production Manager: Kelli Tokos
Composition: Scribe
Copy Editor: Thomas Pitoniak

10 9 8 7 6 5 4 3 2 1

First Edition

For You
Yes, You

Author's Note

This story is true. From 2015 to 2019, I obsessively documented my first non-monogamous and Dom/sub relationships. I'm talking not just journal entries, but hours and hours, days and days of audio recordings. In an attempt to feel some semblance of control, nothing was off-limits: dates, arguments, role-playing, trips to swingers' resorts, moments I was being gaslit, and every single therapy session. Because I'm not only a person who clearly needs said therapy but also a journalist, I conducted many, many interviews along the way. These extensive records mean that people in this book are quoted in their own words verbatim where possible.

Despite this emphasis on primary sources, it's important to remember that my story and perspective have many limitations. As the plot deepens (and darkens), it's increasingly populated with a wider diversity of people and experiences, and with queerer stories. But it's still primarily centered on two cisgender, white, non-disabled, U.S.-city-dwelling, middle-class, child-free, college-educated, thin, liberal, often-assumed-heterosexual, Jewish people in an open relationship. Not only that, but two people in a very gender-normative power dynamic, where the man is dominant and the woman is submissive. I implore you to seek out other non-monogamous and BDSM narratives from people with identities and experiences different from mine. This is in part a cautionary tale; a how-not-to manual as much as a how-to. (Content warning: explicit sex, drug use/addiction, sexual assault, self-injurious behavior/disordered eating, unethical BDSM, threesomes, foursomes, sixsomes, nonconsensual non-monogamy, abuse, gaslighting, misogyny and heterosexism, fuckboys, more fuckboys, Jewish mother savior complex, daddy issues, Disney . . .)

Writing memoir is by necessity an act of approximation. There's a dangerous compounding of that approximation if my specific experience is made to stand as a definitive representation of any lifestyle or identity. I am certainly no perfect role model—I am simply the investigative subject I have most complete access to.

That fact, combined with my myriad privileges in life, drives me to be explicitly honest about my psychosexual reality. I'll weather harassment for it, but I'm less likely to be punished or hurt than most. Almost every non-monogamous person in this book was rightly afraid to use their real first name, let alone their last. There is little legal recourse should they lose their job or children simply due to stigma around our lifestyle. This feels like reason enough to help move the needle of public discourse. Besides, I'm also very curious as to what happens next. In 2022, is "a woman like me" allowed to admit to being this fully a sexual being and remain semi-respected as an "award-winning investigative journalist"? I guess we'll write that part of the story together.

I put myself forward for naked examination because I'm morally opposed to being told to cover up in shame. I am entirely vulnerable. Thank you for helping me find strength in this submission.

Contents

Part 3: Age 29

Part 4: Age 30

Part 5: Age 31

open

PART 1

Age 27

PART 1

Age 27

Once Upon a Time, a Solitary Maiden Believed Only Somewhat Ironically in Being Rescued . . .

6/8/14

Rachel Journal Entry*
Age 26

I let her convince me to have half a carafe but no more because I knew it would lead me to cheating on [Dan]. . . . I would have slept with a woman last night if not for him. . . . I feel resentful of not being able to.

8/3/14

Journal Entry

I'm waiting for someone to come find me. I believe in being rescued.

2/20/15

BROOKLYN, NY

"Here," I said, presenting the bouquet in a casual thrust. "I brought you flowers."

---

*   All primary sources (journal entries, emails, text messages, recorded transcripts) are depicted verbatim. Ellipses indicate where words have been cut; bracketed words are added for clarity.

"You brought me flowers?" I'd managed to disarm him, if only for a moment. I hoped the flowers would send a message: I might be twenty-seven to his thirty-eight, but I was not prey. And I had on the adult-lady-dress I'd found in a giveaway box to prove it.

"Men deserve flowers, too, you know," I said, as if the idea hadn't occurred to me an hour ago.

"Well, thanks. I don't think that's ever happened before." Adam's smile had a slight downward turn to it, amused in a wrung way. It was satisfying to squeeze it out of him. "I think I have a vase here somewhere . . ." I noted his back muscles through his plain white T-shirt as he reached for further proof of his civilized life. Jazz played, and I padded my stockinged feet on his spotless wooden floors as he caramelized onions. I admired titles in English and German, picked books up and put them down like a toddler-cum-anthropologist. I noted the extensive Philip Roth section, *The Professor of Desire* nestled between *Letting Go* and *The Prague Orgy*, the obvious fondness for Updike, Jung, Lacan, Heidegger, Yeats, Freud, and . . . Edith Wharton? *At least I've read all the Diaz and Lahiri.* I'd just broken up with Dan, a guy with neither curtains nor more than ten books—let alone a clean vase. *This is progress.*

Adam and I stood together in a comfortable yet sexually tense silence as he cooked.

"You know, I think the Groupon massage therapist I've been seeing might be molesting me?" *Fuck, why did you just say that?* I could blame the hit of dried-out herb I'd had before I came, but it was more than that. There was something about Adam that was like going to Jewish confession—kneeling felt imminent.

"Uh, what?" His eyebrows furrowed with concern.

"Well, he tells me to get naked, and each session he sort of inches closer and closer to my pussy. Brushing its sides and occasionally over it, but never *fingering* me or anything. Telling me to breathe deeply again and again in this pretty sexual way, kind of moaning to demonstrate . . ." Ironically, I'd treated myself to the Groupon package in the hopes that it would help me avoid making romantic decisions based solely on a hunger for touch, an investment I hoped would pay dividends tonight. "Maybe I'm imagining it? Or I'm giving him the feeling I'm into it, you know? Which in a way I am, until he pushes it too far and I keep pulling away, but then he just does it again . . ." *Why are you telling him this?* "I don't know, what do you think?"

"I think it sounds like you need a new masseur." Adam had a definitive way of closing conversations I already found comforting.

Dinner was skillfully done, but watching him lick rolling paper for dessert was my preferred pornography. His academic research, he told me as I inhaled, was mainly about the psychology of romantic and sexual desire—specifically, the importance of triangulation.

"Like, there being three people?" I asked.

"Often, yes. It's one of the most common stories, the love triangle. *The Unbearable Lightness of Being, Lolita, The Age of Innocence* . . ." *Twilight,* I mentally added. *The Hunger Games.* "But triangulation is also sometimes just an outside obstacle, maybe not even a person. A war, or distance."

"I wonder if that's one subconscious reason people have children," I tried. "To create a safer form of triangulation than another lover, a constant obstacle to being alone together."

"Desire can be understood as a feeling of lack," he said, nodding professorially. "If we believe we have someone in every single way, we usually cease to want them sexually."

"Seems accurate, but a little sad, too, no?"

"No, it's not. It's like physics. Knowing how things work only makes them more beautiful." He held my gaze with meaning. "I study what's most important to me. How I might maintain desire. Not just for me, but for my long-term partner." I nodded, lesson absorbed. I had to admit, I could hardly imagine a topic I'd rather a lover devote their life to studying. My legs were tucked sidesaddle on his wonderfully clean couch. He paused to acknowledge the flesh encased in black tights. "Since your feet are right here and you mentioned earlier you like massage, I'd be happy to work on them for you." *Bold move after my story, and kind of a tone-deaf one? But, I mean, does sound nice . . . just do what you want to do, but don't think that means you owe him anything. You're a grown woman tonight.* I'd promised myself that this evening was about ushering in a new era of Adult Dating. I would no longer feel I owed a certain debt if I received "too much," or placed myself "too deep" into a situation. I would do whatever I wanted and nothing more (*or less?*)—without judgment.

"Okay, sure. Why not," I said, offering my legs toward him like a second bouquet of flower stems.

Adam's touch was subtle, consistent, and sure. An exercise in paying attention to what I wanted and taking not a centimeter more, promising me something attuned, patient, giving. His voice deep and at moments gravelly, his highly grabbable biceps flexing as he continued to steer our conversation, my body the clutch. He had a focus more intense than any I'd felt directed at me before. Not even by a therapist, much less a man I found sexy. As he massaged, he kept asking more and more questions, interviewing me as he had on our first date. It was as if he had to get down to the root of me deeply, thoroughly, urgently. Like there was no more pressing subject.

On that first date the week before, I'd shown up even higher, mostly to prove to myself how little I cared. *I'm just window shopping.* I'd tried to break up with Dan again three weeks earlier, but he'd convinced me to make it a month-long break instead. We could see other people, he agreed, but he insisted we wait a little longer to make it official, "just to be sure." I felt held hostage but unable to say no. I'd squirmed in limbo by reactivating OkCupid. I posted only two black-and-white photos to the profile. Me in a fuzzy shapeless bathrobe looking unimpressed at the camera; me in a fuzzy shapeless bathrobe splayed on the floor like, *Whatever, I can't even muster the will to appease the male gaze right now.* Like I was daring someone to find me attractive and/or exploit my obvious situational depression. Adam wrote to me and referenced only my profile's sparse thoughts.

Since I couldn't find a good reason to discount him like the others, I'd suggested we see some experimental jazz at a small pop-up around the corner. The music took you down deep, dark stairwells into a dystopian existence, a world run by metallic machines. Adam was sober, attentive. For nearly three hours, he barely moved. I shifted and unshifted, by turns riveted and bored and proud and mortified by my defiantly unromantic selection. When I took off my coat, I felt his eyes on me. He was in my peripheral vision, but I could sense it in the hair on my arms like static. The pull of his assessment. *Yes, respect where respect is due.* He hadn't smiled, really, when he met me minutes before the set began. I'd been offended. *What, was he disappointed?* I had something to prove now.

When we went across the street for tea afterward, he interviewed me about my life like a friendly cross-examiner, therapist, and journalist all in one. I'd never been asked so many questions, so directly, so unconcerned with social norms. Usually I drove the first date interview. It was kind of my thing.

"So it says on your profile you're 'mostly vegetarian,'" he'd said, an hour in. "What does that mean?" *Oh, here we go.* I'd actually nearly been able to reject Adam's profile when I saw he was vegetarian. I'd dated a vegan when I was twenty-four; it was the only relationship I'd really ever let myself feel even mildly strung along in. I'd left with a prejudice that men who care about animals must not have energy left to care about women.

"Yeah, well, I don't eat much meat," I said in my own defense. "But I like tuna, some turkey bacon sometimes."

"And do you feel you have a moral right to consume another life for your pleasure when you don't need to?" His tone wasn't angry or really judgmental. He was just asking me what my ethical opinion was, like whether I believed in banning assault weapons.

"No . . . I guess I don't actually believe it's my *right*. Not when you put it like that."

"So why do you do it?" he asked gently.

"I'm not sure," I said slowly. "Maybe I won't anymore." He nodded like this was sufficient answer, and moved on. I didn't know it yet, but that would be the last day I'd eat animals. I'd known vegetarians all my life, but no one had held me accountable like that before. Though we drank no alcohol that night, we closed the bar. When he walked me to my door, I offered him only a hug.

"I'd like to see you again. Would you like to see me?" he asked, blunt as he'd been all night.

"I'm . . . not sure," I answered honestly. He was good-looking and obviously very smart. But something about him made me cautious. Or did I just want to challenge him to be aggressive? "I guess I'd say that I'm open to being persuaded."

He laughed at this good-naturedly. "Okay, I can do that." I later learned he'd literally published papers on the psychology of seduction.

A few days later I was presented with three options for our second date: a museum exhibit with his favorite artist, someone famous I'd never heard of; a flamenco dance performance; or a home-cooked meal at his place. All three ideas sounded much better than the "drinks" or "hanging out" guys usually suggested, but I knew it was the third option I wanted most. *Am I being a slut? No. This is the New Me. A woman, not a girl. I'm being discerning—you can tell a lot about a guy from his apartment. I need to stop fostering boys with lost puppy-dog eyes like I have endless resources and time. I mean, I'm twenty-seven—who knows how much longer I have before my stock/tits rapidly begin to plummet?*

I knew it was unfortunately "normal" I was worried about running out of time to be enduringly lovable at the ripe old age of twenty-seven. But I also knew "normal" is not necessarily the same thing as "natural." I'd have told you vehemently that people socialized as women are taught to think about their life's potential this way, and how this conditioning is (by design) profoundly limiting. I felt the pressure to find my Ideal Other before it was too late regardless.

Yet I also had little genuine desire to settle down. It was hard to imagine being so sure about anyone that I'd want to give up my favorite feeling/drug: falling in love with someone new. Nearly every time I liked someone enough to sleep with them, post-coital armpit hair would mix with Old Spice and I'd latch on till I tired of the smell, roughly eight to twenty months later. In each relationship, I'd gradually lost my attraction and felt stifled imagining a future of kissing only that one person, no matter how well they kissed. I couldn't stand not being able to do whatever I wanted with my life, even when what I wanted was only the abstract possibility of future romantic adventures. I never *cheated* . . . I dumped people when they most expected it. And though I'd loved, I'd never felt fully vulnerable.

———

I was sick of my self-protective romantic pattern, and yet here I was, going over to Adam's house days after my latest breakup so that he could audition for the role of Next Boyfriend. Or ideally, if I was honest, The One Who Would Put My Restlessness to Bed So I Could Arrive at My Adult Life. *So fucking dumb, Rachel. But then again, just to argue the other side, he does seem like an unusually strong contender . . .*

As I lay back like a queen on Adam's couch, I felt myself bloom in his hands. So maybe I *didn't* need to wear tight clothing, ask ingratiat-ing questions, convince myself I was riveted when I was only intrigued. Instead of controlling the ride, maybe I could finally relax and let someone else drive. *I could get used to this . . .* I began to fantasize about a new life, one filled with five-hour foot rubs, surrounded by knowl-edge I'd absorb mostly through osmosis. *Jesus, what the hell is wrong with you? You don't even know this guy. Don't fall for it.*

There was definitely still something hard to read about him, oddly serious and unconcerned with politeness. Granted, he had the angular jaw and strong brow bone of Jake Gyllenhaal, Jewish-looking only in his dark curls and the tasteful smattering of chest hair peeking through his shirt. Yes, he'd seemingly read everything I'd meant to, written two books, was pleasurably tall and muscular, taught at a graduate level. Fine, he was clearly the kind of grown-ass man I'd begun to believe was above my pay grade in Brooklyn, had lamented to my straight girl-friends we'd never find if we stayed in the land of spoiled hipster man-children. But there had to be a catch. There was always a catch.

"What is it?" he asked. "Tell me." I'd learn it was one of his favorite commands: *Tell me.*

"I just got out of a relationship, and I promised myself I wouldn't . . ."

"That's fine. There's no obligation here." His gaze was so hawklike, penetrating yet calm. "I am looking for a partner, someone to share my life with. And I like you—but we're not even close to there yet."

"Of course, I know." I looked down. *I sound like a silly little girl.*

"But since we're talking about it, you should know something else about me." So here it was. I readied myself. "If you were to become that partner for me, I would never restrict you."

". . . What do you mean, 'you wouldn't restrict me'?" I asked cau-tiously.

"I mean that you could still date and sleep with other people, even fall in love again. I don't want to restrict my partners' experiences,"

Adam said, maintaining firm eye contact, speaking slowly like he was delivering good news in a new language. "If you were my primary partner, I would just need to feel privileged and know what's going on in your experiences outside the relationship. As long as you were honest and safe, you would be free. Free to do whatever you wanted."

My stomach dropped. *He didn't mention that on his profile.* "So you're polyamorous," I said, flatter than I'd intended.

"Well, I don't really like labels," he answered. "It's just about the way I want to be in a relationship, not really an identity. But yes, I've been in non-monogamous relationships before. The rest were mostly monogamous, but I've realized now this is the way I want to be towards someone I love. I don't want my insecurities running my partner's life. I don't want to control someone in that way."

"So then you would want to date other people too, right?" Why was the idea already making my cheeks flush and my pulse beat in my ears? I had no claim to him.

"Like I said, I'm looking for a partner to share my life with, so that's not really the priority right now. But yes, I would probably want to have some of the same freedoms sometimes. But I'm willing to be flexible for the right person," he added.

So there it was. *I should have known a man like this would never be satisfied with just one woman.* He'd devoured the hundreds of books in this apartment, gotten rid of many more, was hungry still. Of course I wasn't special. Of course he would need other women—more beautiful, mature, well-read, no doubt—to feel satisfied. Of course everyone who made it to the second round got this dinner, this seductive interrogation.

But there were other feelings mixed in there, too: a sort of recognition, a sense of exciting possibility.

Like many a liberal raised in Oakland and living in Brooklyn, I was familiar with the concept of non-monogamy. I'd read *Sex at Dawn* a few years before, when an ex had mailed it to me a year after our breakup. He'd become polyamorous in his new relationship and sent me the seminal book, saying it had "changed his life" and that he "hoped it would help me, too." Though I'd resented the passive-aggressive implications, I'd devoured it with a focused interest. Its central and heavily sourced argument—that it was not in fact "biologically destined" for me to want to entrap a man to monopolize his sperm—was refreshing.

I'd long before absorbed the "evolutionary reason" sex is viewed mostly as a scarce resource withheld by women. The theory roughly goes that men want to spread their seed, while women evolved to make sure dudes who impregnate us stick around to impale baby rabbits, protect us from ambush gang bangs, open jars we couldn't *possibly* eat the entire contents of, etc. (And of course, under this theory, biological sex is neat and tidy and determines stereotypical gender roles—and intersex, trans, non-binary, and gender non-conforming people don't exist.)

But *Sex at Dawn* argues that the evidence actually points to early hunter-gatherer societies being communal and mostly unconcerned with paternity. It was with the advent of the Agricultural Revolution—and its attendant concern for personal assets—that women's bodies became property to manage. A new paradigm of *"I'll trade my daughter for your cow"* eventually led to a culture with expressions like, *"Why buy the cow when you can get the milk for free?"* According to *Sex at Dawn*'s authors, early evolutionary theorists in the 1800s projected their social norms of monogamy and patriarchy onto their theories—but there is overwhelming evidence that we evolved as a socially promiscuous animal. There are more than three hundred species of primates, and none of them who also live in complex social groups with multiple adult males (like our two closest genetic relatives, bonobos and chimps) are monogamous. In fact, very few animals are—only 3 percent of species even *pair bond,* let alone monogamously.*

After I finished the book, I never saw relationships in quite the same way. Of *course* I'd been sold yet another narrative that reinforced a capitalist, patriarchal system. The idea of breaking out of that sounded radical and right. It also made me nervous. How to begin?

I contemplated this thoughtful man offering me the option to have my cake and eat the pie, too. He was gradually kneading my lower thigh through my dress. His touch still somehow felt devoid of pressing agenda, subtly pulling skin back to create a ripple that reached my pussy as if by happenstance. *Well . . . it's not like serial monogamy can work forever, right? Adam might show me another way. And didn't he say he'd compromise for the right person?*

"What? What is it?" His tone again like he was lovingly reassuring a child scared of monsters. It made me feel little. In a good way.

"I want to lay down next to you, but I'm scared of what we'll start," I admitted.

"I'm not trying to sleep with you tonight. That's not really how it works for me. I prefer to wait several weeks." I raised my eyebrow skeptically. "It's true! I've had women try to break up with me because I wait so long they feel rejected. There's no rush. I *want* to take my time with you." He reached his arms out in that way that makes you see a flicker of the little boy inside the man, the way we are all Russian dolls. "Come here. Lay down next to me." I liked the way he told me what to do. Firm, but gentle. Like it was my choice and not my choice at once.

---

* Not even penguins and swans are sexually monogamous, as is often rumored. In fact, of the few supposedly "monogamous" birds and other mammals, infidelity is present in 100 percent of species examined. We tend to project the social construct of monogamy onto animals who pair bond and raise young together, which is not the same thing as monogamy. J .F. Wittenberger and R. L. Tilson, "The Evolution of Monogamy: Hypotheses and Evidence," *Annual Review of Ecology and Systematics* 11 (1980): 197–232; D. W. Mock and M. Fujioka, "Monogamy and Long-Term Bonding in Vertebrates," *Trends in Ecology and Evolution* 5, no. 2 (1990): 39–43.

We faced each other lying down forehead-to-forehead on the couch, speaking as a one-eyed cyclops in hushed tones. Like two positive ends of a magnet being pushed together, the resistance was as thick as the inevitability of one of our polarities flipping over. Eventually, it was time. He took my chin between his thumb and index finger and lightly moved it forward, kissing me slowly, fluently. I pulled my face away a little, inviting the tension, daring a display of force in a way that felt both new and natural and studied at once. He put his hand around the small of my back and pulled me toward him firmly this time, just hard enough, just the right way, taking a finger and parting my lips as he tasted me. So this was what a first kiss could be. Had I ever been quite so pliant, so well read?

No. I saw now I had not.

And now his hands were making me remember my waist, his back a raft as the couch itself was dissolving, physics and biology working in collusion, telling us to *merge, merge right this minute, you've waited long enough.* I was being lifted into his room, laid on his immaculate bed. A humbled, almost confused awe mixed with determination in his hawk eyes. I was a precious anomaly, a necessary deviation from his otherwise premeditated plans. The ease of it, the inertia, the sudden inevitability.

Oh, so it's you. Is it really you?

A Real Man,
Whatever That Means

---

*"Slowly guided into the fire—why is everyone so scared
to admit how good that can feel?"*
—Kate Elizabeth Russell, *My Dark Vanessa*

End of Winter 2015

BROOKLYN

I don't remember the first time Adam and I said we loved each other. Just that it felt almost redundant, even a little sacrilegious, naming the ordinarily holy. Like pointing out the snow outside was melting. When I told him only a few weeks in that my landlord would be terminating my month-to-month lease, he remarked, as if it was no big deal—

"So move in here."

I blinked, dumbfounded. Even if a part of me had been hoping he'd suggest it, the idea was obviously reckless. "Are you serious?" I asked incredulously.

"Why not?" He shrugged.

"Um, because you barely know me?" I'd never even *talked* about living with someone.

"I've known you a lot longer in soul-time," he said, laughing. "You're not as hard to figure out as you think, you know. I got who you are by our second date, and nothing you've done since has surprised me." This struck me as both arrogant and exciting—like many things he said. I'd felt emotionally a step ahead of every guy I'd dated before him. But Adam seemed to read my subtlest thoughts and feelings, sometimes before I myself felt aware of them. He'd had me take the Myers-Briggs test on my second night sleeping over. Together, our types could be some of the most compatible. Alone, his type was the rarest.

"Plus, you're already here every night anyway. We might as well save the money on rent." He squeezed me, must have seen me contemplating whether this was some elaborate scheme to pay $750 for a one-bedroom in prime Crown Heights, electric and fellatio included.

"If it doesn't work out, so what? You'll just move out. Big deal! Why be afraid of life? Don't be scared. Just *be* with me." Adam held me by both sides of my face, looked me in the eyes. God, I loved that. He was always doing things like this, making me feel swaddled and aroused at once. My favorite was when he would splay his entire hand over the center of my chest and gently rock me in a swirl toward him. He could cover my narrow rib cage this way, his pointer and pinky anchoring small breasts. My heart in the literal palm of his hand, right where we both wanted it. "Look," he said, voice dropping even lower. "I can tell we're unusually compatible as partners. If nothing about you is a big problem I can foresee at this point, nothing will be—at least on my end. I'd have recognized by now which major need I'd be compromising, and there's nothing major I can tell. Sure, you're a little messy. And *definitely younger* than I'd prefer. But you'll get older. There's nothing we can't work on here."

I was repeatedly shocked by his sureness. *Who is this person? And why can't I figure out what's wrong with him that makes him think I'm so wonderful?* His eyes bored into me when he fucked me—and *he* fucked *me,* a fact that made me feel newly smug and secure. Even if I was on top, I was made to feel like a bottom. I might ride him, even temporarily steer my hips. But he was the one with his foot on the gas and brake, the owner of the car, the navigator, all of it.

3/1/15

From: Rachel to [Adam]

Subject: writing . . .

. . . how it feels to be fucked by a man, a real man, whatever that
    means.

Yes, it's a construct—but I feel it. I smell it. I grab onto it for dear
    life . . .

some other times I feel most like a woman:

. . . when a man is out with his wife and kids and checks me out and I
    shoot him back a look that says i'm onto you. Not offended, but
    onto you.

When I feel afraid for the day I am the wife.

. . . when I fear deeply the idea of being tied to one person, yet know i
    want it more than anything.

I asked what made him feel most like a man. I loved all his answers,
but my favorites: Writing me. Reading me. Knowing where he was
going. Dancing. His hands securing my entire back and waist. Holding
my face while he fucked me.

You're my woman, he'd remind me, over and over. No one had ever
called me their woman before. I felt precious and delicately tucked
away, like a porcelain Madame Alexander doll who instead of getting
her hair brushed gets her bush licked. When I turned off the shower,
he'd rush the length of the little apartment just to wrap me in a towel.
He didn't do it once, or sometimes. He did it every single time, no matter what else he was doing. Yet there was nothing submissive about the
gesture. He exuded pure protective dominance.

I found myself having newly retrograde thoughts: *I've found myself
a real man. He's come to claim me, and he wants to keep me, too. I'm safe
now.* I tucked away these feelings like a secret hard candy stored behind
my back cheek. Worried about cavities, but this was sweet.

The concept of "a real man" being someone virile, authoritative, and dominant—it wasn't introduced to me by Adam, of course. But he was the first man I'd dated, or even really known, who so fully embodied these traits. I'd badly craved the experience of being dominated by such a person—and I'd also wanted what I'd been socialized to want: a handsomely-aggressive-yet-sensitive-and-devoted mind reader. With Adam, I actually seemed to have found just that. And there was such satisfaction in it. Finding myself in a play so well-cast that stereotypical gender roles felt almost like no performance at all.

At the same time, I also knew it was dangerous to give in to this kind of thinking. That so closely adhering to what's expected of cis men and women might be seductive and luxurious, filled with benefits and comforts . . . until the bill comes due. That I was also enjoying the same societal constructs used to oppress people who don't fit into these narrow boxes.* People like my best friend Robin.

Within weeks, somehow, my brilliant best friend Robin was the only person in my life I deemed as smart as Adam. The only person whose judgment I might still trust more. I told Robin everything . . . save for the details about my new boyfriend I worried Robin might find problematic, rationalizing that the unspoken power dynamic Adam and I were falling into was just too easy to misconstrue. I'd never hidden things from Robin before. Nor had I ever been subsumed by a

---

*   "The dream of cis-hetero marital bliss is a product of imperialist white supremacist capitalist patriarchy," writer/filmmaker Imran Siddiquee told me. "Throughout history, colonizing forces have used the myth of the gender and sex binaries to justify the domination of Indigenous people, Black people, and other people of color worldwide. Trans and gender non-conforming people, intersex people, and queer people have always existed, and so have various forms of romantic and familial relationships. The obsession with the institution of marriage, with the thin-white-beauty ideal, and with these impossible, made-up ideas of how to 'be a man' and 'be a woman,' are linked to efforts to portray colonizers as more civilized than those they are murdering and stealing from. And that continues to this day." For more on this history, check out the books C. Riley Snorton, *Black on Both Sides* (Minneapolis: University of Minnesota Press, 2017); Sabrina Strings, *Fearing the Black Body* (New York: NYU Press, 2019); Saidiya V. Hartman, *Wayward Lives, Beautiful Experiments* (New York: W.W. Norton & Company, 2019); Imani Perry, *Vexy Thing* (Durham: Duke University Press, 2018).

man this way. I started to tell myself that my best friend, who at the time identified as lesbian, just wouldn't understand this kind of man. That none of my friends would.

My gut told me that hiding details from all my friends was a major warning sign . . . at the same time it urged me to see what came next. My gut sent coexisting and seemingly conflicting messages. *Is this my intuition talking, or my fear of non-monogamy and not having control for once?* * Sometimes, you might know your fear is merited even as you intuit that you'll grow by potentially making a mistake anyway. That's how I remember feeling as I settled into this new life. It scared me to consider being in an open relationship, especially with someone who had all the experience and power in our dynamic. But I also liked the idea of being able to stay with Adam long term without surrendering my future romantic freedom. In fact, now that it had been offered, it was hard to imagine I'd want to go back to my serially monogamous ways again. I was sure I would eventually want to date more than one person at once. Granted, I wasn't sure if I'd be able to not get *confused* by it—but the idea that I could still fall in love endlessly made a lifelong commitment primarily to one person feel conceivable for the first time.

I thought about my first romantic stirrings in a different light now, and what they might foreshadow about my non-monogamous potential. On the one hand, though I'd only "loved" my first, mostly unrequited crush devotedly for a decade, there had been many other boys—and definitely a few girls—who made me feel things. I loved to flirt with all of them in middle school, and each dynamic had been its own sort of relationship.

I also considered the significance of having multiple father figures

---

* The difference between intuition and fear could be explained this way: "With intuition, there's a sense of knowing, there's clarity, there's flowing. Whereas with fear, when it's not coming from a wise intuition, there's a sense of contraction," Buddhist teacher Kaira Jewel Lingo later told me. "That doesn't mean the fear is 'wrong' or totally unfounded, but you experience how it closes you down."

growing up. Not just my dad, but my stepdad and uncle Willie I considered fathers, too. Though none of them were dominant types like
Adam, surely this detail had to be significant. *Could I be excited about
the idea of multiple partners because on a certain level, having three men
in my life feels more normal? But then again, lots of people grow up with
both a mother and a father without wanting both a girlfriend and a boyfriend. Though three boyfriends and a girlfriend does sound fun to me . . .*

Adam continued to remind me that non-monogamy was about my
bodily autonomy, not his hunger for other women. I should be allowed
to make whatever choices I wanted in life. He would never think he
owned my future experiences. "That isn't what love means to me," he
often said. "Plus, I think this is the best way to keep you. You're still
young. You're not done having adventures." I was touched—and I
knew he was right.

The problem was, I didn't at all like the idea of *him* dating other
people, and feared I never would. So to assuage my non-monogamous
anxiety, Adam proposed a generous offer: I could do whatever/whoever
I wished, but he would be monogamous until I allowed otherwise. I
knew the deal would eventually expire, but it felt chivalrous nonetheless. He was holding the door open for me so that I could walk on
through. His offer was meant to ease me into the lifestyle. To let me see
the benefits for myself first, in total safety.

———

One night, reading on the couch, Adam looked at his hand. Even
the way he *sat*, one leg crossed in a square, thumb absently stroking his
middle finger. "You know, ever since around our second date, I stopped
biting my nails," he said nonchalantly.

"Really?"

"Yeah. I tried to stop biting them for years, but I couldn't. And I
realized the other day I've stopped. I don't know why." He shrugged,

put his small wire-framed reading glasses back on, returned to his book. His tone could have been telling me the weather, but I took it as the highest form of praise: His subconscious was telling him he'd found me.

While being so sure was not in my nature, things did feel oddly . . . *fucking awesome*? I'd usually have known by then what the fatal flaw was. My gut would have told me he wasn't kind enough, sexy enough, smart or competent enough in some subtle but irreconcilable way. I was looking for that flaw, hard, but I couldn't quite put my finger on it. Well, besides that he was non-monogamous—a fact I tried to push out of my mind as soon as it surfaced. I would deal with that later, and maybe it would even prove to be a good thing.

I mean, how do I know what I'll be like in the future? Just a few weeks before, *I* was the clean roommate, eating popcorn for dinner, and dating someone whose couch I was afraid to sit on. And now, I was apparently living with a meticulous man who handled just about everything in the house. What was once deemed "women's work" was turned inside out when he wore it. He was the complete master of his domain. He wanted everything his way ("It's just easier when I do it"), and he would handle it. My job was to clean up after myself and otherwise relax and let him take care of me.

And so I'd literally sprint the avenue and a half from the train into his arms and try to relax into this new feeling called contentment. He'd cook us yet another fragrant vegetarian meal, the way he did every night. I'd actually hum to myself in happiness, watching his strong shoulders as he chopped onions, never complaining about the sting. After dinner, he'd usually ask me to dance (he was good; obviously a confident lead). I frequently felt I was living out a very specific dream he was turning lucid. As if his every action was helping me recall a fate already being looked back on. Going to work increasingly felt like a waste of what might be the most precious days of my life.

But for Adam, time never seemed wasted. This was something I'd never witnessed before, in any human: The man somehow never dicked around. Either he was teaching, reading, taking care of me and our home, exercising, or watering a relationship with a loved one. He had an encyclopedic memory, and could eloquently contextualize a broad range of sociology, philosophy, and psychology. He was always up to teaching me, and I told him early that this was exactly what I wanted him to do. He quickly became my most trusted editor.

I now dressed only the way he preferred: tight, simple clothes; no lipstick, no heels, no big jewelry, no lingerie or high-waisted jeans. I grew out my bangs and took out my nose ring, began wearing my hair up in a tight bun instead of down, all to his liking. He never *ordered* me to do any of these things. He made his strong opinions and judgments known, and I started molding myself to his every preference, not wanting to look any way but as beautiful as possible to the man who was so perfect to me.

We were rapidly entering an uncontracted Dom/sub power dynamic replete with language about my being kept and protected, "rescued from the confusion of boys," as he put it. But Adam quickly made clear he disliked the idea of role play or BDSM, for the same reason he found heavy makeup or lingerie unattractive. "Too much artifice," he said.

We're just being ourselves. Role play and rules are for people who are pretending, I thought, beginning to mix his more black-and-white thinking into my marbled palette. *I'm* choosing *to explore this dynamic. And it's not like he's punishing me or doing anything that needs a safe word. Right?*

ROBIN AND RACHEL DRUGGED DISNEY TRANSCRIPT

Drug: Shrooms

Movie: The Little Mermaid

Date: What is time/really/when you think about it?

URSULA:

"I'm not asking for much. Just a token, really, a
trifle . . . You'll never even miss it. What I want
from you is your voice."

ROBIN:

[To TV, shroom trip peaking]

"Yeah, no big deal. Your whole ability to express
yourself; no big fucking deal, Ariel."

ARIEL:

"But without my voice how can I—?"

URSULA:

"You'll have your looks—"

RACHEL:

[Singing along]

—"Your pretty face."

ROBIN:

[Giving full Miami-Cuban shade]

. . . Ariel thinks once she gets to land it'll be
better. Like bitch, on land they'll *rape* you. On
land, you have to fight to vote and shit. You don't
even *know* what's happening on land.

*[Ariel signs contract, trading voice for fuckable
hole/legs]*

. . . Literally [she's] signing her life away and her voice just to go find a dumb fuck. . . . This is an acceptable female in 1989. *This* bitch. Not acceptable. *Idealized.*

RACHEL:

This would never fly now, so it's come a long way. But it's too late for us. Oh my God, when you think about what a magical thing it is that we are where we are; that we have unpacked so many of these things. But what got in there? What's stuck in there anyway, despite our best efforts?
[We reach the end of the movie, Robin grabbing his hair in fists. The film he watched hundreds of times as a child penetrated his subconscious in irreparable ways. Of course Robin knew this already but didn't really know it till now, you know?]

RACHEL:

. . . Watch the last line of this movie.

ROBIN:

I'm going to throw up.

RACHEL AND ARIEL:

"I love you, Daddy."

ROBIN:

[King Triton-like], "I'll allow it. Transferring over my property to you, Eric."
. . . Literally her family members are butchered in the kitchen, but now that she's married to Eric, they're all cool with the genocide of the fish. "Oh,

just some in-law shenanigans, no big deal; half of
the family wants to eat the other half."

RACHEL:

Yep. "*Thanks, Dad, goodbye.*" From one man to the
next.

Yes, Daddy

Spring 2015

BROOKLYN

*"As females in a patriarchal culture, we were not slaves of love;
most of us were and are slaves of longing—yearning for a master
who will set us free and claim us because we cannot claim ourselves."*
—BELL HOOKS, COMMUNION: THE FEMALE SEARCH FOR LOVE

I was buzzing my clit with a vibrator as Adam mined me steady and deep with his usual authoritative ease. It felt so relieving to be fucked by him. He got hard when he wanted, for as long as he wanted. He never came before he meant to. This superhuman, rather freakishly unnerving talent made it possible for me to sometimes truly relax. To move as slowly or forcefully as I wanted to, not worrying about the consequences either way. He made me sit back onto him hard as I got close, gripping my ass in his fists. In his capable hands, I was Adam's rib, fertile earth smoothed to clay.* And now, this originally sinful derivative of man was coming in doggy.

"Yes, Daddy. Fuck me, Daddy!" I tried to play it off in the moment, quickly adding a *"Fuck me, my man."* But like saying your first "I love you," you can't exactly ignore your first Daddy.

---

* "This is now bone of my bones and flesh of my flesh; she shall be called 'woman,' for she was taken out of man." Genesis 2:23.

Afterward, he held me to his chest and flashed that inverted grin. "So . . . Daddy?"

"Ugh, it's so weird I said that! It always creeped me out when people say they're 'daddy's girls,' too." I covered my face with both hands, mortified. "It must be porn culture somehow. *It got to me!*"

Adam whispered in the gravelly night-DJ baritone he reserved for just such occasions. "Don't worry, baby. *I'll be your Daddy*." I laughed and pushed him away, but damn was that delicious.

Though Adam saying he'd be my Daddy thrilled me, I resolved to use the word as little as possible. It didn't work. On the verge of orgasm, over and over like that guy Charlotte dates in that episode of *Sex and the City* who can't stop calling her "you fucking bitch you fucking whore" before he comes, I'd blurt it out. *"Fuck me, Daddy. Yes, Daddy!"* In response, he now sometimes called me his "girl." *My girl,* he'd say, moving his cock around in a highly personalized swirl, a method he'd quickly perfected for making me come. *Yes, my girl.* It turned me on and creeped me the. Fuck. Out. But perhaps I called Adam "Daddy" simply because calling him "baby" or even "babe" seemed so . . . *wrong.* He was anything but a *baby.* Adam was so dominant he'd never call himself dominant. Tasteless and unnecessary, like a guy with a big dick bragging about it.

Naturally, I googled "why women say daddy during sex." I learned there is a dynamic called a Daddy Dom/little girl relationship. (Daddy/ boy and Mommy/girl pairings are also quite common; Mommy/little boy dynamics to a less obvious degree, likely because of how the genders are socialized.) The dynamic could vary in intensity, with some people only using the words "Daddy" and "girl" during sex. Others enjoy the dynamic in everyday life, too, with the Daddy Dom "taking care" of "his girl"—cooking for her, helping pick out her clothes, spanking her when she's been bad, rocking her in his lap, tucking her in. The list of ideas made me cringe. And my pussy throb.

"What do you get when you have a male Dom who's not a sadist and a submissive who's not into pain? Often the result is a Daddy Dom and a little girl submissive in a relationship that focuses not only on domination and punishment, but also on nurturing and adoration for one another," one article explained.* A Daddy Dom, as he's called, will "put the baby girl's needs first," doing everything to make her feel special and cherished and even spoiling her at times—but not letting her get away with being a brat, either. In return, the little girl submissive apparently "worships" her Daddy Dom. The word "worship" made me very uncomfortable. The throbbing grew stronger.

I had to admit this whole Daddy/girl dynamic sounded a lot like me and Adam. Hadn't he promised to protect me? Didn't he cook me dinner every night? Hadn't I confessed I wanted him to be my teacher, and already become a much better writer under his precise edits? Wasn't I dressing only as he preferred, and striving to follow all his many household rules?

Adam would add daily to the list of habits I needed to retrain: the way I spilled water around the sink when I washed the dishes; the way I left fingerprints on the bathroom mirror when I opened the cabinet; the way I forgot which dish towel was for the countertop versus drying; even the way I put the toilet paper on in the wrong direction. "Like this, see?" he'd say lovingly, punctuating his point with a spank for maximum effect. *Yes, Daddy,* I'd think, but never let slip outside the bedroom. And then, judging myself, *Jesus, I really like to bring the armchair to the analyst, don't I?*

It was obvious to me why I was drawn to Adam's strictness. There weren't explicit boundaries, rules, or punishments in my upbringing.

---

* "Daddy Doms Explained—The Softer Side of BDSM," Normandie Alleman, *Goodreads*, Jun. 2, 2014.

There were subtly shifting emotional expectations, and yelling/guilt trips when my parents' only child failed to meet them. Don't get me wrong, I'm in most ways very lucky—my biological parents were and are loving and well-intentioned, engaged, open-minded. But the quid pro quo always felt clear: *Be a brag-worthy mini-adult attuned to easing our moods, and we won't do inane things like give you a bedtime or make you go to school when you don't feel like it.* My mom often said I was her "do-over," destined to live out the achievements her own poor and traumatic childhood had prevented. There was a lot of love and admiration, and a lot of implicit pressure/blurred lines/sudden outbursts I felt responsible for quelling.

My parents divorced before I turned three; their custody agreement had me passed back and forth each day or two. There was a constant shift not just between homes, but between the different sides of myself that most pleased each parent. If I fought with one, I could always run between my two rooms without consequence (literally, they lived a mile apart). Either "authority figure" would readily agree that the other was nuts. It should be no surprise then that throughout my twenties I did not take to monotony or feeling hemmed in. I was hypersensitive to being micromanaged—or really, managed at all. I continued to feel caged in by walls and regular working hours, claustrophobic in my total lack of privacy within open office plans. Being glued to a computer all day, no matter how potentially influential my position as an editor at a major women's website, felt like a capitalist trap.

All I really wanted was to be a full-time writer. But that dream seemed too rare, too precious, too unlikely to financially pan out. I was lucky to work as close to my passion as I did, to be paying down my student loans . . . even if I dreaded Sunday nights and my morning alarm and many of the hours in between. At least, with Adam, less time felt squandered. My weekends were officially a Netflix-free zone. We read and danced, ambled in Prospect Park, went out for Buddhist Chinese food. I only smoked weed socially. We went to the Blue Note monthly, along with all the other shows Adam bought tickets for without asking. (I liked that he didn't request permission, even though we split the cost on the shared card he had us get as soon as I moved in.) We had dinner with his fascinating friends, mostly academics whose stunning wit and kindness reaffirmed his specialness. We made heroic subway voyages home from Target. Though I was expected to pull my weight, bags were never carried evenly. I just tried to keep up.

————

In this way especially, I knew Adam was also a long-fermenting rebellion against the first and maybe only dating advice my dad gave me. We sat in the car at a stoplight as a man tugged on his girlfriend's arm when it was time to cross the street. "Never let someone treat you like that. Like you're a dog," my dad said, uncharacteristically paternal.

"Okay, Dad, sure." Still in high school, I couldn't imagine I'd date a *jerk* like that anyway.

Now, not only did I enjoy the way Adam lurched me around the city, but he often joked that he was "training me." I was surprised to find this idea was actually deeply relieving. Like it was no longer my sole responsibility to arrive at a destination—or even my own life. Adam never seemed lost in a way he couldn't quickly correct. Insecurity appeared to elude him completely. In this shared illusion of his infallibility, I felt safe. I worried, intellectually, that this was problematic as hell. But oh, how relieving it felt. To fully trust, for the first time since I was a very little girl, that someone knew better than me which way to walk. That someone was lovingly monitoring me.

And Adam was interested in every detail. How I often unconsciously placed my mugs on the farthest edges of tables, as if daring them to fall. How I added a bizarre array of toppings on my ice cream and oatmeal alike, opting for variety and novelty and uniqueness over vanilla with sprinkles. How I left drawers ajar and toothpaste uncapped, perhaps afraid of wasting the cumulative seconds of my life. Though he still only brought up non-monogamy abstractly, the potential implications for these traits of mine were obvious to both of us—I liked pushing limits, ample variety, advancing quickly.

"You can tell a lot about a person by the way they brush their teeth." Adam would smile at me, amused. Now I saw what he meant: my mouth foamed haphazardly, toothpaste often dribbled on my chin. I was quick, childlike, unconcerned with any reliable or couth methodology so much as the *feeling* that I had reached clean. He, on the other hand, was almost self-punishing; contained, effective, bicep bulging. No mess escaped his mouth. These were the kinds of character details I imagined people dissected in MFA writing workshops. I wasn't willing to go into further debt to attend a grad program myself. But oh, did it sound luxurious and liberating to be tasked with *only writing*. Being analyzed by a professor felt like more than a consolation prize, then. It was like absorbing wealth by proxy.

———

When Adam very quickly took me home to meet his parents, I was already presented as his Partner with a capital "P." I felt immediately at home in this happy, liberal Jewish family; they made it so by being incredibly *hamish*,* breaking out their vintage bong as we watched *The Daily Show* and feasted on organic snacks. I saw the difference an extra generation of assimilation and college can make. Under their upper-middle-class wings, we'd never have to worry, Adam assured me.

I'd never dated someone who made much money. But securing a more stable future was also an important element of the pressure I felt to find "The One"—The One to Help Me Manage My Mom. I'd long felt emotionally responsible for taking care of my now-single mom,

---

*   Yiddish for warm, relaxed, cozy, unpretentious, homey.

and her inevitable financial dependence could only be staved off so long. How would I manage it alone when she could no longer get by? That constant question had in many ways also driven my professional ambitions—I needed to climb the success ladder quickly (she had me at forty-one). When I confessed my fears about the future, Adam told me to stick with him. We would figure out her situation together. No one had ever said something like that to me before—lover or family member. I'd felt alone with the worry for so long. But now, apparently, I had a Partner.

Wait, is this what wanting to get married someday feels like?

And What Would That Give You?

Spring 2015

BROOKLYN

I'd started wearing the turquoise ring on my left ring finger shortly before I met Adam. The idea was that I would become engaged to myself, that I would give myself the symbolic maturity a talisman on your ring finger seemed to afford you. "I swore that married women used their left hands more than their right when they spoke, gestured, or wiped a stray hair out of their eyes, just to rub it in," Melissa Broder writes of the phenomenon in *The Pisces*.* "They seemed to be saying, 'Look, someone wants me this much. I have safely made it to the other shore.'"

As I'd been trying to break up with Dan, I wanted to see if I could give some of that safety to myself. Indeed, I found I enjoyed the light presence of the ring on my finger, the way it gave me reassurance that wherever I go, there I am. Rings on other fingers didn't seem to have the same effect. But after Adam appeared, I started to wonder if it held certain powers: *Wear it, and he will come.* It was a small silver band, with five vertical turquoise rectangles lined up neatly like dominoes. I began to mythologize that my self-induced engagement would go on five years, one for each stone, until he gave me a new ring that symbolized something new, something like earning his lifelong commitment. When Adam asked me about my ring, I told him I was engaged to

---

*   Melissa Broder, *The Pisces* (New York: Hogarth, 2018).

myself, and more or less left it at that. I suspected he was amused but largely indifferent.

He still had his old wedding band. He wasn't sure why he'd kept it for a decade, but he had. He knew he would never wear a ring again—it felt wrong to him, being marked like that as someone's property, even if only for the year he'd been married. His ex-wife had been "crazy," according to him; violent and jealous, though they were monogamous. (I noted his use of the word "crazy" and filed it under my growing internal list titled Misogynist Red Flags I'll Worry About Later.) He explained that he'd been trying to adhere to what he thought he was supposed to do when he got married. Plus, *she'd* proposed to *him*. It happened impulsively, after they landed on the ground from the literal adrenaline rush of skydiving. He wouldn't be making *that* mistake again. Often, there's nothing like someone's disregard to get you interested.

One night, I surprised myself by asking him to put the ring on while we had sex, "just so I could see." As he slipped it on, it was almost like sleeping with a stranger; the silver band made him look like a cow with his ear tagged. Normal, perhaps, but not natural. And yet when I saw him grab my thigh with it, put his fingers in my pussy and take them lightly in and out with it, I felt I was sleeping with him in another life, and it made me very wet.*

It became a recurring request. Afterward, he'd pull it off before he went to take a shower, like it was just more postcoital residue to clean. Sometimes he (*carelessly or on purpose?*) left the ring by the bed, next to the rose quartz votive holder his mom had given him "for positive energy." I wondered if we were inviting in bad juju, using his failed mar-

---

* "Weddings are so kinky. . . . You put a woman in a special elaborate outfit, and then one man gives her to another man like some kind of BDSM scene, and then they put like a symbolic collar on the woman's finger, and then the man lifts her dress to show everyone there—maybe hundreds of people!—her garter and lingerie. . . . It's so dirty." —Torrey Peters, *Detransition, Baby* (New York: One World, 2020).

riage for sexual pleasure. That risk, as if I were daring the universe to curse me, was of course also part of what turned me on.

When I lost my self-engagement ring one night that spring, I asked him what it might symbolize. "Maybe it symbolizes the beginning of you not making everything symbolize something," he answered.

"Do you know me at all?"

"Oh, I know you. But I also know it's your choice what meaning you assign symbols and events." He shrugged. "I think you should let the ring go. I mean, if you want to." That was invitation enough for me. *Perhaps he has the hope to one day buy its replacement after all.*

The Paraguard is copper, and so in a way, that was a different sort of metallic commitment we made together, right? He'd quickly encouraged me to have an IUD implanted. I hadn't wanted to go back on hormonal birth control, and he hated using condoms. So we'd used the withdrawal method our first month together, a newly reckless technique I'd never entertained before.* *I choose you. Over every other woman. I want to mix us into another person,* he'd tell me before coming as romantically as he could on my tits. I knew he didn't actually want children—but he also refused to get a vasectomy, "just in case." It certainly wasn't part of my five-year/maybe-ever plan to have kids. But the fact he couldn't help imagining procreating with me anyway? It felt like a feat. *If I'm good enough, maybe I'll prove the exception to all his rules. What satisfaction it would be, to achieve unrestrained desirability at his level.*

With Adam's total control over his orgasms, I wasn't worried he'd accidentally come inside me. But I did *want* to feel him come inside very much, and so did he. So I got the IUD, and, now protected for ten years, was glad I'd been encouraged to do something that scared me. Granted, we'd gotten in a fight after I felt pressured to have sex with

---

* The pullout method is officially termed "coitus interruptus" (lol); 1 in 5 people with ovaries will become pregnant after a year practicing it (Planned Parenthood).

him only a day or two after implantation. He'd said past girlfriends hadn't "thought it was such a big deal" or "seemed to be in much pain," or "had a problem with it" (I wasn't the first girlfriend to get an IUD with him). He got upset and defensive when I accused him of being coercive.* *"That's not what I was saying at all!"* he yelled at me for what might have been the first time. "Repeat back to me what I said!" It would become a familiar exchange—as if all that mattered were his exact words, not their subtext.

He just can't get enough of me, I rationalized. We had sex after all, and though it hurt, it wasn't as bad as I'd feared. *He's just trying to help me mature by bringing up past girlfriends.* Because of him, I too was now a woman shielded by the most reliable form of long-term birth control. I even now used more environmentally friendly non-applicator tampons because *his ex* had been able to, briefly overachieving with bloodied menstrual cups. Before Adam, fear and squeamishness around my own reproductive system were valid excuses. No more. I was his girl, and that required an effort in a direction I respected.

But non-monogamy was like the Grim Relationship Reaper, hovering in some shadowy corner of my mind. Whenever Adam reminded me I was free (as he seemed to every few weeks, as if to not let me get too comfortable in a delusion) I'd redden and feel immediately defensive, putting space between our bodies. When he stayed out late one night with his very attractive friend Ayesha, who was also polyamorous, I became worried he was trying to date other people while promising

---

*   Sexual coercion is when you do not feel that it would be possible to say no to sex without harmful emotional fallout, punishment, resentment, or physical danger. Coercive behaviors can show up in any kind of relationship, but polyamorous relationship coach Dedeker Winston told me she does see it in unique ways in certain non-monogamous scenarios. "A person may feel that they have to say yes to group sex, for example, out of fear that their refusal will ruin the evening for multiple other people involved. There is also the classic example of a person who is staunchly monogamous feeling like they have no choice but to adhere to their partner's non-monogamous preferences, lest the relationship come crashing down." The reverse of this also happens, where a polyamorous person feels coerced into being monogamous.

me otherwise. He corrected something I did around the house the next day as usual, and I picked a fight, claiming it was about his controlling tendencies. And indeed, I was also afraid of the power dynamic I was now embedded in. He had more experience in every area, and it was clear he would be setting the pace, however he might insist it was all up to me. We were still only two months in, officially living together for only one. But an implicit pressure for me to catch up was already felt in the background.

4/13/15

Reply: Rachel to [Adam]
Subject: A Few Promises

it really worries me the groundwork we're laying here, where i have to adjust to all your methods . . . i know it's coming from a good place, but i think if other people who care about me saw our dynamic play out they would say i don't seem like myself, like i'm making myself smaller.
. . . you're establishing a power dynamic where i reveal everything . . . and you get to always be the perfect, calm one in return. you get total control.

He replied that I seemed to be interpreting everything through the lens of power. That I was afraid of being in the first relationship where I wasn't in full control. With him, I didn't have the upper hand I was used to. If I couldn't handle some loving criticism, I was correct that I would not be well matched with him. Rarely one to turn down a dare, I proposed I move out. I suggested we stay together but simply have a little more space. He warned he'd essentially have to demote me from Potential Life Partner if we "went backwards," and with his preference for polyamory, I wasn't about to call his bluff. But I looked at one place in Astoria anyway. He called and emailed me nonstop dozens and dozens of times that day. It was scary and bizarre . . . and a little oddly flattering. He was apparently desperate to keep me, seemingly out of control for the first time.

When I came back home, he got on his knees and begged me not to leave, his eyes watering with a tasteful fierceness. No one had gotten on their knees for me before. It was thrilling to see him lower himself, to realize how terrified this otherwise indomitable man was of losing me. *"My girl, don't leave, please!"* It made me want to see him get on one knee instead. Some version of this began to happen periodically. I'd feel that I was being manipulated in a way I couldn't quite pinpoint, he'd say I was acting emotionally out of fear and social conditioning, the fight would escalate, I'd try to leave to get some air. Usually he didn't let me, even blocking the door. He'd tell me to stop running away. To let him touch me as we spoke so we didn't stay "needlessly distant." It made me squirm. But then it worked. I was finally living in a home filled with rules. There was no mistaking who had authority now, and there would be consequences to running away.

Once we'd nearly reconciled, he'd pull me up to dance. He never tripped on the beat, knowing exactly what came next, and why he'd picked it. In his arms I felt like a rag doll come to life, soft and summoned. Breaking form for the special occasion, he'd finish off by dipping me low and deep, a secret promise the only space between us. His grip left no question: He'd never find me too much to hold. Nor would he attempt a move he couldn't execute in total confidence. I needn't worry about him at all. So long as I agreed to follow his lead, my body and mind could finally rest.

Ah, yes, rest.

––––––––––

The psychologist and Buddhist teacher Tara Brach suggests that when you have a strong desire or addiction, it's useful to question yourself until you get to the true heart's longing that is its very source. So, say the yearning is that someone will rescue you and deliver you to your adult life. You can ask yourself: *And what would that give you?* And when you think you have the answer, you ask the same question again. You keep digging deeper and deeper, until you get to the innermost wish.

If I were rescued, I'd feel loved . . . protected . . . safe . . . accepted . . . chosen. Worthwhile.

And then what would that give you?

I'd feel like I was really alive. Like I could just be happy, because I made it. Like I'd played my life right. Like I was allowed to exist just as I am, in that moment. Without having to change or anticipate anything.

And what would that give you?

I'd feel like I could finally, really, fully rest. Just rest in presence.

The idea, then, is to practice giving that feeling to yourself, right now, regardless of circumstances and conditions. To try on believing you've had what you seek inside all along. If you didn't already have its potential within you, Brach says, you wouldn't be able to conceive of it.

But simply submitting to Adam in order to rest felt easier, and relaxing. "Submission psychologically changes you from a person to an object and helps to take you out of your head. This is something that may be appealing to people who are easily distracted or tend to be anxious during sex," sex researcher Dr. Justin Lehmiller writes in *Tell Me What You Want*. Women report more anxiety during sex and in life in general—I certainly experience plenty in the bedroom and out. So it makes sense that we also report more discipline, submission, and masochism fantasies,* Dr. Lehmiller writes, "because unquestioningly fol-

---

* Some traits that also make it more likely you're into BDSM, according to Dr. Lehmiller's survey of more than 4,000 North Americans: If you're a Democrat. If you have a high level of neurosis and anxiety. If you're a woman and/or younger adult. "I think the way we should think about BDSM is that it's this adaptive tool," Dr. Lehmiller told me. "A coping mechanism for getting out of their head and not letting anxieties, insecurities, and worries disrupt their se ence." Justin Lehmiller, *Tell Me What You Want* (New York: Hachette Go, 2018).

lowing orders, submitting to others, and receiving pain are all experiences that depersonalize us to some extent—they transform us from persons to objects." Being an "object"—consensually removing choice—can feel like a big relief.

After all, this is how I'd been socialized to see my body and worth: Was I a successful object of desire, or was I failing? In Adam's arms, I felt secure validation. Like I'd done my job. I'd elicited and submitted to a dominant man's desire for my body, and I was a worthy sex object. For a moment, maybe I could forget about trying to control anything. I'd been commanded to rest in presence.

Ah, yes, rest.

But also, maybe don't get too comfortable.

I May Be Bisexual

_____

2/18/08

Journal Entry
Age 20

I realized a few things last night that are very important.

    I am not in love with [Oren] b/c i was still tempted by [Max] and even entertained the idea of cheating . . . I need to remember that means I'm not in love yet . . .

    I may be bisexual . . . I must not settle. I must have adventures. I must live!

4/10/08

Journal Entry
Still 20

I had a dream last night that men of many different races were pursuing me, and I wanted to date them all at once, not [Oren]. It was a free feeling, and the opposite of the commitment I felt last night.

    Explain that.

Spring 2015

BROOKLYN

One night, when I asked if there was anything he desired in bed that I could be giving him but wasn't (implicit: besides another woman), Adam confided in me his most powerful fantasy—seeing me have sex with another man.

Well, *this* didn't sound half bad. Being doubly taken, doubly helpless under the weight of masculine virility? Of all the kinks he could have, I felt I'd hit the deviant jackpot. *So maybe he isn't even really that interested in sleeping with other women! Maybe this whole non-monogamy thing is about seeing me with other men!* Now this I could get behind, or on top of, depending on the scenario. "So, but, is it just about seeing me with the guy? Or, do you also want to . . ."

"No, I don't want to have sex with the guy. And I *definitely* want to have my turn with you." He smiled. "I don't like humiliation, or just watching. It's more about inviting the competition and potential pain, while seeing your pleasure intensified. Then reclaiming you as my woman after."

Though Adam didn't use the term, this kind of fantasy is generally called "hotwifing." A "hotwife" is defined (heterocentrically, though of course the dynamic exists in all possible sexual and gender permutations) on Wikipedia as "a married woman who has sex with men other than her spouse, with the husband's consent. In most cases the husbands take a vicarious pleasure in watching their wives' and the other male's enjoyment, or enjoy watching, hearing, or knowing about their wives' adventures. Husbands may also take part by engaging in threesomes, or arranging dates for their wives." Cuckolding, which might be more rare as a fantasy but is the more commonly known term, is when someone enjoys elements of being dominated and possibly humiliated as they watch or hear about their partner having sex with others. They may or may not be allowed to touch their partner while the other per-

son is present. While we don't have numbers on how many people actually *enact* cuckolding or hotwifing scenarios, the genre consistently
ranks in the top ten categories of porn on most major sites.*

But I'd certainly never heard a man admit his interest in this fantasy
before. Had a boyfriend suggested it earlier, I'm certain I would have
been interested. Anyone who's even heard of YA knows the fantasy of
two guys fighting over you can run early and deep. "So . . . you *like*
jealousy?" I asked, taking in this welcome news.

"Well, the jealousy makes everything more intense. It's a good kind
of hurt I can channel into the erotic." Indeed, jealousy triggers the
amygdala, a portion of the brain that also initiates sexual activity. "I
mean, I'm speaking about how I *imagine* it will feel. I only know this is
something I want because I started getting turned on in the middle of
sex in college, when my ex admitted she was cheating." Instead of getting mad, the fantasy to see her with other men had emerged. I later
learned some researchers use "eroticization theory" to explain this kind
of response; the excitement might be an adaptation to trauma. The
unconscious mind transforms negative feelings (like the humiliation of
finding out you're being cheated on) into sexual arousal. This makes
the ego bruise less painful and helps a person regain a sense of control
over the experience.† But hotwifing fantasies could just as easily also be
an adaptive strategy designed to mitigate the trappings of long-term
commitment: boredom, the possibility of cheating, loss of novelty and
desire, and feelings of power imbalance.

"It's hard to believe you could have wanted this since college and
not had it," I said.

"Well, I saw Molly make out with someone at Chemistry once,"
Adam said nonchalantly, referencing a partner he'd once taken to the

---

*   PornHub.com; Ogi Ogas and Sai Gaddam, *A Billion Wicked Thoughts* (New York: Dutton, 2011).

†   Uri Wernik, "The Nature of Explanation in Sexology and the Riddle of Triolism," *Annals of Sex Research* 3, no. 1 (1990).

Brooklyn sex party. "But yeah, no one has really fulfilled the full fantasy for me yet." Like I needed more incentive.

———————

Adam had been in one long-term open relationship, with a woman he'd dated seriously for four years, Ramona. During that relationship, he had two other secondary partners,* Molly and Faith, whom he saw roughly once a week each. Eventually, Molly wanted a more serious commitment than he felt he could give. By then, he and Ramona were barely having sex anymore due to Adam's lack of desire for her. All three women eventually left him. The story read to me like a cautionary tale, reaffirmed the stereotype of non-monogamy being employed when a person isn't attracted to their partner but doesn't want to leave them. Adam said non-monogamy had "nothing to do" with why he realized he wasn't attracted to Ramona anymore. *As if having hot sex with two new women wouldn't throw your lack of desire for the one at home into starker relief.* I wasn't buying it, and resented and noted his denial.

He reassured me—often, because it had become a fear, another sub-catch—that the same thing wouldn't happen with me. He "loved my basic shape too much," he replied, as if it were simple mathematics. Even as I grew old, or if I "gained some weight," he would be able to recall and build upon his desire for me over a lifetime. Like a building's foundation, I had good bones. I was obviously skeptical. One thing was for sure, or so I thought: I would never be able to suffer the same indignity—to watch my partner go to two different women's beds twice a week when I had no one else, only to have him return to me without sexual desire. *Nope. No way am I self-assured or masochistic enough for that shit.* But I understood the impulse to do whatever it

———————

* The term some polyamorous people use to define partners you don't share the bulk of your time or resources with. The primary/secondary model of non-monogamy ranks one partner as, well, of primary position and concern.

took to keep him, his ability to persuade. The desire he evoked to please. That I did understand.

"Well, your fantasy definitely sounds fun to me," I said, straddling his lap. The whole idea felt subversive and primal. In fact, I could hardly imagine a fetish I'd rather share. Or a more ego-safe way to wade into the waters of non-monogamy. We both came that night imagining making his kink a reality.

———————

But a few weeks later, when Adam again casually mentioned us trying a sex party, the familiar face-burn began immediately. I could only compare this new and very physical feeling to when you can't not cry at work, but angrier. Had he only been buttering me up when he'd confessed his fetish? "I thought you weren't going to do anything with anyone else for now," I said, trying not to sound panicky.

"I won't do anything, if you don't want me to," he reassured me. "I just think you'd find it interesting to see a sex party. It isn't even that arousing. You realize how we're all just animals. It's an experience I know you'll find fascinating."

I was annoyed, but also glad he was pushing me. Of course I'd always *wanted* to experience an orgy. It was one of my most obvious life goals I just hadn't gotten around to yet. And judging by sex researcher Dr. Justin Lehmiller's landmark survey of more than 4,000 North Americans' sexual fantasies, you can probably relate: Group sex came in as the most commonly reported fantasy for both cis* men and cis

———————

*   This study, and many others in the book where I reference only "women and men," did not include data on trans and non-binary people. "While I did have some participants who were trans or non-binary in my original study, they didn't represent a particularly large part of the sample, which made it difficult to draw firm conclusions," Dr. Lehmiller later told me. A follow-up study he did included findings from trans and non-binary participants, and it showed that their sexual fantasies were quite similar to cisgender people's, although they were more

women.* After group sex, the next-most-common fantasies in his survey were, in order: power, control, and rough sex; novelty, adventure, and
variety; taboo and forbidden sex; partner sharing and non-monogamous
relationships; passion and romance. A sex party with Adam, then, was
my chance to have all of the toppings at once.†

*But what if seeing the desire in his eyes for other naked women ruins
something essential for me, the belief that I'm special? Then again, no risk,
no reward. I mean, I want to see and touch other naked women, too . . .*

———————

Ever since I first got that good-throbby feeling from watching mermaid Ariel turn into a naked human, there whatever I was . . . was. I'd
masturbated furiously to even the abysmal last season of *The L Word.*
But that doesn't prove anything, I'd think to myself. Not because I didn't
(consciously) want to like women—but because I worried I simply
wanted to want them and had tricked myself into homoerotic feelings.
*This is probably what happens when you're raised in the Bay Area—you
think there's something wrong with you if you're not queer.* But then someone would appear and—*bam!* I was suddenly blushing, trying not to
stare at breasts. It was maybe one in fifteen women this happened with,
since middle school. Often these women had a boyfriend or said they
were straight. But there was some sort of mutual recognition there, too.

———————

likely to fantasize about physical transformation—becoming another person or creature—than
cis people. Lehmiller, *Tell Me What You Want.*

* Eighty-nine percent of people in Dr. Lehmiller's study reported the fantasy of having a threesome, and 74 percent fantasized about orgies. Lehmiller, *Tell Me What You Want.*

† I certainly wasn't alone in my adventurousness as a twenty-seven-year-old woman. A 2017
study showed that women ages 25–29 were nearly twice as likely as men to have gone to a
dungeon, BDSM, or sex party—and equally likely as men to have tried a threesome or group
sex. D. Herbenick, J. Bowling, T. J. Fu, B. Dodge, L. Guerra-Reyes, and S. Sanders, "Sexual
Diversity in the United States: Results from a Nationally Representative Probability Sample of
Adult Women and Men," *PLOS ONE* 12, no. 7: e0181198. https://doi.org/10.1371/journal
.pone.0181198.

Like we could see in each other's faces something not quite totally gay, but not not-gay, either. Maybe I was projecting.

Lesbians and queer women had long been some of my closest friends.* I didn't know what this said about me, other than that I had good taste. Though I'd never fallen in (once again, yet-conscious) love with any of these friends, my periodic crushes on other women were oddly stupefying. Sometimes they lasted years. Since I was twenty-two, I'd alternated saying on dating profiles that I was bisexual, or queer, or pansexual, or heteroflexible, or even straight—I tried all the labels, but felt only one really suited me: imposter.

The first time I had the chance to perform cunnilingus, when I was twenty-two, I'd frozen. I barely understood how I wanted someone to eat my pussy. I felt certain I'd "fail." To my own great shame, I was also afraid I wouldn't like the taste. *How can I really even like women if I have that fear?* Still, I was thrilled to have touched a naked woman for the first time. It felt like getting into a warm bath, like, *Why don't I do this all the time? Just one more hour, please? It's so cozy and sexy and warm and amniotic in here . . .*

But cis women (I was not yet super conscious I was also attracted to trans and non-binary people) never seemed to pursue me the way cis men did. And I didn't know how to pursue them. Or clearly not very well, judging from the lack of responses in my inbox. It led to a sort of inertia. Plus, I'd commiserated with my friends over the years about the "bicurious" women who "used them as experiments" or left them for men "once the novelty wore off." I really didn't want that to be me. But how could I know unless I tried acting on the feelings that had always been there? I felt stuck. Now, I was doubly mortified imagining a woman's face when she found out that not only was I a "virgin," but I was also in an open relationship with a man.

---

* Out of care for these friends of mine, it feels important to note that some of them later came out as trans or non-binary and no longer identify as lesbians or queer women.

I knew a sex party might be the easiest way to gain some queer confidence/experience and reconfirm to myself that I was "legitimate" in my desires. I also knew this party was clearly what Adam wanted, even required, eventually. And so feeling I both did and didn't have a choice, I agreed to try it.

Was I going to a sex party because I felt pressured to please Adam and become the woman he wanted? Yes. Was I going to a sex party because I'd wanted to ever since I was a teenager masturbating to naked women in *Eyes Wide Shut*? Also yes. Adam was my guide into a world I'd long wanted to enter, the heteronormative/patriarchal/dominant-culture life raft to cling to when I feared drowning in my queer and slut-tastic depths. I later learned that white supremacy culture tends to value (among many other more direct forms of oppression): either/or binary thinking, perfectionism, worship of the written word, paternalism, quantity over quality, speed, objectivity/rationality, and the idea that progress = bigger/more.[*]

Adam was "paternalism, worship of the written word, perfectionism, and rationality," personified. To please him was to adhere to what was expected of me as a white, assumed-straight cis woman in my culture—and to benefit from the myriad privileges that come with falling in line. But pleasing Adam *also* meant I would secretly be subverting what was expected of me. And that rebellion reinforced my self-image as a "unique person" rebelling against oppressive patriarchal and proprietary systems.

So, let the record show: He handed me the brew, urged me to sip. And I deliberately chose to chug and fall down the rabbit hole.

---

[*] Tema Okun, "White Supremacy Culture," (dRWORKS, https://www.dismantlingracism.org/uploads/4/3/5/7/43579015/okun_-_white_sup_culture.pdf); Rachel Ricketts, *Do Better: Spiritual Activism for Fighting and Healing from White Supremacy* (New York: Atria Books, 2021).

When in Roman Orgy . . .

The Williamsburg loft was large, with a few huge rooms that had the feeling of secret attics. Many people were dressed in the circus theme for the night, steampunk corsets and top hats, sipping from red Solo cups. Everyone was responsible for bringing their own alcohol, but bottles were kept behind the bar (you were given only a couple of drink tickets in order to ensure no one could get too drunk). The lighting was flattering, but the ambiance wasn't shady or exclusive; no candelabras, no cult vibe. A lot of half-nakedness, tattoos, a majority (maybe 60–70 percent) white people in their twenties, thirties, and forties. Overall, my fellow sexual deviants were better-looking than I'd expected. People smoked joints inside freely, but not cigarettes. No phones allowed. Nothing seemed so unusual, save for one man dressed as a giant baby—diaper, very creepy Halloween infant mask that still haunts me, giant rattle and all. His mistress pulled him by the arm.

The large camping tents in the corner and the dozen white mattresses in the "playroom" upstairs were still pristine and empty. I inspected a bed that hadn't been laid on yet. It looked clean, but I was as nervous about the idea of sharing a bed with a stranger as I was potentially sleeping with them. It was so *unhygienic,* not knowing who you were jumping into bed with, or even who had been on that bed before you. I was only mildly reassured by the baskets of condoms in every corner.* I was more phobic about the plagues that couldn't be entirely prevented by prophylactics—bed bugs, lice, genital warts, and HSV 2.

A little cherub of a millennial walked up to us, merrily introduced himself.

"Hi! I'm Rob!" His pants were sagging and belted so that his front was covered but his entire bare-naked bubble butt was hanging out. "Are you guys new?"

"I've never been here before, but he has," I answered.

"Ah, I knew I would have remembered *you*. Well, you should know me and my girlfriend then. We are sort of *unofficial ambassadors* here. We've been coming to Chemistry for years."

"That's cool. Have you guys always been non-monogamous?" It was refreshing to be able to ask this so quickly. Was I one of them yet, or was non-monogamy more verb than relationship status?

"Yeah. I was like, 'I love you, but I still like to fuck other people.' And she was like, 'Oh my god, me too!' And we've been coming here and happy ever since. We play with couples and date outside of parties too, if you guys are interested . . ." He looked me up and down. "You're very sexy."

"Ha, thanks," I said in a polite deflection, as if he were offering to buy me a drink instead of fuck me in a pile. I was already "doing my job" of being coveted by other men in front of Adam, and for that, I was relieved. Rob scampered away, perky pale rear bouncing like the Coppertone girl.

A live jazz band started playing, and we could have been at any artsy

---

*   Not unlike in more normative hookups, I'd learn it's standard that most people at sex parties forgo protection for oral sex. But they tend to be more religious about using condoms for penetration (and soliciting consent). One study also found that people cheating on their partners used condoms at a rate 27–35 percent lower than those in open relationships. Terri D. Conley, Amy C. Moors, Ali Ziegler, and Constantina Karathanasis, "Unfaithful Individuals Are Less Likely to Practice Safer Sex Than Openly Nonmonogamous Individuals," *Journal of Sexual Medicine* 9, no. 6 (2012): 1559–65. https://doi.org/10.1111/j.1743-6109.2012.02712.

Brooklyn loft party, except that in certain corners, many people were beginning to fuck. Adam was right—it wasn't that erotic, but it was interesting. We stared, and it was allowed. Encouraged, even. The women moaned loudly, and watching the way the men were fucking them (rabbit-like, unskillful to my eyes), I resented their overdone performance. Mostly because I probably identified with it. *Oh God, is that how we look, too?* Either way, it was abundantly clear—humans are definitely apes.*

Finally, I saw something appealing: a blindfolded woman on a massage table being rubbed by at least six pairs of hands. Men and women fondled her breasts, massaged her thighs, teased the borders of her pussy. I wanted to be her in that moment—sprawled, pinned, and wriggling under all those coveting fingers. To my immense relief, that Adam was looking too didn't bother me. *So we can do this together. I could even fuck someone else tonight, if that's what I want to do. I'm free, but I'm not alone.*

I kept coming back to a memory from before I met Adam. Decidedly solo and undoubtedly stoned at the small live music club Barbès, I'd watched a couple dance. The wife was graceful in a way only tall women over fifty can be, and a man in the crowd, decades younger, was riveted. She broke away from her husband and bestowed herself upon the younger man, seducing him effortlessly with her hands and hips as her husband watched. As she danced, her eyes briefly caught her husband's in silent, secret laughter. I couldn't look away. It was clear that nothing, no one, could touch their love—no matter who touched their

---

*   Chimpanzees and bonobos are humans' two closest genetic relatives. Chimps get more of the attention (they are also the more violent and patriarchal species). But bonobos are just as genetically close to us, some argue more. Bonobos are matriarchal, bisexual, diffuse conflict with sex, kiss and cuddle and dry hump, and female bonobos enjoy sex at all points of their cycle, fertile or not. For more on this fascinating species—and why study of them has been in many ways systemically tamped down—I highly recommend anthropologist Dr. Amy Parish's interview on the podcast *True Sex & Wild Love.* And if you would like to support the conservation of this endangered animal, give to Bonobo Conservation Initiative, https://donate.bonobo.org/.

bodies. Their fidelity felt bound not by society's rules but by the weight of their own mutual investment. Their love knew wide-open space, so many memories and experiences that no one could ever be their undoing.

So that's what I want, I remember thinking. *Something so untouchable everyone wants to touch it, and anyone and no one can.*

Adam went to the bathroom, and within twenty seconds, a tall, handsome man swooped in Edward Cullen–like and introduced himself. I hoped he didn't leave before Adam could see proof I was instant prey. It felt very important he know this. (This didn't usually happen to me in the spaces we moved in.)

"Hi," the man said, looking down at me. "You look very beautiful tonight."

"Thanks. Are you here with someone?" I asked reflexively, though I knew men were not allowed to attend alone.

"Yeah, but she's playing with someone else right now. We're just friends, though." This was an odd brand of small talk, to be sure. Adam returned, extending his hand in a way I found pleasurably dominant, if a little less possessive than I might have preferred. The tall man turned to me.

"So, do you want to go to the playroom?" *Well, that was quick.*

"Um . . ." I looked over at Adam—for permission or instruction, I wasn't sure.

"Whatever you want," Adam said. As he would always say. But I felt both the men's energies silently building behind their eyes, rooting for me to say yes. *What the hell,* I thought. *We can just make out, and he is cute. When in Roman orgy . . .*

We went up to the playroom, where about half the beds were now occupied with other couples having sex in dimmer light. The tall man sat on a chair in the corner and I stood over him, nearly the same height now. He kissed me and as we made out I straddled his lap in excitement and reflex. He grabbed my ass, picked me up easily to carry me toward the nearest bed. Everything was happening so quickly. But it was exciting knowing my boyfriend, not to mention a whole group of strangers, was watching. I looked up at Adam. He nodded seriously, intently.

Not wanting him out of arm's reach, I motioned him over to the bed, too. Adam kissed me and smoothed back my hair, stroking my breasts as the tall man worked the rest of me. The sensations were wonderfully saturated. And just like that, after the mandatory 2.5 minutes of passable cunnilingus and soliciting my verbal consent, the handsome stranger got a condom. I'd never fucked someone so casually, knowing so little about them, barely remembering his name. He came on top of me in under 90 seconds and promptly left, embarrassed. But Adam now looked possessed. He pinned me and felt purely primal, a male animal coming to take his dinner. He growled and grunted, looked into my eyes like I was a miracle he had to gain sense of. I could feel a crowd of voyeurs enjoying us, and I liked it. I felt nasty and treasured at once—gourmet sloppy seconds.

I realized that, if I wanted to, I could still sleep with someone else that night. I'd never had sex with two people in one night, hadn't even hooked up casually more than a couple of times. But instead of feeling dirty or "like a slut," I now felt how I imagined men are encouraged to: as if, by simply allowing a stranger's latexed genitals to rub up against mine, I'd accomplished something of value. Something that enhanced rather than potentially degraded my mystique and lovability. This possibility turned me on. As did the growing fantasy that the men watching us would further encroach and each take their turn with me.*

Later that night, I was getting naked again with a different man. It

---

* In Dr. Lehmiller's study, he found that 69 percent of the men and 54 percent of the women had at some point had a gang-bang fantasy. One could say the gang bang is also an extension of what's called a "consensual non-consent" fantasy, which two-thirds of women reported as well. (More than half of the men reported imagining being forced to have sex, too.) Being consensually "forced" to have sex in a way that does not actually violate your consent can be a way to feel you have "no choice" in the matter and relax. Add in multiple people, and you might imagine being extra powerless and extra desired. Lehmiller, *Tell Me What You Want.*

felt so right to be able to experience kissing someone new without having to give up the man I still loved kissing. I understood now that experiences with other people didn't have to take anything away from Adam. If anything, they made me want to keep him more. Adam spooned me and rubbed my ass as the new stranger and I made out. I was in a man sandwich just like that scene in *Y Tu Mamá También*, only preferable because I didn't secretly have terminal cancer. Soon, yet another new man came over and asked if he could also play. *Sure*, I said, in a tactile haze of attention. *Disease, schmizease. I'm so brave, overcoming my fears!*

With my consent, the first man wrapped himself up for delivery. His weight was heavier than Adam's, new big arms and different tattoos holding me firmly in place. He thrust his tongue just right in my ear as he stretched me. I wasn't sure what Adam and the other guy were doing to me, but it felt like drugs. Here, finally, was the proper amount of hands and mouths required to have almost every fleshy part of me grabbed and sucked at simultaneously. *If three men feel this good, what about six men and women, all taking turns with me? Maybe then, I'd really be able to forget myself. More. More. More.*

Suddenly, all the lights came on. They were fluorescent and jarring, an alarm waking you from a wet dream.

"It's 3 a.m., everybody out!" The party had a strict turning-into-a-pumpkin policy. (So long as they stick to zoning laws and don't sell alcohol without a license, there's nothing actually illegal about an organized sex party.)

"I'm Carlos, by the way," the man I'd just had inside me said. "I hope we see you guys again." I saw him rejoin his fiancée and noted that she was just my type—voluptuous, barefaced, seemingly at total ease in her queerness and self as she kissed another woman goodbye. My type was a woman unlike me. *Maybe next time I'll get to touch her. And another woman, too. I was just warming up, so of course it was still easier to just let men come to me. But I'm definitely coming back.*

"Get ready. *You're going to get it,*" Adam growled with approving menace in my ear. I felt like I'd stepped through the dirty looking glass. I could now see the world as I imagined a man might: brimming with the potential for anonymous sex in every moment.

Once we got home, I could barely rinse off in the shower before Adam threw me back on the bed. He thrusted with a force that almost scared me, coming inside me with a moan that sounded like a real live beast. Within minutes, this thirty-eight-year-old man was somehow ready to go again. And again.

In the days to come, I reveled in the romance of Adam's reclaiming. He seemed high, like the intensity of falling in love had been consolidated and snorted from my pussy. He couldn't get enough of me—and he couldn't stop telling me, either.

"Maybe we should get married, huh? *Huh?* I want to get you pregnant. I want to put a baby in you. Mine. You're mine. My woman. *My girl!*" He'd said these things before, but never so effusively, like it was an emergency. He held me by my back and neck, moving me down onto his firmness with each declaration.

Adam later explained the reasons he entered this trancelike state: the good-painful fear that I might like another cock more. That I'd made sounds of pleasure with the other man he'd never elicited in me. That I had an insatiable desire for sperm competition. That I'd been proven a prize he'd have to continually work to win. That he felt powerful knowing his jealousy could be controlled and channeled into a hyperarousal that benefited us both. That afterward he felt like he was falling in love with me all over again, filled with an animal drive to impregnate me and "lock me down." That with this heightened vulnerability he experienced an unusual lack of control, a sense of feeling "torn open, ravaged, and raw."

What a Slut

After we went to one more sex party, I told Adam I'd prefer to have more foreplay woven into the experience. To get to go on dates, dress up, flirt. I still didn't want to sleep with anyone else alone, so we set up an anonymous profile for threesomes together. Because I wasn't ready to see Adam have sex with another woman, I said I was open to MFMs, and threesomes where another woman would only touch me (a scenario I unsurprisingly had no takers for). In explicitly seeking out de facto MFMs online, I felt open to men I'd usually written off as incompatible in the long term for being "too conventionally good-looking," "too buttoned up," or "not boyfriend material" (read: more likely to reject me/identify as fiscal conservatives/cheat). Pursuing MFMs seemed to make more men "open" to me as well.

When I met John Smith (his pseudonym of choice, and it suits him), he was more stereotypically good-looking WASP than I'd normally go for, wearing a button-down shirt to match his impressive finance job. Maybe it was the fact that his profile promised dominance and surreal abs, or that I was editing roughly eight "features" about the new *Fifty Shades of Grey* movie all day, but either way, I was feeling it. Sipping overpriced cocktails he would definitely be paying for, John Smith told me he'd been in monogamous relationships before. But at thirty-four, he wasn't sure they were in his DNA. He could form at-tachments, but he couldn't imagine having sex with just one person for the rest of his life, and admitting this proved an issue. Whenever he'd try to bring up the idea of being able to have outside experiences with a girlfriend, he said they'd "flip out" and want to break up with him. For a while, he'd try to do it their way, but eventually, he'd either cheat or leave.* He seemed resigned to being alone, an L.L.Bean model con-demned to wander the pages of his catalog single forever.

Sitting there with John Smith, I could feel the immense privilege-that-shouldn't-be-a-privilege to be able to make a different choice. But I knew so many can't. It's not just a matter of fearing society's judg-ment; so many people live in situations where being non-monogamous or otherwise outside sexual and gender norms risks their safety, job, children, or even life. "I think the term 'ethical non-monogamy' is ar-rogant and inaccurate. You're either *disclosing* your non-monogamy, or *you're not disclosing* it," Dr. Wednesday Martin, author of *Untrue*, later cautioned me. "Plenty of women 'cheat' as a strategy to get sexual sat-isfaction, while having a primary partner who might kill them for being non-monogamous. People with the incredible privilege of being able to

---

* Roughly 21.9 percent of people in America have engaged in consensual non-monogamy at some point in their lives—but cheating is also as prevalent as ever. In 2013, women married to men were roughly 40 percent more likely to report cheating on their husbands than in 1990, and an estimated 20–37.5 percent of people will cheat in their lifetimes (and that's based on numbers of people who admit to it).

Siddiquee later put it to me this way: "Within the dominant white Christian culture of the United States we're actually expected to go through a period of life when we're non-monogamous, it's just the expectation that dating around will end and you'll choose one per-son. But then half of the people who do settle down get divorced, sometimes due to cheating or wanting to date other people. So the marginalization of non-monogamy here is perhaps more a reflection of the discomfort we feel with our own inability to maintain a lifestyle of monogamy that is so stringent—or rather an expression of an oppressive system maintaining its hold." M. L. Haupert, A. N. Gesselman, A. C. Moors, H. E. Fisher, and J. R. Garcia, "Preva-lence of Experiences with Consensual Nonmonogamous Relationships: Findings from Two National Samples of Single Americans," *Journal of Sex and Marital Therapy* 43, no. 5 (2017): 424–40; General Social Survey.

be non-monogamous without threat to their physical safety need to wake up and stop acting like they have the moral upper hand. They're just luckier."

And here I was, the luckiest of the lucky. I knew Adam was currently hoping I was having a good time. That he'd want me immediately after this date. In this new paradigm, admitting my desire to stray was accepted as not only perfectly natural, but preferred. I'd never felt this before—cherished, kept—yet encouraged to be as adventurous as I pleased. *Everyone should be able to experience this kind of freedom without shame, if that's what they want,* I remember thinking. I was also beginning to realize there's nothing so weird about being a woman who has trouble with long-term monogamy, either. After all, despite the stereotype that men are more likely to cheat, they might just be more likely to get caught. Studies have shown that women cheat and crave multiple partners at a rate equal to or higher than men.[*]

"Why don't you only look for people online who are non-monogamous then?" I asked John Smith, feeling perfectly tipsy now. "I think how much monogamy feels right for you is on a spectrum, like the Kinsey scale."[†] I was aware how silly it was for me to already be giving advice on the topic, but this was part of the fun—improvising my way into the future.

"I can't put that I'm non-monogamous on my profile . . . if that's even what I am," John Smith scoffed. "I don't work at that kind of place. What if someone saw me?"

"Well, your profile only had your abs on it, so . . ."

---

[*]   The 2013 General Social Survey also found that women in the United States ages 18–29 reported an even higher rate of cheating than men the same age.

[†]   Sex researcher Dr. Lisa Hamilton told me her yet-to-be-published survey found that self-reported monogamous orientation falls on a natural bell curve. The majority of people fell in the middle of the spectrum, meaning they have both tendencies, and might be flexible with how monogamous they are depending on the relationship. Certain personality traits, such as your degree of openness or extraversion, might predispose you to more consistently fall on the curve where you do. Of course, the importance of monogamous social conditioning should also not be underestimated.

He smiled. I could tell he liked being called out. I usually did well with this kind of man. "You're right. Maybe I do need to look for those women." He looked at me meaningfully over his drink, taking a sip but maintaining firm eye contact. "I mean, you're one of those women, right?"

———————

When Adam and I went over to John Smith's rooftop the next weekend, the two men got along easily, which was rather disappointing. I was hoping for more of an undercurrent of rivalry or competition, ideally being the rope in an attention tug-of-war. But with Adam, I'd learn any interaction with these other men would be mostly friendly, even fraternal—it was only once we were alone that he indulged in the competitive spirit.

In classic threesome-rookie-style, we all drank a little too much and couldn't seem to decide who would make the first move. At 2 a.m., Adam went to the bathroom, leaving us without "supervision" so that John Smith could finally kiss me. When Adam came back into the room, John Smith pulled away and looked over at him, waiting for permission to proceed. Adam nodded seriously, that burn again beginning to overtake his eyes. That these men were negotiating me wordlessly was quite welcome. Paradoxically, the more sexually liberated I was seemingly becoming, the more I wanted to feel like Adam's property. I now thought of myself as a dog off-leash. Loyal to her master, she returned because she was given the freedom to stray.

As we all migrated to the bed, I could feel the gathering pulsation of male sexual force directed straight at my body. Together, they could do terrible things to me more easily, but instead, they would join forces to pleasure me. Everything was going as I'd fantasized—John Smith eating me out against a luxurious Manhattan skyline as Adam sucked supportively at my neck. I lay back, inviting the familiar high I'd experienced at

Chemistry. In this sensory flooding, I could almost forget myself. This was the sound track I craved: the music of the present moment, so loud it might finally drown out my mind. John Smith put a condom on and got inside me in missionary. He kissed me passionately, thrusting hard while Adam exuded pure protective lust. *This is kind of romantic, actually! I am so living my best life right now.* I remember little about the actual sex, more the feeling of being desired. Well, until it happened.

"Yeah, *you little slut.* Yeah, *you slut,* you want two dicks, don't you?" John Smith purred, wilting my clit faster than you can say "enchanted rose." If a record had been there to scratch, a whomp-whomp button to be pushed—so there it was. Because I was in bed with two men, I was a slut. He continued on and on with the pornspeak from there, the details of which my memory has seemed to selectively erase.

———

John Smith had clearly watched considerable MFM porn, in which themes of group rape, humiliating wives, and calling women "whores" or "bitches in heat" are common. That isn't to say that women can't sometimes get off on those words or fantasies, or even request them. Hotwifing can be a way of playing with misogynistic taboos. After all, "the fantasy is really built on a history of heteronormative sexism," psychologist Dr. David Ley, author of *Insatiable Wives,* later told me. "That's not to pathologize it. I just think the strength of those taboos is part of what makes this fantasy so powerful and erotic."

Indeed, it seems that ever since women started being considered property, adulterous or cuckolding women were treated as if their sexual autonomy were a form of theft. Common punishments (some even endorsed by the Bible*) included being stripped and shamed before the

———

* "But if you have gone astray while married to your husband and you have made yourself impure by having sexual relations with a man other than your husband here the priest is to put the woman under this curse—'may the Lord cause you to become a curse among your people when

town, banished, stoned and flogged, burned, made to miscarry, and killed. (Adulterous or non-monogamous men, perhaps needless to say, were a given.) Sadly, these kinds of punishments are also hardly past-tense: Women around the world are frequently burned, beaten, and killed for suspected infidelity.* More than half the women in the United States who are murdered are killed by romantic partners—and at least 12 percent of these homicides are associated with jealousy.† Hotwifing and cuckolding as a fun fetish can sometimes subvert this violent patriarchy by turning a foundation of I-Own-You-Woman into a vehicle for extremely guiltless female hedonism. Or not.

———————

I was too inexperienced with kinky sex to know I had to communicate my preferences and boundaries ahead of time. I'd failed to even consider John Smith might dare do something I found icky, what with Adam there to protect me and all [*flutters eyelashes, clasps hands to cheek*]. But here Adam was now, looking as turned on and unoffended on my behalf as ever. To be fair, I was still halfheartedly moaning. I felt an internalized obligation that the show must go on. At least I could complain to myself. *If I'm anyone's slut, it's Adam's. You haven't earned the right to call me that. God, I just wish you'd just shut up,* I remember thinking as John Smith prattled on, "cumhole" this, "slut" that. There would be no recovering my orgasm now, but instead of telling him to stop or fully feeling my disappointment, I worried instead I was letting

———————

he makes your womb miscarry and your abdomen swell. . . . This, then, is the law of jealousy when a woman goes astray and makes herself impure . . . or when feelings of jealousy come over a man because he suspects his wife. . . . The husband will be innocent of any wrongdoing, but the woman will bear the consequences of her sin.'" Numbers 5:11–31.

*   Dr. David Ley, "Do Cheating Wives Really Deserve Lashes and Death?" *Psychology Today*, Jun. 3, 2010.

†   Olga Khazan, "Nearly Half of All Murdered Women Are Killed by Romantic Partners," *The Atlantic*, Jul. 20, 2017.

both these men down by not coming. It became clear to me that night: Fucking two men at once provided the possibility to lose myself twice as hard, but it also meant twice the potential worrying about their egos and my performance. Wherever I went, there too would go my societal conditioning and subsequent neuroses.

Ugh, he's lasting forever. And there's still Adam to handle at home. I don't need to get raw from this, too. Shit, I hope they aren't disappointed I can't come. What's wrong with me that even an MFM with two hot guys can't get me off? And so I reverted to the most reliable way to make it end. "I want you to come," I purred in my best porn star falsetto. Like a dutiful little soldier—they often remind me of eighteen-year-old cadets in these moments—John Smith mounted me and came in my "tight little fuckhole." *Oh well. The aftermath is what I want anyway, the reclamation.*

"You're gonna get it," Adam growled like déjà vu in my ear on the way home. He never bluffed. While his ravenousness after MFMs could sometimes feel (literally and figuratively) smothering, I would take the soreness, that's for sure. The showering of verbal validation; the verb "ravishing" made tangibly realistic; the way his dick felt like a punishing plunger removing the imaginary residue of another man. It was like handing this love addict a speedball. That Adam invited the competition only made him read to me more confident, more the dominant alpha no one could possibly beat.

Until I met Liam.

Pure, Uncut Kryptonite

Summary 2015

BROOKLYN

I found Liam shortly after John Smith. He was holding a small chain saw and looking askance, like you do when you're white* and ridiculously handsome and can get away with things that on most people would be considered creepy as fuck. So minimal was his OkCupid profile's effort that there was only one other blurry photo and a few outdated lines about being "on the road." Yes, the red flags flapped—but when I saw him holding that chain saw in the forest I had a feeling, you know? Like he'd *definitely* have a valid reason for cutting down trees. (They were already dead, he later told me, and he was building a raft for kids at a summer camp. *See!*)

He spoke humbly of himself on our first date. None of the facts of his life felt calculated to impress me, but neither did he seem uninterested or superior. He taught poetry to incarcerated people and college

---

* If you're noticing I keep mentioning everyone's race, it's likely because white writers often only name the race of people of color in their books, thereby making white people the standard default by omission and reinforcing white supremacy. In Matthew Salesses's book *Craft in the Real World,* he suggests that if you name any major character's race and/or ethnicity (as I have by making clear both Adam and I are white and Jewish) it's best practice to make clear every major character's race. So that is what I have tried to do throughout for every major character, either outright naming their race or making it clearly implied through context. Matthew Salesses, *Craft in the Real World* (New York: Catapult, 2021).

students (be still my heart!), bartended (of course), spoke fluent French (*ooh, oui!*), once had his heart broken by a successful foreign film actress (also of course), often slept on the sailboat he liked to fix using his big man hands (how much of my waist could he grab in one fist)?

It was immediately clear he was a rare mythical creature: the finest salt of the earth, oozing literate-yet-rugged masculinity. His protruding brow ridge presenting eyebrows that connected lightly, as if to underline his structure's solidity. A smile that crinkled around genuinely green eyes, like James Franco's calm cousin. A deep voice to match the intimation of his long, thick throat. A few short curls of soft brown hair atop a heavy-yet-proportional head. A slightly crooked front tooth, the kind of inconsequential imperfection that only serves to make a handsome man more endearing. (He thinks that tooth is the first thing people notice about him. He's very wrong, but therein lies another layer of his appeal.) Yes, if Adam wanted sperm competition, this man was the stuff accidental pregnancies were made of. Liam held my gaze that split second too long, a nonverbal overture as sexy as it was relieving. I blushed, and felt an intense desire compound in me. Not just this moment, but the almost fearful anticipation of what my attraction would elicit in Adam.*

After a second "date" where I watched Liam prep bar and passively swat off other women like flies, I knew I had to move quickly. I invited him over later that week and told him what I wanted: us alone first, then Adam coming home to find us, watching before joining in. It was refreshing and a little terrifying to be so direct, but I wanted to get the most romantic juice out of the experience I could. In the beginning, Adam preferred I not have another dick in me without his supervision.

---

* "No. I was not afraid of him; but of myself. I seemed reborn in his unreflective eyes, reborn in unfamiliar shapes. I hardly recognized myself from his descriptions of me and yet, and yet— might there not be a grain of beastly truth in them? And, in the red firelight, I blushed again, unnoticed, to think he might have chosen me because, in my innocence, he sensed a rare talent for corruption." —Angela Carter, *The Bloody Chamber* (London: Vintage, 1979).

Having him play voyeur, then, was mostly just a way to orchestrate experiencing Liam alone.

———

I put on the white slip I'd owned since senior prom and took a hit off my pipe to calm myself. It didn't work, but it was a good nervous, the sort of unease I was grateful Adam still let me have. Picking out what you're going to wear, the excited anticipation of checking even for toe hairs. Knowing someone wants you back, but not for sure how much. Feeling your heartbeat in your ears when the doorbell rings. *What am I doing? Am I really going to answer the door in a slip? I guess I am a slut.* Everything about premeditated casual sex/non-monogamy (and they were one and the same new experience for me at this point) felt like playing high-stakes dress-up.

And then there he was at our door, in a faded vintage T-shirt Adam would never wear, effortlessly stretched by the kind of shoulders you get from swimming or building things. I wanted to grab on to them like his little monkey, wrap my legs around his waist, and feel his big arms bounce me however he wanted. He complimented my "dress" sincerely and I immediately felt utterly ridiculous, like a nerd the hottest guy in school had been paired with in science class. We sat on the couch and I began to high-ramble.

"I've been thinking about the judgments I used to have about people. I mean, I thought sex parties were cool, but I never really thought I'd be 'the kind of person' who regularly went to them and had sex with strangers. But I guess I am?" I needed him to know: I may have answered the door in a slip, but it was *white* and not sheer. I was more of a Madonna-whore combo special, then, a literary lady in the streets and a freak in selective sheets. "And I didn't think I'd be the kind of person who sets up an anonymous profile for MFM threesomes, but I guess I am, too . . ."

He put his hand on my thigh reassuringly. I got the sense he was used to women trying to justify their erratic behavior around him. "Is this okay?" That he asked if it was okay to touch me, even if it was after he did it, was (in this pre-#MeToo-and-still-in-my-twenties era) deeply moving to me. I nodded appreciatively, like he was some sort of hot Mother Teresa.

"You know, I've never kissed a guy first?" I said, newly emboldened. "I mean, I've made it clear I'm ready to be kissed. But I never just went for it first."

"Oh yeah?" When he smiled, the crinkles drew his face up like the curtain before a symphony. "Well, maybe you should."

Yes, he could kiss, and we could kiss each other. To me it felt like more chemistry than a lab—to him, maybe just another day at the hot guy office. And now he was popping my tits out of my bra one by one, sucking on my nipples while my breasts were still half-bound, leaving them offered toward him as he kissed my entire torso on his knees. *His goddamn knees!* He was just a perfect man, taking his time savoring me. (*Me, of all the women!*) Slowly, he made his way to my pussy, asked me if he could take my underwear off. (*So thoughtful to ask!*) It was much farther than I'd intended to go before Adam got home, but it was technically "allowed." I was committed to not crossing Adam's boundaries, but liked the idea of pushing them very much.

I'd always told myself that men who looked like Liam were probably unskilled or selfish in bed anyway. As he began to lick me, I saw I'd only been telling myself that to preemptively avoid rejection. *This is really happening. Oh my god, he is so damn*— I soon took his pants off, suppressing an actual gasp. His dick was . . . well, of course it was like that. The most beautiful I'd ever seen. Straight and perfectly smooth as his deep voice, a present within a present. As thick and long and tan as his neck had foreshadowed. Pure, uncut kryptonite.

We were hungrily 69ing in bed when Adam came in the door. As

I'd requested, he pulled up a chair and watched. I wanted to stay eating each other that way until Liam acquiesced to falling in love, but having Adam there felt like romantic cockblocking. I looked at my boyfriend for permission to have sex as he defined it, though (to my horror) I still didn't particularly want him to join us. Adam nodded, eyes familiarly overtaken.

As Liam slid on top of me, I now understood how some women might come in missionary. The virtue of a big dick and a handsome face is unearned but palpable. Opening to his thrusting weight inside me felt emotionally reckless. Eventually, I got on top and looked down at his fern eyes, silent and almost solemn. Liam didn't make a sound during sex, making it all the easier to project whatever you want onto him. He barely had to work for my orgasm, such was his inheritance. It was the first time since I started dating Adam that I came with another man. The only time I'd wanted someone else just as badly, if not more. As I collapsed forward onto Liam's broad chest, a hormonal wave of attachment rushed over me. *But I want to keep him! I want to feel him without a condom someday, too.*

Sensing this, Adam came over and began to fuck me fiercely, almost painfully, putting me on my stomach, getting as deep as possible. My head turned toward Liam's face, and I held on to his disconcertingly thicker bicep. Liam kissed me softly, almost with sympathy, as Adam thrusted. *Save me, Liam,* I thought. *Please, save me from him.* The words kept echoing in my head, and I realized that this must be part of the fantasy I was having. Not just that these two men would fight over me, but that Adam was dangerous and I was his captive and Liam had come to rescue me. I wanted to be able to live out all the potential lives—the one where I ended up with the protective beast who liked to loan out his girl *and* the one where Liam would pitch a tent for me under the stars and implant me with his genetically perfect offspring. That you can't live out infinite interesting paths simultaneously is what made me begin to cry silently.* But I wasn't unhappy—no, this was exactly the kind of intensity I chased. The more I sensed life's inescapable brevity, the more alive I felt.

After Adam was done, Liam got up to pee and offered some flimsy excuse for "leaving us to it." As the aluminum door slammed shut, I wanted to sob. *What a fucking weirdo idiot I am for crying, even if (hopefully?) prettily. What if I never see him again?* I let Adam, hard already again, begin to reclaim me. I shut my eyes, and thought of the man with no interest in rescuing me.

In the ensuing days and weeks, I couldn't stop thinking about Liam. Suddenly, my Big Strong Man felt diminished, some illusion that no one would feel as attuned to my body, broken. *What have I done?* I'd get on top, and Adam would see me close my eyes.

"Tell me," he'd command. "It's okay. You can tell me." But it felt cruel to tell the truth. How could my love for Adam—the most profound I thought I'd experienced, if only six months old still—prove so fragile? For the only time I'd witness, Adam lost his stiffness, came sooner than he meant to. Clearly, my new infatuation had shaken him—how could it not? I let him fuck me as hard as possible, hoping it would reset things to their natural order. It wasn't working.

Later that week, in his first display of insecure jealousy, he looked up Liam's poetry online. "Have you *read* his writing?" Adam laughed bitterly. "I'll tell you one thing, you're crazy if you think he can write better than me." His throat caught and his eyes welled before he quickly swallowed his feelings back down. Seeing him this way, I felt guilty and repulsed at once.

Meanwhile, Liam only wanted to see me again on my own. I'd later find out that something about Adam and our "almost violent sex" made him uncomfortable. I asked Adam what he thought I should do,

---

* "Monogamy is a way of getting the versions of ourselves down to a minimum. And, of course, a way of convincing ourselves that some versions are truer than others—that some are special." Adam Phillips, *Monogamy* (New York: Vintage Books, 1996).

but he always had the same response to that question: "Do whatever you want." Only this time, he added bitterly, "I'll have to clean up the mess when the confused dude disappoints you, but I will." He might have been telling me to go with my desire, but his tone and newfound erectile issues made it clear what his actual preference was.

I knew logically that Liam would be a disaster as a boyfriend, and more humiliatingly, that he would probably never consider me that way. But I still didn't trust myself not to "self-sabotage" or "get con-fused" if I slept with him alone. I very reluctantly decided not to see Liam again. My body went into mourning, a withdrawal that never fully left.

Yes, I was tempted. Very tempted. But it has to mean something that I didn't risk ruining my relationship by being alone with the hottest guy ever. That I still sort of knew all along who would actually be best for me. Real-izing I'd "chosen" Adam after all, his unspoken yet near-total domina-tion of me began to return with credibility. With enough reclaiming he regained his confidence and seemingly perfect control over his body, actions, and mind. And increasingly, over mine as well.

PART 2

Age 28

Open on Both Sides

"That was the year, my twenty-eighth, when I was discovering that not all of the promises would be kept, that some things are in fact irrevocable and that it had counted after all, every evasion and every procrastination, every mistake, every word, all of it."
—Joan Didion, "Goodbye to All That"

April 2016

BROOKLYN

A little over a year into our relationship, we got scabies. Though Adam said you can also get these invisible critters from hotel beds, I was relatively confident our forays into sex parties were to blame, and felt biblically punished for my Jezebel ways. (John Smith and Liam both said they were clear and were now almost nine months in the past, so it was likely the only other non-monogamous experiences we'd had since—three or so sex parties.) Considering I'd had a relatively severe phobia of head lice and bedbugs for much of my twenties, the idea that *literal bugs were hatching under my skin* was certainly upsetting.

Adam pulled us through both practically and emotionally. Within a few weeks, we were in the clear. He'd promised to protect me, and he had. "Let your man handle that shit," he'd often joke. But it wasn't a joke—it was what he did. He thoroughly, quickly, reliably handled shit. *If we can confront my phobia and get through it, what else do I have to be afraid of?* Perhaps life was trying to send me another sign: This intimacy, this protection, you can trust.

The smell of Adam's peanut noodle stir-frys dancing in the air to jazz had become home. I now felt I could barely remember what adulting B.A. was even like. We split all our expenses, sure, but he was the one who handled the bills, cooking, and nearly everything else I found tedious. "What would you even do without your man to take care of you, huh?" he'd ask. It was a joke that was also our still-uncontracted power dynamic. "What would you even *eat?*" He'd laugh, drawing me into his chest by the back of my rib cage. *Popcorn and cereal and salad and Arctic Zero in a binge/exercise-purge cycle, mostly.* But I didn't get the urge to punish myself that way anymore. I was vegan now—and for the time being, that major paradigm shift (along with Adam's excellent cooking) appeared to have cured my disordered habits.

———————

Adam and I had watched the documentary *Earthlings* the summer before. I felt compelled by its central argument: Thinking a certain group is "just different" and designed for our exploitation is the same logic that sexism and racism runs on. Eating animals and their secretions is how most of us first learn to rationalize that another body or life can have less value, or is somehow "made" for our use. Dismantle this premise—that any life on earth doesn't deserve full freedom—and what other systems of human oppression might also crumble?

Little by little, as I started sharing with people that I was in an open relationship, I noticed that the reaction was frequently the same as finding out I was vegan: "Oh, I've wanted to try that, too . . . but I'm too weak." But it was only about my veganism that some New Yorkers were immediately defensive or antagonistic.* When it came to finding out about my open relationship, most people seemed to feel relieved, as if they could now be honest with me about their inner lives. Usually, when straight cis men learned I was non-monogamous, they smiled at me knowingly, appraisingly, and acted more interested (occasionally also confessing they were secretly bi or kinky). When straight cis women found out, they often began to admit all their secret longings in hushed tones, the ways they felt bored, trapped, and listless; the things they were afraid to tell their male partners (and were almost always newly flirtatious). When queer and/or trans people found out, they usually said something along the lines of "Oh honey, good for you," or, "Yeah, me too" (and seemed to find me less basic).

I began hanging out at our neighborhood Rasta restaurant, Ital Kitchen, almost every weekend. I'd started up a friendly flirtation with the waiter, Mohammed,† a tall, Black, very sweet stoner. I liked his big hugs, the way he made me laugh, his obvious admiration and kindness, his French-African accent. A few months in, we kissed by a fire he'd made. We started consistently making out in the restaurant's backyard on my way home from work. It quickly started to feel unfair that Adam was at home in a monogamous cage of my making, an unnatural cuckold. Sure, he liked the idea of my having solo experiences, but this was

---

* "One survey found that vegans are viewed more negatively than atheists and immigrants, and are only slightly more tolerated than drug addicts. . . . Many omnivores understand the toll that meat wreaks on the planet, and we can't help but feel the tension between loving animals in the abstract while eating them with abandon on the plate. All of this creates feelings of defensiveness, so when a vegan comes along, their very presence seems like an affront." Farhad Manjoo, "Stop Mocking Vegans," *New York Times,* Aug. 28, 2019.

† I let most people in the book choose their own pseudonyms. This was Mohammed's choice, and he likes Mo for short. Not trying to make any religious references in this case.

something new. It wasn't serious, but this was almost like I was *dating on my own.* (Mo wasn't into the idea of an MFM threesome.)

Each time I returned to Adam of my own volition—doubly horny, grateful, and filled with surety that he was the right primary partner for me—I saw how, ironically, allowing him the same privileges was more likely to ensure his continued devotion. Being open also seemed like the more generous way to be. It felt like an ultimate act of love, to sacrifice your ego in the interest of a partner's bodily autonomy. And I wanted to give that loving generosity back. That even the idea of Adam being on a date with someone else made me nauseous also made me curious.

One night, as I watched Adam cooking dinner, I watched an old myth solidify: *True love isn't supposed to be easy. It requires real transformation, right? It's time to do my part.* I came up behind him and smelled his neck. "Yeah? You love me again, huh?" he asked playfully. It was one of his phrases. He seemed to sense when I'd even been contemplating our future compatibility. I often felt he was telepathic.

"I never stopped loving you," I answered as always.

"Uh-huh." He oozed security and stirred.

I took a deep breath. "Okay, let's do it."

"Do what?"

"Let's be open on both sides," I said. "I'm ready to try. I want to give this to you. For us."

I could feel him smile toward the pan. I'd done good. "You'll see, you have nothing to be worried about," he said, turning around to kiss me. "You know you're my only girl, right?"

"I do." I was the ticking antique clock he patiently took apart and reassembled every night, polished and placed upon his highest shelf. He did this not because he had to, but because he was fascinated to see how the many tiny gears inside worked. To understand all of it.

He smiled, giving me an approving spank. "Now let me finish making our dinner." *Yes, Daddy,* I thought, but didn't dare say aloud.

... And Here's What Happened

May 2016

MANHATTAN

I decided to come out as being in a non-monogamous relationship in my writing. Though my closeting had been brief, I felt a palpable relief. Much of my life was immediately synthesized and published then. It was incentivized for me to be that way. There was a formula that performed well on the site where I was a writer and editor, and I was good at writing this rapid-fire, highly personal immersion journalism: "I Tried [XXX] Experience/Experiment & Here's What Happened."

Every piece of first-person writing had to be accompanied by at least three photos of yourself (it increased reader engagement time, which affected Google's algorithm). It was a rule I hated, then quickly became seduced by. The number of eyeballs on anything I published was immediately visible and ranked on a site called Chartbeat. Sometimes, I could see that thousands of people were at that very moment reading something I'd written or edited. This was a recipe for some truly egoic delusions to form. I was the half-naked woman in the photos reviewing period underwear, and I was not. I was the woman telling the internet about her mental health and drug habits, and I was not.* I drove enough traffic that I was rewarded with a second writing

* Katherine Angel writes that one could argue "honing a persona—one who is 'me and not-me'—[is] the necessary condition for writing good first-person material, for being able to make a story out of a mere situation.... [But] the more accurate formulation, for me, is that writing

day. I had to churn out three to four roughly 1,200-word articles in those eighteen hours (compared to the eight I was expected to edit in one editing day). I was up to the challenge. I'd been training to be a tempting and ultimately disposable commodity since puberty.

Working in digital media was a nearly perfect exaggeration of the same system I'd already been conditioned to feel rushed within. Those of us who are socialized as women are set up to believe from a young age that our clock is ticking faster. To feel we must work to secure our future before our market power expires. We're cast as anxious Cinderellas; exactly when our chariots will turn into pumpkins is unknown but it's certain to happen. So whether I was being desired by a group of men at a sex party—or literally having each click on my face and frequently half-naked body tallied in real time—it felt good because I was "achieving" exactly what was expected of me, and experiencing a (often misguided) sense of power by working within, and sometimes subverting, those oppressive systems.

I was both proud of and mystified by what I'd helped create: a website that for several years had significantly more pageviews than NYTimes.com. I was the one who'd convinced our founding team that the site had to be explicitly feminist . . . using the argument that Beyoncé had proven feminism could be both popular and profitable (*oy to the motherfucking vey*).

Many of the articles I wrote and edited I still feel good about. The majority, however, I wish I owned the rights to take down, and feel a deep regret over hurriedly spewing ignorant mistakes in permanent ink. But that is a sort of gift, too: I'm already embarrassed by a large swath of my digital footprint; I have less to lose. I know I will, in retrospect, continue to prove myself naïve or worse in my attempts to tell

---

is how I experience my experience. Until writing, in mere living, everything is out of focus; in mere living, I comply with demands." Katherine Angel, *Daddy Issues* (London: Peninsula Press, 2019).

the truth of where I'm at. I try much harder to mitigate against this now than I did then, by seeking out many other perspectives and early readers, by slowing down. But missteps are inevitable anyway. Living life on the record means learning from them publicly, hopefully in a way that's ultimately more beneficial than harmful.

I began saving some of my most interesting ideas and experiences instead of immediately publishing them. I started documenting as much of my non-monogamous journey as I could (soon quite literally) stomach. Perhaps one day I'd write some sort of book about . . . *whatever the fuck is happening to me in this relationship*. I created these ground rules for myself: I wouldn't do anything (or anyone) simply for the sake of potentially writing about it. I resented those kinds of stories anyway, the ones where journalists scribbled judgmental notes from the corner of a sex party and then maybe made out with someone so they could conclude it was not for them. I made the very same sexist knee-jerk judgments, in many ways, that some people make of me—that an adventurous woman writing about her sex life is probably bragging and only doing it for the material/attention.*

But for me, the fermenting idea of a future book was more an attempt to process my already rapidly piling experiences. My hedonistic, exhibitionist, and novelty-seeking tendencies had combined forces with Adam's strong desire for me to be polyamorous. I was already incentivized to go all in. But the belief/coping mechanism that my life

---

* Olivia Sudjic points out that as a female writer, "Either you won't be believed or people will assume they know your life story. Either you're a narcissist or you don't know what you're talking about. Either you expose your myriad, contradictory, imperfect selves, or you conceal and dissemble and appear inauthentic or unrelatable and then someone exposes it for you." Olivia Sudjic, *Exposure* (London: Peninsula Press, 2018).

could be viewed as an artistic anthropological record allowed me to sometimes dissociate and push myself even further. To approach the limits I was determined to reach for myself and Adam. To also imagine working and processing in a less rushed way. If I was going to potentially write about people living on the margins of mainstream sexual culture, I wanted to genuinely be on those margins myself. To approach it otherwise felt unethical and boring. So I had to take my time with this story, aka my life, until I knew where it led. But maybe not so much time that I'd be going slower than the pace Adam seemed to expect. The motivations fed one another symbiotically.

And so it was in this context that Adam and I recorded a podcast on our newly mutual open relationship. In the audio (which I've since taken down in order to protect his identity) you can hear Adam's professorial tone, and my hedging, clarifying that I don't know how things will go when it comes to jealousy.

That night, to celebrate, we went to Ital Kitchen to eat and hang out with Mo. Sandwiched between these two men, I was more than content: *I'm alive. Dare I say it, modern? Yes, but also somehow ancient. Like a biblical rewrite where things are even.* It felt so communal, more natural than pretending the entirety of my body or attraction could or should belong to one man. The fun tension of feeling both their pull, and having to hide none of it. I wondered how many people it would take to satiate me. What if my desire was only bound by time and space, like finding a toy that let you come and come until you either got too sore or passed out or needed a snack?

And that's when Life flashed her wise smile. *Okay, my dear. You want to be all publicly progressive and enlightened? Cool, but let's keep you humble. Here you go!*

A petite white woman with short blond hair, a beautiful face, and a great ass sauntered in the door and turned all our heads, literally stopping the table's conversation midsentence. A group of regulars, we'd never seen her before. I don't remember having felt that another woman must be ovulating. But I thought it now as I watched her outlined cat eyes scanning for prey. The way she in no way deferred to who I might be as she asked if she could sit with us and plopped herself down next to the most handsome and confident man in the room. This *stranger* was flirting with *my man* with the drive of a competitive athlete. I recognized her behavior from similarly raw moments in my own life: This woman needed some male validation, *stat*. But it was more than that. She was on a mission to prove to herself that she was free. I later found out she had just left her husband.

I want to cut this motherfucking cunt. That the phrase entered my mind instantly shocked me, since I'd honestly rarely even *thought* the c-word before. I felt suddenly brimming with insults I'd seen on TV, phrases and sentiments that didn't quite feel like my own, yet seemed embedded. I watched them angled toward each other intently, a bad waking dream. I'd enjoyed seeing Adam flirt before, but knowing he could *act* on it now seemed to change my entire response. I retreated to the corner to breathe deeply by the backyard fire.

That's right, Life cooed back to me from the flames. Not smug, but amused. *You can dish it out, but can you take it?*

"—Ugh, I can't believe he's acting like this in front of you!" Mo interrupted my low-grade burning-bush hallucination, coming over to offer me more of his spliff. Mo's distaste for Adam would soon become well-established and venomous. I was suddenly grateful for his protectiveness, even found myself wishing he would fight Adam right about now. If only for the diversion.

"No, it's okay," I muttered. "We just opened up the relationship on his side, too. I just didn't think . . . so soon . . . but he's allowed to. I'm okay. I'll be okay." I felt I might vomit up my Ital coconut curry, actually, were marijuana not keeping it at bay.

Adam might have come over to check on me at some point, I'm not sure. Mostly I just remember feeling abandoned by his abrupt absorption with this more novel and lovely interview subject for hours, this new *slut* named *Simone* (*pretentious bitch name!*). I tried to breathe deeply and remind myself I had chosen to ride this ride. I stayed that way, gripping the edge of the bench, trying to appear normal, until Adam got her number and we could go home.

Why So Pathetic

"During the road of trials a woman transcends the limits of her conditioning. It is a particularly harrowing time, an adventure fraught with fears, tears, and trauma. As a child and adolescent she is shaped to fit a role determined by expectations of parents, teachers, and friends. To move beyond them she must flee the captors of her conditioning. . . . It is a perilous journey."
—MAUREEN MURDOCK, *THE HEROINE'S JOURNEY*

Summer 2016

HELL

A complex brew of pungent emotions the English language lumps together as "jealousy" arose with a vengeance that suggested it had been fermenting all my life.

5/28/16

Journal Entry

> Sex want anal why so pathetic . . .
> Already plotting escapes walk and cry cry cry
> 'You should be rooting for me' he says
> i feel like a hypocrite
> . . . List of reasons he's fucked up:
> . . . I submit myself too much
> I wear things just to please him

... He's going to want to date other people
And i'm not even old and ugly yet
And i'll have to watch
I hate him
List of reasons he's not fucked up:
He's loyal (in his way)
He loves me (i think).
He's smart (but not as smart as he thinks)
He's honest (sometimes too honest)
He wants to make a good life (so long as he can
control it)

I'd never had anal sex before, but I felt a sudden urge to push my physical limits in a way that hurt. A desire to be "degraded," or at least further topped. I wanted sex to match what I was feeling: at Adam's mercy, stretching my innermost anal-retentive nature. I'd told Adam it was all right if he went out with (*that tacky blond freak!*) Simone, but on the inside, I felt like I was now possessed by a tangible if invisible demon. I had violent, venomous thoughts—a capability I previously didn't know existed in me. I had diarrhea. My whole body ached like I had a flu. *And all this before they've slept together? Fuck!*

Adam would kiss me upon the head in reassurance. "Don't worry, you'll adapt. It's just hard at first. You know you're still my only girl, right?"

"I know," I'd sniffle, shuffling off to the bathroom with a mercifully loud fan.

At the same time, the immersion journalist in me was *really* curious what the fuck was happening. I would employ research and reporting to beat this nonsense! I searched desperately for a book that would

lt most polyamory guides spoke to jealousy in a way that

. optimistic. Until I found Kathy Labriola, a polyamorous

d author. Her excellent book, *Love in Abundance: A Coun-*

selor's Advice on Open Relationships,* contained the best dissection of non-monogamous jealousy I've found to this day. Freud was wrong about plenty else, but in my experience, he was right that there are four major components to jealousy, explained perfectly by Labriola in the context of open relationships:

> First, he believed, we experience grief, the terrible pain of losing or believing we are losing someone we love. Second, we are flooded with the very distressing realization that we cannot have everything we want in life. Third, we are gripped with feelings of enmity towards the successful rival who has won the love of our partner or who we fear will succeed in stealing our partner. Fourth, we turn our anger on ourselves in a belief that our own inadequacies as a partner will cause our partner to leave us. . . . So, as you can see, Freud viewed jealousy as a nightmare driven by our most primal fears of inferiority, loss, and abandonment.

This powerful combination then triggers a set of five fundamental fears:[†] that of abandonment *(I knew he'd replace me with a shiny new toy!)*; losing face or status in the community *(you fucking idiot, Rachel, coming out on the internet as non-monogamous!)*; fear of betrayal *(I knew I couldn't trust him, resting dickface!)*; fear of inadequacy *(it's because I'm an ugly used-up slut!)*; and envy *(I want to wipe her heavy mascara right off her smug, pretty little . . .)*.

I'd learned only a few facts about Simone, all of which my mind labeled DANGER: She was getting out of a monogamous marriage

---

* Kathy Labriola, Love in Abundance (Eugene: Greenery Press, 2013).

† Ayala Pines, *Romantic Jealousy: Causes, Symptoms, and Cures* (New York: St. Martin's Press, 1996).

she'd been unsatisfied in. She had no experience with open relationships. She also practiced yoga seriously, and soon went with Adam to
class. *I hate her,* I would think out of nowhere, terrified by my own
anger. I'd never felt like I hated anyone (besides myself). And yet, a
higher awareness also watched and didn't believe these thoughts fully.
Simone's name had become a dirty word in my mind, but I was simultaneously cognizant that she was really not so different from me: a
woman attracted to Adam on the tails of a breakup. A woman perhaps
also craving protective dominance. A woman who might want to steal
his heart "away," the way I might have if Adam had been in an open
relationship when *we* met. So I would also chastise myself, mortified to
wish another woman (literal) ill. I wanted to overcome these basest of
impulses.

Here was an opportunity for personal growth as emotional extreme sport—my favorite pastime, next to dancercizing stoned. I ate
binding foods and kept reading and journaling, hoping that what I
was going through was both normal and hopefully temporary.

Date: 6/5/16

Reply: Rachel to [Adam]
Subject: In the air. . . .

. . . this feels like shit and it comes out of me like shit. i want it to feel like
sex and light and sky and puppies and compassion. it feels like anger
and hate, and hypocrisy, and ugliness and competition and resentment
and fear, the oldest kind of fear i didn't even know how much i had . . .

I hit myself a little and that felt good . . . then i hated my own
melodrama so i stopped and went back to just crying . . . . i sucked my
thumb. i went back somewhere very old.

If you like *that,* you should have seen the *other* ten pages. Jealousy is
made all the more infuriating by how you watch it invite exactly what

you're trying to prevent. I could see logically that my grotesque insecurity was extremely unattractive, and risked making Adam grow tired of me more than his dating someone else—yes, I could see that quite clearly. I was filled with self-aversion at my apparently threadbare self-esteem. *Why can't I just get a handle on myself?*

The thing we initially value most about our relationship is often the very same thing we fear losing most, and therefore feel most jealous over. "During this initial transition, the partner who is feeling 'demoted' often reports experiencing sadness, betrayal, distrust, a sense of loss and grieving, and fear of abandonment," Labriola wrote of my current state. "The other partner often makes the situation worse by denying that there is any loss, ridiculing or dismissing their partner's fears, and stressing that this new development will enhance the primary relationship . . . it is bound to backfire by making the partner feel invalidated. Instead, it is important to acknowledge that their partner has lost something: they have lost the primacy of being the one and only lover." I underlined that last line several times. *This is exactly what Adam won't acknowledge! Asshole!*

Adam kept saying I was "making things harder than they had to be." He reminded me that if I looked at it *logically*, I'd see that nothing about his behavior or feelings toward me had actually changed. Anyone else would be a "romantic friendship" at most, about a desire that "wasn't really even about sex or love," he explained. It was more his curiosity about life, "a desire to access the intimacy only romance affords you." Intimacy meant stories, understanding the human experience so that he could better write and teach about it. This desire for continued romantic inspiration I related to, and didn't want to deny him.

But despite what had happened with Liam, Adam couldn't empathize with—or even admit to understanding—my jealousy. That he presented himself as above these feelings reinforced the idea that he was the more mature and enlightened one in the relationship. "Suited to non-monogamy" had become synonymous with positive traits; "struggling with jealousy," with immaturity and pettiness. "What Adam wants" and "ethical non-monogamy goals" had become conflated as one and the same in my mind.

————

Several weeks later, Adam still hadn't slept with Simone; he hadn't been lying about usually taking it slow. But his "marathon dates," as I came to bitterly call them, felt worse than if he'd just been having casual sex. He'd spend half a day or longer with her—*cooking, cuddling, no doubt massaging her, fucking slut.* I tried to distract myself with weed or Mo, whom to my horror I seemed to have mostly lost my attraction to. *Why can't I just attach to Mo the way I used to as soon as I had sex with someone?* I wasn't sure why, but it would prove to be a new pattern: fantasize about someone new, have sex with them hoping to override my jealousy, watch my attraction almost immediately vaporize when they failed to best Adam and/or sufficiently erase my overwhelming anxiety.

After one jealousy attack he deemed "a tantrum," Adam said he could stop seeing Simone, if that's what I really *wanted.* But his tone made it clear this would be a self-sabotaging failure on my part, a temporary offer.

"No, I don't want you to stop," I said.

"Are you sure?" he asked unconvincingly.

"Well, I *do,* but not *rationally.* I know that's not fair. And I'll have to do this at some point if I want to be with you no matter what."

He'd grimace sympathetically but not reassure me otherwise. "It just takes time," he said, softening. "But can you see how I'm even more committed to you now? I mean, *I'm* the one who's been talking about marriage, right? It just makes me more serious about you."

"I know. I want to do this, I do. I just feel . . . *I feel fucking crazy.*"

"My little jealous pain in the ass, huh? What are we going to do with you? Come here." He held out his arms. "I *love* you. You know I love you, right?"

"I love you, too." *Also I fucking hate you for doing this to me,* the new voice inside would spit. *You fucking liar. You said you'd protect me. You said I was special.* I also noticed what Adam didn't say: "I will prioritize you no matter what. If this doesn't work for you, I still want to be with you. This isn't a test. I'm willing to really compromise for the right person, and that person is still you." Now that he'd been granted his freedom, it was clear he'd never intended to give it up long term. This had been the plan all along, to ease me into an open relationship. He readily admitted it, and on a podcast I'd recorded, no less. Though I'd known this, I still felt duped.

It also certainly didn't help that society had deeply conditioned me to feel betrayed by Adam. In the culture I was raised in and many others, fidelity and commitment are considered synonymous with monogamy. Jealousy is more prevalent in cultures with a strong emphasis on property rights, getting married, and knowing paternity.* It also seems to correlate with cultures where sex is viewed as a scarce and (potentially immoral) resource.

Labriola named the core societal beliefs about love that had set me up to feel scorned:

> Core Belief #1: If my partner really loved me, (s)he wouldn't have any desire for a sexual relationship with anyone else.

> Core Belief #2: If my partner were happy with me, and if I were a good partner . . . [they] would be so satisfied that (s)he wouldn't want to get involved with anyone else.

---

* Bram Buunk and Ralph B. Hupka, "Cross-Cultural Differences in the Elicitation of Sexual Jealousy," *Journal of Sex Research* 23, no. 1 (1987): 12–22. https://doi.org/10.1080/002244 98709551338.

Core Belief #3: It's just not possible to love more than one person at the same time.

If I was going to adapt and be happy with polyamory, I would have to unlearn what most every movie and song had taught me about what love and commitment means. I would have to eventually grow a new set of beliefs, a new paradigm. Kathy suggested:

New Core Belief #1: My partner loves me so much that (s)he trusts our relationship to expand and be enriched by experiencing even more love from others.

New Core Belief #2: My relationship is so solid and trusting that we can experience other relationships freely. My partner is so satisfied with me and our relationship that having other partners will not threaten the bond we enjoy.

New Core Belief #3: There is an abundance of love in the world and there is plenty for everyone. Loving more than one person is a choice that can exponentially expand my potential for giving and receiving love.

These new beliefs certainly sounded more mature and less possessive, what I *wanted* to feel. But my bowels couldn't seem to catch up to my values. Adam tried to reassure me that neuroplasticity was real, but took time. Or maybe it was more like prolonged exposure therapy to a phobia.

One day, Adam simply sent me a quote from a *New York Times* article that was going viral, "Why You Will Marry the Wrong Person," by Alain de Botton.

6/6/16

From: [Adam] to Rachel
Subject: apropos our situation

"We are looking to recreate, within our adult relationships, the feelings we knew so well in childhood. The love most of us will have tasted early on was often confused with other, more destructive dynamics . . . How logical, then, that we should as grown-ups find ourselves rejecting certain candidates for marriage not because they are wrong but because they are too right—too balanced, mature, understanding and reliable—given that in our hearts, such rightness feels foreign."

The message I was supposed to take away was clear: I shouldn't trust my own fear-based conditioning. I should try to trust in Adam's "right-ness" instead. He was the best person for me, he was saying, but being a child of divorce made me confused about what romantic happiness looked like. *He has a better map—his parents are still in love forty years later. And he's definitely calmer than me, way less irrational. I'll just keep working at it. I'll even interview Kathy Labriola, goddammit.*

Meeting the Mentor

"In life, there are godmothers everywhere.
Strangers who step forward—poof!—when they're needed most."
—Diana Clarke, *Thin Girls*

Summer 2016

PHONE INTERVIEW

When I interviewed Kathy over the phone that first time, I learned that she's in her sixties and lives in Berkeley, California, that infamous city next door to where I was born and raised, and that she is a white bisexual woman with two live-in long-term partners, and has been polyamorous for over forty years.

The woman who'd written the only book I'd felt spoke to the roots of my jealousy was indeed someone I immediately adored. I started out our interview by asking about trends she saw in her clients when it came to jealousy. Kathy told me that though rates of jealousy are similar for both cis men and cis women, the manifestations are different.

"Men tend to get angry, women to feel rejected and abandoned, more anxious and fearful. Men tend to be much more jealous about a female partner having sex with someone else," Kathy told me. "Women certainly can get insanely jealous over sex, too, but they're much more likely to be alarmed by a relationship becoming more than sex, being replaced or displaced or demoted in a big way. Of course, these are broad generalizations. But I'm willing to make them if I can say with some certainty that two times out of three it's true of my clients."

"What about jealousy among your trans and non-binary clients?"

"I have non-binary clients, but not enough yet to notice any patterns. As for trans clients, I mean, trans women are women and trans men are men, so duh, they would be jealous in situations that would generally make cis women and cis men jealous. But there is one unique component of jealousy for straight trans people. In my experience, they're more likely to become extremely jealous and insecure if their partner has a relationship with a cis person of a different gender. Trans people constantly receive negative messages from a transphobic society that they're not a 'real' man or woman, so it's very understandable that their partner's involvement with a cis person would provoke a strong fear of abandonment and trigger their own body dysphoria, bring back past feelings of inadequacy, and remind them of past rejection."

"What about jealousy among gay couples? Does that change anything about gendered trends?"

"My experience is that gay men as a group are much less jealous than anyone else. It's partially due to gay men's broader understanding that sex and love are not the same thing, and having established community norms around non-monogamy. Lesbians I counsel tend to experience jealousy the same way straight women do. But while straight women can often learn to tolerate the man having casual sex much more comfortably than the man having another relationship, my lesbian clients have tended to remain equally jealous over both casual sex and emotional intimacy."

"What about bi or pansexual people?"

"I've noticed bisexual women tend to have jealousy nearly identical to straight women, but bisexual men tend to be much less jealous than straight men. And there's a very clear pattern among straight guys not to be very jealous of their bi female partner having a relationship with another woman, while they may go totally ballistic if she sleeps with a man.* But there doesn't seem to be any pattern for women who have bisexual male partners. Some are much more jealous of their partner having a relationship with a man, afraid maybe he's really gay and will abandon them, and some are less jealous."

In these generalizations, Kathy was drawing on more than thirty years of what she's witnessed as a counselor. Unlike many higher-charging "polyamory specialists," she operates on a sliding scale; you can pay her as little as forty dollars for a ninety-minute session, if that's all you can afford. Most of the time, people reach out to her for relationship advice that doesn't have much to do with polyamory. If there is a non-monogamy problem they're reaching out about, it's going to be one of four things, Kathy told me: 1) a polyamorous person has fallen in love with a monogamist; 2) a couple wants separate, different models—one really wants primary/secondary, the other to pursue other relationships more intensely; 3) issues around time and energy management; or 4) jealousy.

"I remember you writing that jealousy is like a smoke alarm—there to alert you that there might be a fire. It's going off for a reason, but it's up to you to detect whether you're actually in danger of being hurt, or whether you just need to change the batteries," I said like the teacher's pet I was.

"Exactly! I encourage people to push past your comfort level somewhat, but to say no to things that you just know are going to make you miserable. It's not always easy to tell exactly where that line is," Kathy added.

"I know that I really struggle with that . . ." I said. I was tempted to talk to her about it more, but asked instead if there were other gender-based trends she'd noticed. She told me that twenty years ago, men were into non-monogamy more often for sex; women, for intimacy.

---

*   Sometimes known colloquially as the cis-hetero "one-penis policy."

But now, things have leveled out somewhat. More women are enjoying casual sex, more men are looking for relationships.

"But in straight relationships, women are still much better at polyamory than men are. It's not because we're *innately* better," she clarified. "It's because we're so trained to be relational and attuned to the nuances of a relationship; to be caring about other people's needs and to do the work of caring and feeding a relationship. Women are still better at being the emotional guardian of the relationship, whether it's monogamous or polyam." Kathy said that when she speaks with cis straight couples, the men are driving an open relationship "ninety-nine percent" of the time. The exception is usually when the woman is caught in an affair and decides she doesn't want to give either relationship up.

Though Kathy told me she has clients all over the world, a lot of calls are from people in the South—Texas, Louisiana, Florida, Georgia, the Bible Belt. They can't find support in their area, so she usually sends them to kink meetups, which tend to have polyamorous contingents. Most of her clients are in the closet. "I mean, people here in *Berkeley* are afraid to be out as non-monogamous. But in the South they are especially worried, very frightened they are going to lose their kids.*

---

* There are generally no civil protections for people in non-monogamous relationships. In most places, you can lose your job or kids if you're found out, and usually have little to no recourse, lawyer Jonathan D. Lane, an expert in this area of the law, told me. If you are raising a child with two other adults but you are not one of the biological parents, you might not have rights to partial custody if you decide to break up. You can also lose your kids even if you aren't breaking up. In one case, a Tennessee judge accused a woman with two live-in male partners of "trying to have her cake and eat it too" and said he couldn't "get the image of the three of them in bed out of his head." The woman's child was placed in the custody of the grandmother who'd brought the case, despite four different court-appointed experts testifying the child's existing family was in no way unhealthy.

In some places, however, legal rights are expanding. In 2020, two towns in Massachusetts passed ordinances allowing groups of three or more people who "consider themselves to be a family" to be recognized as domestic partners. Laws allowing for three or more legal parents have passed in Canada and a few US states and are under consideration in other places. Elizabeth F. Emens, "Monogamy's Law: Compulsory Monogamy and Polyamorous Existence," *New York University Review of Law & Social Change* 29 (2004): 277; University of Chicago, Public Law Working Paper No. 58 (2004).

Even afraid of potential violence, or feeling so ostracized that they would have to move out of town. And they're not being paranoid.* There is definitely a lot of hostility in society around being polyamorous."

A year after that interview, in 2017, I asked Kathy to be my counselor—with a twist. I wanted our sessions to be recorded and on the record, with the caveat she could approve/veto any of her quotes if I used them one day. She was game. In the years of recorded phone sessions to come, Kathy never seemed to expect me to reach out to her with any certain regularity. Sometimes we went months without speaking. But when I did email her, often in the heat of some crisis or another, she'd reply within hours, making herself available as soon as possible. I often wondered how she was so enthusiastically caring. I was tired of listening to myself, let alone dozens of other fretful permutations of me. But that's Kathy. A benevolence when summoned that makes me believe in real-life fairy godmothers. And why shouldn't they be compensated for their labor?

---

* In one study psychologist and researcher Dr. Ryan Witherspoon conducted, he found that over half of non-monogamous people reported experiencing at least one type of discrimination or harassment because of being non-monogamous. About a third reported experiencing three or more types of discrimination. That can be anything from internet and verbal harassment, to job and child custody loss, to sexual harassment and assault. Of course, being non-monogamous can also often overlap with other identities, like being queer and/or kinky. Ryan G. Witherspoon, "Exploring Polyamorous Resilience and Strength Factors: A Structural Equation Modeling Approach" (PhD diss., Alliant International University, 2018), 214, 10841959.

Hardly Homeostasis

Summer 2016

BROOKLYN

Journal Entry

Last night I came in and he must have known that i
might have seen [Mo] and he gave me a real kiss
and said,

   'i kind of feel like i wanna marry you. you know,
just lock down this feeling.'

Journal Entry

He says 'you wanna be my wifey?' and I say 'kind
of, yeah'. . . . he says 'How about we do the domestic
partnership here and consider it a sort of
engagement, then get married in California?' We
share a couple kisses. 'Enfianced,' he says . . . I fall
asleep with my head on his chest, his lovely chest I
love.

That day he suggested we become domestic partners, I answered so immediately I felt possessed: "Okay, but I want a ring."

"Sure, you can have a ring." His tone was placating and mildly amused, as I expected.

"Don't worry, it won't be expensive," I said, feeling the warmth of Jewish stereotypes course between us. "I'll even pick it out for you." *Actually, I already have.*

I'd found it on Etsy, where all one's dreams come true. With a dozen small turquoise stones lined up, it was the evolution of the five-stoned ring I'd worn during that very brief engagement to myself. You could inscribe this new ring with a single, hidden word. I decided I liked the idea of this collaboration: I asked for what I wanted, he picked the time and meaning. I hoped this magic word would break my deepest of spells. I wanted not so much the promise of "forever," but the symbolic security I imagined the ring and marriage would afford me. If I had to share Adam, I at least wanted to be marked his primary original sin.

7/11/16

Journal Entry

I twisted my foot chasing him [as he was rushing] down the subway stairs and his first impulse seemed to be not to believe I'd actually hurt myself and was exaggerating. Later when I could show swelling he believed me.

[Same night] he says 'do you want me to just be w/ you? Not see anyone else? I will.'

I say 'don't offer that and marriage stuff if you don't want or mean it.'

He says 'I don't want it but I want to be with you . . . Just stop being upset, just be mine and just

be happy. All the getting upset just makes it worse.
Things can just be good.'
   . . . [Doctor says] I broke my foot

                                                7/16/16

Journal Entry

   [What] echos in my head trying to reclaim him
[after his date] is 'will you be my daddy' or 'are you
still my daddy' 'don't leave daddy.' 'I'll be your
daddy' he says, [reading my mind]

                                                8/2/16

Journal Entry

Cried on the bathroom floor hitting myself* and he
said 'stop throwing a tantrum'. . . My head is dull
like I'm hungover, my eyes swollen from all the
crying. Why do this? Because I love him and I'm not
ready to say I can't . . .
   He said 'I've tried it when I restrict myself and I
know it doesn't work out, I at least need to know I
have the option.'. . . This is the catch. The question is
now whether I can deal with it.
   'You're my woman,' he says. 'Unless you leave
me, then I'll have to get a new woman.' Another
veiled threat . . . I called him a monster. And then I
cling to him in the morning.

---

* Self-abuse like this was new to me, but increasingly common. Its appearance or resurfacing as a
behavior is a common symptom of an unhealthy relationship. A. Boyle, P. Jones, and S. Lloyd,
"The Association Between Domestic Violence and Self Harm in Emergency Medicine Patients,"
Emergency Medicine Journal 23, no. 8: 604–7. https://doi.org/10.1136/emj.2005.031260.

The more intense my fear of abandonment, the harder I latched on.* Jealousy seemed to activate my desire for Adam even more strongly—along with a newfound fury. *Up-down, lust-rage.*

It's interesting to consider what was happening from a physiological perspective. Though it might not feel good, when you're jealous, it's in many ways a similar physical state to being highly sexually aroused— your heart rate and blood pressure rise, your breathing becomes heavier, the amygdala is activated, and you create a lot of endocrine activity. It's part of why couples can get so addicted to the fight-and-makeup-sex cycle. But the body naturally "wants" to return to a resting state— homeostasis. If you start consuming more cannabis, for example, your body responds by creating fewer of the receptors that the cannabinoids bind to, resulting in a directly proportional need to consume more and more THC to feel high.† Homeostasis is also a reason we chemically adapt to the initial lust we feel for a lover. That falling-in-love high goes away over time because your body perceives it as stress and wants to return to homeostasis.

I was hoping that the same principle would apply to my jealousy exposure therapy—the more I experienced its triggers, the more my body might eventually learn to tamp down this unwanted and extreme fight-or-flight response. Hopefully, my baseline feeling of "normal" would adapt. But in the meantime, I judged myself for my "irrational feelings"—and so did Adam—*hard.*

---

* According to attachment theory, people with an anxious attachment style have brains that react more strongly to thoughts of loss—and are also less able to "recruit" regions of the brain that help down-regulate emotions. This can create a vicious cycle where it's harder to get rid of anxious responses once they're activated. Also not helpful is that anxious types/our culture often tend to conflate this kind of activated emotional state with passion. N. Barbaro, M. N. Pham, T. K. Shackelford, and V. Zeigler-Hill, "Insecure Romantic Attachment Dimensions and Frequency of Mate Retention Behaviors," *Personal Relationships* 23, no. 3 (2016): 605–18. https://doi.org/10.1111/pere.12146.

† Julie Holland, *The Pot Book: A Complete Guide to Cannabis* (Rochester, NY: Park Street Press, 2010).

Around this time, Simone broke up with Adam. His explanation as to why seemed to imply that he'd taken things too slowly, mostly on my behalf (they still hadn't had penetrative sex). She'd found a guy she wanted to date exclusively, and that was that. My relief was brief, a deep exhale followed by a shallow held breath.

Miranda, Spiral, Explode

Summary 2016

Summer 2016

BROOKLYN

Miranda was feeling a little conflicted about being paid to shit into a guy's mouth.

"I wouldn't usually do it, but it's such easy money. He wants to be blindfolded and tied to the hotel bathtub then left there alone . . . But it's three hundred bucks and takes me like five minutes." Miranda took in the ever-present joint between us. Ital Kitchen's backyard was a sanctuary for us both, but somehow our paths hadn't crossed before she started dating Mo. She exhaled thoughtfully as a song by Cymande played in the background. "The thing that gets me though is, how does he get untied? And how long does he lay there like that?"

"Someone in this city is a very good friend," I said, taking a hit. I hoped the effect was more Carrie Bradshaw than Groucho Marx. Miranda was beautiful, inside and out, and I was *crushing*. Half-Jewish, half-*goy** with protruding cheekbones, straight dark brows, a strong nose, smooth ivory skin, heart-shaped bow lips, and brown bedroom eyes, she really had no use for makeup.

I contemplated her dilemma. I could understand her temptation as easily as her ambivalence. Pop a squat and get paid $300 in cash? I sold roughly twenty office-and-subway-confined-hours of my life for the

---

* Yiddish for non-Jewish person.

same sum. She didn't have to touch him or be touched, even be seen. If a dame could make that kind of money *and* get her morning BM in, why wouldn't she? Well, this I understood just as easily. It wasn't the shitting—it was the desire to do no harm. The same instinct, ironically, that seemed to drive Miranda as a dominatrix. Long recovered from heroin and opioid addiction, this is why she was also in grad school to become a social worker. What ultimately mattered to Miranda was whether she was helping people.

Taking a thoughtful pause, I asked what was obviously the most important question: ". . . But what if you can't go on the spot?"

"I know how to plan it so I can," she said with a wink, always a lady.

"You mean coffee, or—"

"—Ugh, stop! I don't want to hear this anymore!" Mo moaned, pulling his beanie down over his entire face. We smiled at him like you do a boy who can't handle his parents kissing.

"You're so *innocent,*" one of us said. We loved to gang up on him like schoolgirls.

"I'm not innocent," he mock-pouted, in on the joke. "And I'm not sweet, either. *I'm badass.* You guys don't know who I turn into at night."

"Yeah, you watch MSNBC."

"And play computer games and code."

Though I hadn't been interested in Mo romantically for months now, with Miranda dating him, I saw him anew. She was polyamorous and queer, and Mo told me she'd already floated her interest in a three-some with me.

Perhaps she is the one! Lumière the candlestick's French accent exclaimed in my mind. *The one to break the spell!*

———

As I'd hoped, the sex parties I'd been to in the last year had built my queer confidence. Interestingly, with women, it seemed I was a Top.

These women were also larger than I was, so why was I so different with them than with men?

First, I suspect societal conditioning had taught me that "the woman is the submissive one"; perhaps I wanted to act out that dominance over women, rather than always being on the receiving end of it. As if I'd internalized that with a woman's body, "this is what you do"—you dominate it. Second, I was also following my instincts to touch women the way I'd often wished men touched me: slowly, commandingly, teasingly, with reverence; an attuned dialogue filled with intuitive listening and creatively assured responses. Third, there was a surprising feeling that surfaced when I touched women around men: I felt a strong resentment toward guys well up, and a desire to show the women (and I'm sure myself) that we shouldn't let them rush us. That we didn't need men to feel a sense of surrender at all. Each time I climbed atop a woman (Adam claimed in one case obliviously "pushing her boyfriend out of the way") a large part of me felt like, *Any way he can top, I can top better.*

In the symbiotic infinity loop I felt coursing between our bodies, I could sense more acutely how women are too often made to limit our potential; to adhere to a trajectory and timeline that isn't designed around our bodies or emotional experience at all. Something linear rather than spiraling, deepening down and up and to all sides. "There's power in a wave, its sense of beginning, midpoint, and end; no wonder we fall into it in [structuring] stories," Jane Alison writes in *Meander, Spiral, Explode: Design and Power in Narrative.** "But something that swells and tautens until climax, then collapses? Bit masculo-sexual, no? So many other patterns run through nature, tracing other deep motions in life."

And yet a part of me was also reassured by the men watching us in the periphery and eventually interrupting. Because I'd waited too long

---

* Jane Alison, *Meander, Spiral, Explode* (New York: Catapult, 2019).

to lose my virginity with a woman at a sex party. To do so would be another capitulation to a culture of acceleration. I wanted my first time to be with someone special, someone I cared about.

Someone like Miranda. I saw now I'd been waiting for someone just like Miranda.

It's About Power

"My decision not to use my real name in this comes not from a place of shame but a need to protect myself from potential job insecurity or negative social impact. My choosing to obscure my name should be a testament to the sheer lack of protections non-monogamous people have, and the degree of stigma that surrounds the way we live and love."
—STATEMENT FROM AYESHA (2021)

Fall 2016

BROOKLYN

We were several months into Adam dating other people now. Non-monogamy both was and wasn't a big part of our lives—we went on a date with someone else once a week, or even every few weeks. As a rookie, this still felt like a lot to me. He reminded me that he hadn't even *slept* with anyone else yet (oral sex didn't "count"). Most of his prospects went nowhere or fizzled after a few weeks, when the women met someone they wanted to be monogamous with. That, or he said "they were confused about what they wanted," and left it at that. I didn't ask for details. But now that he'd been dating a woman named Leah for several weeks, a certain momentum began to build. He'd asked her to get tested (though our agreement was to always use condoms with other people, we also now tried to ask for a recent STI test to be extra careful).

During a bad jealousy attack of wanting to flee, I'd go talk to someone who was Adam's friend, but who also took no shit from him:

Ayesha. Though Ayesha actually went to college with me, I hadn't dared penetrate their* aura at that time. But when Adam and I got together, Ayesha turned out to be one of his many friends in academia. Several of these friends were also queer and polyamorous, and their mere association with Adam reassured me of his fundamental trustworthiness.† During Ayesha's divorce the year before, Adam had been a great friend. He'd taken Ayesha to Ikea to furnish the new apartment he'd helped them find and move into, counseled them nearly daily. So it felt safe to say my fears to Ayesha. They could understand my reasons for loving Adam, but they shared and validated my worries.

"You know, I'm polyam because it makes me feel *safe*. But that doesn't mean it will make *you* feel safe," Ayesha said, looking at me bluntly. South Asian from Paris, they've lived in New York for over a decade and lost most of their accent, but the French remains in their riveting monologues and graceful hand gestures. Our sessions together were part therapy, part theater, part interview, part symposium. "And there's nothing wrong or unevolved about you, if you feel unsafe. I don't give a *fuck* what Adam says otherwise."

"Well . . . why does being polyamorous make you feel safe?" Maybe Ayesha's reasons could rub off on me.

"It comes down to possession and control," they answered. "Men in my life have treated me like something to conquer, tame, and hold in their pockets. After this fucking marriage, *nobody* gets to believe that I belong to them anymore. At least not beyond what I give them to hold. That I do not feel controlled, limited—I feel I could live a really full life this way. I'm not a possession. It's very soothing."

"Did your ex know how you felt about monogamy before you got married?"

---

*   Ayesha's pronouns are they/them, and they are non-binary.

†   I'm happy to say these people are still some of my most trusted friends and editors. This book has Ayesha's fingerprints all over it, lucky for me.

"Oh yeah, I identified as non-monogamous when I met him. My ex-husband just wasn't having it, and I got bullied out of it. But I've felt this way since high school. Then the big bad world happened, and all of a sudden it was like, '*This is what it means to be a good girlfriend, and to be a girl.*' I became convinced that non-monogamy wasn't viable. I wanted to be loved in a particular way and felt like I had to fit in to receive love." Ayesha sighed. "Low self-esteem will do a lot."

I grimaced knowingly. "Do you think there's any way you would have been happy with him if it had been an open marriage?"

"I thought about this a lot. Ultimately, no. Because he and I were not compatible to begin with," Ayesha answered. "We knee-jerked into marriage in a way that's very typical to South Asian young people looking to figure out their identity, especially when you're diasporic. I thought, *Maybe together we'll be able to make something that doesn't feel oppressive, but will serve all of these other cultural purposes at the same time.* Needless to say, that did not work."

I considered whether I was doing my own version of this: finally settling down with a Jewish guy in a seemingly normative "straight" dynamic, the way my family might prefer—but on my own sexually subversive terms. "See, the thing is, I do believe being non-monogamous makes so much more sense for me, *logically,*" I thought aloud. "But then it also makes me anxious, the feeling that things could shift with Adam at any moment."

"Look, there isn't a person in the world who may not one day walk into a bookstore and meet someone and be like, '*Well, things are different now.*' That's not a polyam thing—that's just a *human being* thing. If it happens, it's just going to," Ayesha said.

"That's true, I guess . . ."

"I think the bottom line is, we have sexuality, and we should get to express it safely, and be safe toward other people while we do it," Ayesha said. "For some people the safer option will be monogamy. For others it's non-monogamy. And I am *not* ashamed of being polyam.

Seeing it as a deep, dark secret connotes that I'm doing something wrong. But what am I admitting to? That I am radically honest? That I aim to be as vulnerable and loving as possible in the world, to be honest about what I can and can't give, and not feel like I ever have the right to own anybody's time or body, and vice versa?" Ayesha shook their head firmly. "I am *not* ashamed of that."

"Nor should you be," I said. "You know, ever since I've come out publicly as being in an open relationship, strangers keep pulling me aside at parties and work events confessing they're also secretly non-monogamous. And I've noticed some of the reasons people give me for why they can't be out about it are in some ways pretty similar to why some people don't or can't come out as gay.* They're worried about being seen as overly sexual, or deviant, or not fit to be around children, losing their jobs. Or they'll say, 'It's no one's business what I do behind closed doors,' you know? 'It's my private sexual life.'"

"Those things are all true, and I'm certainly not out as polyam at work or forthcoming with strangers, especially seemingly hetero-monogamous strangers, because of the stigma. But I feel like I should be as out as is appropriate or comfortable," Ayesha said. "But I also happen to have a lot of privilege in being able to live as polyam as a queer brown person in a relatively accepting community in Brooklyn."

"Because being able to choose to be non-monogamous is a privilege, right?" I thought about my ability to broadcast my open relationship all over the internet. Sure, I was trolled sometimes, but nothing so scary. But a colleague who simply wrote about being a plus-size woman was so harassed she decided to change both her address and legal name. As potentially distasteful as being a Jewish vegan non-monogamous

---

* We know from decades of research on queer populations that internalized homophobia is very real, and a very real predictor of psychological distress, relationship problems, and other negative effects. We also know from research on queer populations that concealment of one's sexuality is a direct internal source of stress that independently contributes to negative mental health outcomes.

feminist was, trolls still seemed to consider it less offensive than if I were simply no longer thin.

"It's definitely a privilege to practice polyamory,"* Ayesha answered. "I live in a country and city that is not kind to queers like me, particularly Black trans folk, but that usually, so far, isn't killing them outright in their homes with most of society deeming it justified. Which is not the case in many places—including India, where I'm originally from. Plus, even though I'm increasingly understanding that I'm genderqueer, I don't read as masc.† So that makes it easier to be out as polyam, too, I think."

"What do you mean? Why would it be harder to be polyamorous if you looked more masculine?" I was confused.

"Well, first off, that I don't read as masc gives me privilege that more obviously androgynous people and trans folks do not have. But also, I mean that there's also a history of women, and femmes, and queers talking about their sexual liberation. But then sexual liberation is still really unavailable to male and masc people, and we don't talk about that, except in some butch communities. We talk about masculinity in terms of damage, violence, toxicity. We don't have enough of a conversation about how to help *free* men and mascs from that, provide loving alternatives.‡ Polyam cis men are seen as dangerous, and

---

* "So, when do you engage in all that valuable [polyamorous] relationship-affirming communication? In the limited space between your full-time, minimum-wage shift, and your part-time, minimum wage shift? Do you find time on the phone, while taking public transportation to pick your children up from school or daycare? . . . Do you see the problem here? . . . Logistically, it takes spare resources to make polyamory function. Time. Lodging. Disposable income. It stands to reason that communities that have been generationally, often intentionally, left on the short end of the stick, will have trouble keeping up with polyamory's version of the 'Joneses.'" Kevin A. Patterson and Ruby Bouie Johnson, *Love's Not Color Blind: Race and Representation in Polyamorous and Other Alternative Communities* (Portland: Thorntree Press, 2018).

† "Masc" is a term for a person whose gender identity is masculine, but who is not necessarily a man.

‡ To get involved in this conversation, check out the Good Men Project and watch the documentary *The Mask You Live In*.

they're seen as manipulating cis women into more sex. Sometimes that's definitely happening, but that's such a limited narrative. I have a lot of sympathy for that."

"See, that's part of why I'm scared about this idea of writing a book someday about non-monogamy," I said. A literary agent had by now approached me, having read some of my articles. I knew I wasn't ready to write a book yet, but the seed I'd already planted in my own mind had now been watered by someone legitimate. I started to imagine a book as a light at the end of the jealousy tunnel. "There are so few mainstream representations of non-monogamy that it feels like Adam would represent Most Polyamorous Men. And we *know* he wouldn't always come off well . . ."

"No, he would not," Ayesha said. "But you have to trust the reader, and yourself, to be nuanced. I mean, I think the reason there is less stigma around homosexuality now is because people chose to educate about what it actually is, and what it isn't, destigmatizing it. So just contributing one story to the hopefully future *pile* of polyam narratives is valuable, even if it's not the perfect representation of 'ideal' non-monogamy. Plus, our having to be in perfect relationships in order to be respected is its own cage."

I nodded, feeling more excited about the idea by the minute. It helped me think less about Adam, and more about my future. I toggled to reporter/student mode. "So, but, if for you being polyam means a rejection of these gendered constructs designed to control you, does that mean monogamy is inherently restrictive?"

"No. I think that historically imposed *constructs* of monogamy, with their unequal gender dynamics, specifically in heterosexual relationships, can be very, very oppressive. But monogamy that's based on two people just always preferring one another over everyone else? Yeah! I'm super here for that! But monogamy, patriarchy, marriage—telling people how they're supposed to live, making legal marriage a way to get more rights and protection, *is* social control. It's a political choice to refuse conscription to certain kinds of living." Ayesha looked me square in the face. "You know, this isn't about sex. It's about *power*."

"Right." I nodded, knowing they were referring to my relationship as well. "So . . ."

"So stand up for yourself. Don't take Adam's shit. Just tell him he's being an arrogant patriarchal prick if he makes you feel weak or illogical for struggling with jealousy. And you can tell him I said so, too."

————

Having been reassured I was no unaware dummy, I would take myself home. Adam would be there, waiting. Ready to make up again.

"You smell like cigarettes," he'd say.

"I know. I'll take a shower . . ."

He'd grab my hand before I could sulk away, turning me toward him. "Just *be* with me already. Just stop running away," he'd say softly into my eyes. "It hurts me that you still don't trust me. Things could be so good if you just relaxed. Why don't you trust me still?"

"Well, maybe because you make me feel like I'm stupid for having trouble adjusting to you dating. Ayesha said you shouldn't be telling me I'm too emotional."

"I'm *not* telling you you're too emotional. When have I used those words?" he'd demand, growing suddenly angry. *Is that true? I need to remember to point it out to him in the moment so he can't deny it. Or maybe he does use different words? But that's what it feels like . . .* "Look. I know it's not easy, adjusting to this. I know that," he'd concede, calming himself. "But I also know you're strong. I wouldn't be pushing you if I didn't think this would make you happier in the long run. I *love* you. We're going to be together until one of us dies, right? Right?" He'd laugh, bend down to my eye level. "Come on . . . don't smile . . . don't smile. Aw, *so serious.*" I'd smile, caving. "Go take a shower and be my girl already. It's way past time for bed."

I'd let the feeling of safety encircle me. Just like the towel he would surely wrap me in as soon as I got clean. The way he always did. The way, if I continued to do my best and be good for him, I trusted he always would. "This is the female's first lesson in the school of patriarchal thinking and values," bell hooks writes in *Communion.** "She must earn love. She is not entitled. She must be good to be loved. And good is always defined by someone else."

---

*   bell hooks, *Communion* (New York: W. Morrow, 2002).

FFM

I was nervous and high off a vegan weed cookie Mo gave me when I rang Miranda's buzzer that first time. I remember my outfit, because I chose it both carefully and easily: baggy olive cargo pants and a white shirt that fell off my shoulder, an unusual look for me then, Adam-unapproved. But I was dressed for something else. Tonight, I was going to lose my queer virginity. So help me Goddess.

After Miranda's signature greeting of a closed-lipped, puckered kiss, we sat in her kitchen at a comfortable distance drinking tea. I could see her many arm tats—one commemorating her deceased mom, a rose, a smiling moon. Her perfectly naked face, the black tank top with no bra. I was spellbound, but not stupefied. Miranda put me at ease, a natural counselor already. We seemed able to easily flow between interacting as friends and potential lovers. When two sexually fluid people combine, it's a brimming thing.

"I don't know, Mo's so sweet, but it's an issue that he doesn't like me to talk about work," Miranda confided. "Like, this one time, I got a rose from a guy at the dungeon and Mo got all hurt. And I was like, 'Dude, if you only fucking *knew*! This rose came from a guy in a dress and blond wig. An eighty-year-old man. *Literally.*'"

"Did you tell him that?"

"Ya, but he still got jealous." She grimaced. "He knows I'm polyam, but not exactly a good sign for long-term compatibility . . ."

When Mo buzzed hours earlier than expected, you could feel the energy in the room shift toward the masculine. I was a little resentful of it, suddenly—the unearned, disruptive pull of a tall man with a deep voice.

"What up, Rach," he said, giving me a big hug. He kissed Miranda's ear, and I got an immediate contact high, almost like a static shock. It was easy to feel compersion* in this situation—I felt no sense of ownership over Mo or Miranda. Adam, who was on a fifth date tonight with *that strictly dickly straight bitch Leah,* was another story. But I wasn't going to think about that now. And if being on the brink of my first threesome/below-waist experience with a woman I really liked wasn't distracting enough for me, I was truly fucked.

I sat between them on the couch. We were getting stoned(er), as usual.

"So, how's work been?" I asked Miranda.

"Good! Me and the girls, we've been making sandwiches for people living on the street and passing them out on our breaks. Or, really, we get the sissies† to make them, or at least to pay for the supplies, and then we pass them out."

"That's so sweet!" I smiled, charmed. "What made you decide to do it?"

"The work makes you notice the suffering around you a bit more, I think. It's so funny, when the people ask what organization we work for we're just like, '*Um* . . .' and we all laugh."

"You see that painting?" Mo said suddenly, pointing straight ahead.

---

*   A popular polyamorous term for "pleasure in your partner's pleasure."

†   BDSM term for someone who enjoys feminization as part of their submission, often involving feminine crossdressing.

"That was made by the *Boogeyman Dom*." He used a ghost story voice, and it was admittedly cute. "Do you know what she did? *She nailed a guy's balls to a board. For real.*"

"Yeah, she's done a lot more than that, too, but it's because they *wanted* her to." Miranda laughed. "He's talking about the woman who was my girlfriend for years. But in private she wasn't like that at all. She wouldn't even dominate me because she doesn't like power play over women."

"Is that why you broke up?" Miranda had mentioned she was more submissive in her romantic relationships, and I'd diligently taken note.

"No, we broke up because of the live-in sissy." Miranda sighed.

"Um, go on . . ." I suppressed a giggle.

"At first, it was great. He did all the cleaning, errands. But then he fell in love with my girlfriend and would try to sabotage things between us. Eventually, it worked." She shrugged and looked down at my foot, took it in her hand. "Look at your feet, they are so tiny! You could make a ton of money just making videos of your feet next to stuff. If you were at the dungeon you'd be the Foot Dom."

"Wow, that would be nice. Do you think I could find clients remotely? How would—"

"—I'm tired of talking." Mo sighed. By now, they each had one of my thighs in their grasp. He turned and kissed me. And with that, I turned my head to the left and kissed Miranda. I had the same two thoughts I always have with women, which is that they are so much softer, and that it feels like switching back to your native tongue. She liked little nibbles, she told me wordlessly, and as I obliged I began to listen to the rest of her. Shyly at first, then gripping, I explored her inked arms and waist, her hot and fragrant neck.

Befitting a Sapphic devirginizing, Miranda's room smelled like freshly smoked Mary Jane and essential oil potions. Her ceiling was painted to look like the sky; a bird-mermaid-angel-demon mobile liked to watch. Her bed seemed to go on and on, our wide raft floating down a lazy river. I lay on top of her, pressed my pelvis into hers as we moaned and kissed each other.

"Okay, I guess I'll just watch you two," Mo said after a while, not a little bitter.

"Don't worry, you're here, we care about you, too," she said, taking some time to kiss him. "Rachel and I just haven't had a chance to connect yet the way we already have with you is all." I inwardly rolled my eyes at the need to babysit the male ego. I wanted him to be there, I was pretty sure, but I resented the pace demanded.

Miranda began to lick me for a good long while. It was skillful and exciting, but to my disappointment, the fact it was a woman eating me out instead was no silver-bullet vibrator. At moments, I thought this would be the time I'd finally come again this way—but as usual, as soon as hope entered, orgasm vaporized. However novel and intense my sexual explorations were becoming, there seemed to be no escaping my interior narrator. She followed me everywhere, whispering self-conscious nothings in my ear, my best frenemy forever. Finally, I admitted to Miranda that I hadn't been able to orgasm from oral in years. "I get it, don't worry about that," she said, popping her head up to smile before returning to finish her meal.

"I want to go down on you, too, but I'm afraid I'll be bad at it," I admitted after she was satiated. "This would be my first time. I should have told you that earlier. I'm sorry."

"Oh honey, I'm honored," Miranda purred in that way she had about her, maternal and sultry at once. "Whatever you want to do is great. *You're* great. I'm just so glad you're here."

And so I obeyed her, and did what I wanted to do.

First, I admired her grooming: narrow bush on top, impossibly smooth lips. I felt a certain relief at her clear canvas and (because Jewish and feminist) a swift guilt at that relief. I myself rocked a mostly full

bush, but here I was, no better than the men who I'd suspected preferred my vagina somehow sterilized. *What are we so afraid of? Disappearing into the organic wilderness from whence we came, probably.*

Beholding someone's pussy, I now realized, was like staring down
the barrel of a gun in reverse: *I gave you life, and I won't take it away.*
Had I ever understood our power so acutely? Certainly not by examining myself. I pulled apart her lips delicately, assessing her with my eyes
over many minutes, following the Golden Rule. *Stay with her,* I thought.
*Worship her until she remembers she's like the sun, always doing its radiant
thing whether or not someone's there to see it. Communicate it's a privilege
she lets you soak her in.* I put my palm over her entire vulva, massaging
gently to get blood flowing.* As she began to grind into the bed, my
arousal went in a straight line down my body, throat to root. I took my
hand away and stared into her.

"You have a really pretty pussy," I said. It was symmetrical in a
way I thought no one's actually was, ironic on a person who so accepted others' irregularities. I delicately pulled up her hood and inspected her clit, a raw pink planet unto itself. Only when she was
begging did I take a deep breath and begin to interview her. I knew
the first step was to let her know she could trust me, to ease her in
until she felt safe enough to tell me the most important stories. I
started with a confident, low-pressure question, recorded her answer,
created a dialogue. Most important was to listen carefully and erase a
sense of separation, to stay tethered to the source. There was no rush,
no rush at all.

As if on cue, Mo's dick slipped into me. I don't remember if he
asked. His large rubbered penis swiped right, which made it perfect for
hitting my G-spot at certain angles and more like a pap smear in others. I got a wave of that "go away dick" feeling. It's the one I assumed

---

*   One of many tips I'd studied up on in Allison Moon's excellent guide, *Girl Sex 101* (Lunatic
Ink, 2014).

was a universal experience among we-the-penetrated, no matter our gender or sexual orientation. A sudden strong aversion to having a penis or dildo inside you, sometimes without a clear trigger. Could the feeling be the result of previous less-than-consensual experiences I'd repressed, or was the sense of déjà vu a collective memory passed down through generations of dickspreading? Maybe it was just the emotional vent through which all the microaggressions men had committed against me sexually—usually without malice or intention but simply unexamined privilege—attempted to pass.

Either way, for not the first time that night, I wanted Mo to literally and figuratively stop inserting himself. It was unfair of me, I scolded myself—he just wanted to be included. But it was harder to hear Miranda's wordless cues above his phallic interjections, and that held immense symbolic weight, too. My tongue began to go faster and faster, to become less skillful, though she didn't seem to mind. I worked my tongue up and down in little pointed licks like I was a cat lapping milk. *Ah, pussy! How did I never get that before now?* I laughed into her, and as I did, Miranda began to shudder on my face. As she came, I felt satiated in a way I'd not quite absorbed from making a man orgasm. The empathy felt somehow embedded, our bodies melded. It was easier to sense there was no separate self.

———

My stomach plummeted when I finally walked into our apartment at 3 a.m. Adam was still out with Leah. He'd told me they'd probably be sleeping together for the first time that night. Another milestone—only this one I'd dreaded. And so as I waited for him to come home from fucking and cuddling and cooking dinner for that *whore-slut-bitch-cunt-don't-think-that-she's-just-like-you-Rachel,* I did the thing that almost always helped, the ritual I would continue to enact for years to come. I journaled everything I could remember about what had just happened, my fingers struggling to keep up with the recent past in order to prove my presence worthwhile.

When Adam came in the door and found me writing in child's pose, I kept typing. I was pretending to be too swept up to care what he'd done, and in this enactment it almost felt true. He knew better than to say too much. He stood behind me and made parentheses of my hips, cupping my ass in a way that made me hope I was still his most finely crafted sentence yet. He spanked me, firm—not to hurt, but to remind me how this worked. "Come to bed," he commanded. He'd been inside another woman not hours—maybe minutes—before, and the thought of it made me want to cry, scream, fuck, and be his wife at once. I assumed the position of a tabletop, his favorite.

"Did you fuck him?" he asked my back, working deep and slow. I knew the experience with Miranda—not Mo—was what really merited reclaiming. But it had to be a man for him to enter that state we both chased.

"Yeah, and his dick is so big," I answered. This was important to Adam: that the other man's dick might satisfy me more. He dug even further into me. It stung a little, but that felt right, like being punished and savored simultaneously.

"Do you want to know what I did?"

"No, not yet," I answered in a little voice, my throat tightening. I already knew. I could feel it. I pushed back onto him harder, wildly aroused and grieving at once. So I didn't even have a monopoly on this now. How could something that was breaking my heart make me come so quickly and hard? *I'll never be enough for him, and I never was. He told me I was special, but it wasn't true.*

He seemed to read my mind, the way he always did, like my thoughts were a story he was predestined to author himself. "*You're* my girl," he reminded, scooping me out till I was empty.

The Divine Feminine

10/17/16

Text Message

> **Rachel:** I wouldn't mind coming over and cuddling for a bit, if you're in the mood.

> **Miranda:** Sure! You can meet my sissy maid :)

10/17/16

BROOKLYN

The morning after, Miranda was in sweats and no bra again, and I found her doubly beautiful. She led me to the bathroom, where a slight, fair-skinned man was on his hands and knees cleaning the bathtub.

"Rachel, this is sissy. Sissy, this is my friend Rachel."

"Hi," he said in a small voice, looking down. They had an arrangement: He wanted to serve her in a maid's outfit, she wanted to have her apartment cleaned for free.

"Hi, nice to meet you!" I said. "It looks really clean in here!" *I hope I don't sound patronizing . . . unless that's what he wants? He really is doing a great job. Miranda is some kind of brilliant.*

"Honey, we're going in my room for a bit," Miranda said to sissy.

"Here are the rags for the kitchen, and when you're done you can pol-ish the floors. The wipes are under the sink. You can use those to clean the countertops, sweetie." She didn't say please or thanks, but she was completely gentle in her commands. *So this is what domination can look like.*

We lay down, and I let her hold me like a sick child. My head throbbed like I was hungover, though I hadn't drunk alcohol. The morning after sleeping with Leah, and Adam was already out on a first date with someone else today. We seemed to be out with other people at least twice a week now, sometimes more. A momentum was building that I wasn't comfortable with, but since we were moving to Los Ange-les in a few weeks, it felt mutually understandable. We were both end-ing a decade-long love affair with New York, both ready to be around trees and Adam's family. I also wanted to move so that I'd have to work from home instead of the office. I'd seen a few women say they had to relocate because their fiancé or husband got a job. I did the same, and told my boss I was engaged for extra hetero/mono-normative credibil-ity. Though Adam hadn't given me the ring yet, the plan was to get domestic-partnered when we moved and then engaged to be married, as he'd suggested.

In Miranda's bosom, my headache began to fade. "You were so kind and firm with sissy just now," I murmured. "I think I had this image, before you, of domming being harsh or mean. But you're so sweet. Sweet—but in total control."

"Yeah, that's how I prefer it. I want them to *want* to serve me, to worship the divine feminine."

"*The divine feminine,*" I said, repeating the phrase like a precocious kid learning a new word. This little sub feeling wasn't only coming out with Adam now; a part of me felt like Miranda's girl in her arms, too. I tried to go back to my more adult side. "I guess your work as a dom must have also taught you a lot about how to be a social worker," I observed.

"Oh, *so* much. I've learned to hold space for people, not to be judgmental, or let my surprise or laughter show. I've also had to be good about setting firm boundaries." I nodded like I understood, but "boundaries" were still an abstract concept. Setting them was a nice idea I could conceive of, but when I sat down to do the math, it all felt blurry. Like explaining the theory of relativity or something. *Sure, it's about gravity, right, yeah, of course, I know.**

After a while, Miranda went to go check on sissy. "Oh sweetie, you took a nappy!" she squealed, laughing. I heard her mutter to herself that he was curled up like a kitten on the floor. "Show Rachel your new outfit!" Silence. Sterner, but still kind. "Come on. Show her." He had changed from the latex maid uniform into stockings and a pretty black bra.

"You don't seem fazed by any of this," he said shyly, looking down. Maybe he wanted me to be. I wasn't sure.

"I'm not," I said. *Interested, sure. But not really fazed.* "I don't have any lingerie that pretty anymore. I'm jealous! You look great."

"Thank you," he said, blushing, eyes still downcast.

"Okay, honey, you can go now," Miranda said, shutting the door in his face gently.

I began kissing Miranda all over, sucking on her breasts with a slow reverence, fingering her gently, teasingly. No man was there to escalate

---

*   Dedeker Winston, who's also the author of *The Smart Girl's Guide to Polyamory,* later helped me understand how a person might go about figuring out their boundaries: First, you should look at your past for examples of behavior that ran counter to your values. Use that to ask yourself what your guiding principles are. The difference between a rule and a boundary, she emphasizes, is that you impose a rule on someone else. A boundary, on the other hand, you make clear to someone else, but are personally responsible for enforcing. If a behavior crosses your boundaries, it is your responsibility to speak up for yourself and give yourself permission to say no—or potentially even leave the relationship.

"To figure out your hard lines, you can start from a place like, 'What do I not want to have happen? What's not okay with me? What goes counter to my values?' Then, also, think about the positive side. 'What kind of relationships do I want to foster? How do I want to feel in my relationships? How do I want to feel in my life? How do I want to feel around the people that I'm intimate with?'" she said. It can be a lifelong process of adjusting your boundaries by paying close attention to how they might evolve.

our rhythm now, and I was so glad, if a little nervous. I loosened my grip on the construct of linear time, my search for a destination. I found it was much easier to do this with a woman alone. I was in no way surprised. When she came again on my lips, I still didn't feel like I needed or wanted an orgasm myself, the normal tendency to keep score. Again, like my body was already her body. She seemed to understand this intuitively. I rested my head on her leg and curled up into her inner thigh, breathing her in. I went from topping her back to feeling little, comforted by the fecundity that seeped from Miranda's pores.

"Adam slept with someone else last night," I said quietly. "It was the first time. I know it doesn't mean he loves me less, but I can't help feeling like something is lost . . ." She stroked my hair, and I let myself grip harder on to her leg. "Either way, it's worth it for this freedom, right? I mean, I wanted this for so long, and it's because of non-monogamy I was finally confident enough to be with you."

She was silent for a while. "I sometimes think about what my mentor, a ninety-four-year-old woman, told me," Miranda said slowly. "This woman led our psychedelic journey group for decades, and she was lucid in the weeks before she died. We'd sit together in these long, comfortable silences." Miranda paused, let us rest there, too. "And when she came out of one of those long silences, I'll always remember she said to me: 'The best way to truly love, and know yourself, is through the romantic love of another woman. And my men have honored that.'

"I'm polyam *now*," Miranda eventually continued. "But I'm guessing I might like something more monogamish in the long run, if I have kids. But if I end up with a man, I'd need to have the freedom to be with women in some way."

I now felt the same. Now that I knew for sure what I'd been missing, I didn't want to have to choose. I realized for this reason alone, I'd likely never want to offer someone total monogamy again. Though my queer imposter syndrome lingered, I knew for sure now being with women was not some bucket list item for me. It was like turning on music I'd been subliminally told to mute since before I knew how to operate a remote. Music I also loved, but that Adam would never be able to dance with me to. A tone his ears couldn't even register.

———

While those elder woman's words resonate for my life—that there would be no "true" knowing myself without experiencing romance with women—they are also an example of a certain idolization of queerness I'm dangerously prone to. As if being with women is somehow more evolved or interesting than being with men. As if women who don't at least try being with other cis women, trans people, or nonbinary folks are simply fearful of fully understanding themselves. In addition to being rude to straight people, this way of thinking actually puts queerness on a dangerous pedestal. Idealization can flow easily into tokenization and appropriation. Like non-monogamous relationships, queer ones are no more inherently noble or sophisticated. But when I was rejecting certain societal constructs to engage in either, it was easy to feel smug in the rebellion. My need to prove to myself that my own queerness was legitimate or "strong enough" was the engine behind this misguided tendency. I knew I was frequently attracted to women, and had now finally become romantically involved with one. But I still felt like I'd snuck into a club with a fake ID. *Look at my record of dating cis man after cis man! I could be kicked out at any moment.* That feeling of inferiority was easy to confuse for queer people's inherent superiority.

———

A few days later, I stood in the middle of Mohammed and Miranda, linking arms around our inside joke as we walked down Eastern Parkway. "You know, I feel like I wouldn't mind having a sister wife, like that would be ideal," Miranda said, smiling down at me.

"Are you trying to ask me something? Because I accept." I grinned. I didn't want us to commit to Mo, but I did like the two roles embedded in the term: sister and wife. With Miranda, it felt so natural to float back and forth between these feelings—sexual and sororal. But now, when we were just getting started, I was moving to LA. At least I was sure we'd keep in touch.

Savor the season, for this too shall pass, Brooklyn's autumnal leaves confirmed. One of many things that make fall in New York so poignantly beautiful is the knowledge that winter is coming. And it'll get you every time.

I Didn't Say No

10/24/16

BROOKLYN

"You're even wearing my favorite outfit," I pouted, seeing Adam get dressed for Leah. He smiled, came over to give me an enveloping hug.

"My beautiful Jewish woman," he said and laughed. "Of course she's going to be a little pain in the ass."

"When was the last time you dressed up for me and took *me* out?"

"We go out. We'll go out again soon, okay? Come on, don't be like that. Come on! We're moving to LA to start a new life together! Aren't you excited?" He got so unusually giddy before his dates. I hated myself for having an image of wiping his smile right off. *If I really loved him the way he loved me, I wouldn't be so selfish. I'd want whatever made him feel this free.* And so I tried to mostly perform this future self.

Adam told me he loved me, and left. I drank and smoked and word-vomited a venomous journal entry in an attempt at catharsis before Mo arrived. Miranda wanted to hear about us alone together. I sensed this wasn't going to be a strong enough numbing agent for me tonight, Mo minus Miranda. But her wish was our command. We kissed as I let Mo do *whatever, don't really care.* Some indie song with the sarcastic chorus "Jesus Christ is your friend" played. "Mohammed fingering a Jewess in the ass to a song about Jesus Christ! Like a joke that needs no punch line," I said wryly.

I was only half there. High and drunk in an effort to forget that

Adam was probably having romantic sex with Leah at that very moment. I felt sick about it on all levels—sick imagining it, and sick with myself for still having that "illogical reaction" *a whole six months* after opening up the relationship on his end. *I need to learn to be more rational already.* But the jealous demon was only getting stronger. "Do you want to go to the bed?" I asked Mo.

It was my most immature and petty move yet. I was violating Adam's one rule in the apartment: no penile penetration in our bed without him. *But he said I could do "whatever I want" with Mo tonight, and isn't he breaking my heart at this very moment, and aren't we moving to LA in a week and going to have a different bed anyway?* I came twice on top of Mo, but I didn't feel better. It was late now, and Adam still wasn't home.

"I just had sex in our bed," I texted him. "Come fuck me with Mo? He finally suggested it." We hadn't had an MFM since Liam. I wanted to feel worth reclaiming again, shiny and new.

"Wtf????" he texted back. Adam almost never used acronyms or superfluous punctuation. I was in trouble. The idea made me feel nervous and reassured at once. "I'll be home soon," he wrote. "And no."

When Adam walked in the door a half hour later, I could see he was indeed pissed. Again, I tried to initiate a threesome, still intoxicated and desperate. Both men were dressed as I sat naked on the couch. That felt sexy and scary, too, like I was being handed back for cleaning— ("I believe this hot mess is yours?")—but perhaps it would make up for my transgression if I could redirect Adam's anger into lust. *Plus, didn't he say when he found me 69ing in bed with Liam (and why did that not count as sex?!) that it was a "good hurt," and that a part of him "almost did want to find us fucking," even though he'd be pissed? Can't he see I'm trying to give him a stronger high than boring Leah could? That I'm acting out because I'm so not okay, but I'm trying to be what he wants anyway?**

---

*   In psychology, this is called "protest behavior." It's a way of trying to reestablish a sense of connected security by forcing your partner to pay attention to you when you feel ignored or misunderstood. Amir Levine and Rachel S. F. Heller, *Attached* (New York: Tarcher Perigee, 2011).

"Sorry, man, but you have to go. Rachel and I need to talk," Adam said, not yet looking at me. I apologized to Mo and kissed him good-bye, still naked. As I shut the door I knew I was in for it. I'd finally managed to give Adam a taste of what I felt when he left me—uncomfortably betrayed. It was thrilling and dangerous, like getting caught in the West Wing.

"I had one rule," he said slowly.

"I know but—"

"One rule—"

"—But you said I could do anything I wanted," I muttered. "I thought you'd like it. That it would be that good-bad feeling."

"You *know* you're just justifying your manipulation now." I was. But it was also the partial truth.

"I'm—"

"—Just. Shut up, Rachel. Give me a minute." He almost never said my name unless I was my Best or Worst. This was bad. He put his head in his hands, took a few deep breaths, closed his eyes. I saw him decide to gather himself above jealousy. A useless and counterproductive emotion, as he deemed it. Or maybe he wasn't even jealous; maybe he was just pissed I broke a rule. Either way, watching him regain control was like watching a computer reboot, and it left me astounded and terrified. He walked into our room, looked at the sexed bed. "Get on top of me," he said, stern. I obliged, glad he might want to reclaim me. Changing his mind, he flipped me over and began to fuck me the way he liked best, the way that hurt, like he was excavating my cervix. He was going even harder than usual, which was saying something. My pussy was already raw from Mo's size and condoms.

This hurts, but I deserve it. He's punishing me. I was bad on purpose. I bit down on the comforter, turned my head away, and started dissociating. *Miranda. Miranda, save me from this man,* I began to pray. *So he will hurt me if I act out badly enough.* Everything inside and out ached. I began to cry. Quite loudly, not in any way cute or controlled. He was used to me crying lightly during sex sometimes, feeling moved. But this was straight-up *ugly scream-sobbing*—something very different than ever before. I was heaving snotty, yelling cries, like full-on losing it. I was drunk, high, tired, and miserably jealous that my boyfriend had just had sex with another woman.

"Are you okay?" he finally asked in an annoyed tone, still thrusting. I could tell he thought this was a tantrum, more behavior not to indulge. I didn't answer his question with words. Instead I kept sobbing wildly into the blanket, hoping that if he really loved me, he would see *I was obviously not at all okay.* That he would want to stop and hold me, protect me from his anger, tell me I was still his only girl, that he didn't want to hurt me. Instead, he kept pumping punishingly as I scream-cried and floated further away than ever before. I imagined him fucking Leah lovingly, and the image made me want to hurt myself. *I deserve to be degraded. A used-up, unspecial, wasted slut. A bad girl failing every test that matters.* When he was done, he turned away from me and fell asleep quickly, wordlessly, as if nothing had happened. Another unusual punishment.

I went to the bathroom and tried to pee, but was so raw nothing came out. Something in me had clamped unusually shut. I looked in the mirror. My hair was a mess, mascara smeared down my face, my eyes swollen. I looked like . . . *What the fuck just happened?* I cried softly now, holding on to the sink, dizzy. I tried to come back to myself, my body. I felt like I'd been seriously violated, like . . .

. . . Don't you even think *that word, it's disrespectful to people who actually have been! You know you provoked him on purpose. He asked if you were okay and you didn't say no or tell him to stop . . . Then again, just to argue the other side, you* were *sobbing and screaming and that was obviously not normal, and you didn't say you were okay when he asked . . . he definitely should have stopped instead of going even harder than usual . . . so he wanted to hurt you? How could he love you and also want to hurt you*

and think it's okay to fuck a sobbing-screaming person? Stop it, don't pre-
tend you're some victim. Wasn't this exactly the kind of punishment you
were asking for?* You have no right to feel . . .

I thought of a personal essay I'd edited earlier that year: "I Didn't
Say No—But It Was Still Rape." It was one of the most argued-about
articles we had ever published, and described a similar experience to
the one I'd just had. Most of the people slamming the anonymous author were other women. I remember one comment in particular: "Oh,
please. If not saying 'no' when you realize you don't feel like sex is rape,
then I'm raped by my husband every night."

I'd initially consented to sex with Adam. But I was deeply violated
when he didn't stop as I began to clearly signal intense distress. I certainly didn't give affirmative or enthusiastic consent when he asked if I
was okay, just the absence of a verbal no.† A "no" given in hysterical
sobs and screams.

I stared into the mirror at my now-common sex bruises, once a
source of pride. I looked into my puffy eyes and asked myself a question I'd repeat over and over in the years to come:

So, Rachel, is this liberation?

———

*   The so-called "rough sex" defense "is being used more and more often in the UK, up by 90%
over the past decade, according to one estimate. The website We Can't Consent to This has
found 59 women killed in so-called 'consensual' violence in the UK, and the defence was successful in almost half of the 18 cases that came to trial in the past five years, leading to a lesser
verdict of manslaughter or an acquittal." Joan Smith, "The Rough Sex Defense Is Indefensible,"
Guardian, Nov. 22, 2019.

†   But even a verbal "no" only really works, as Angel writes in *Tomorrow Sex Will Be Good Again,*
if you actually have a partner who "is already fully committed to the complex autonomy of the
other. It all depends on whether the woman feels she has the option to refuse . . . [can her
partner] countenance a no? Will he flare up, cajole, bully, punish? Any model of consent can
prove itself worthless if a man is not open to his sexual partner's no, or her changing desires, and
if he responds to either of these with a rage borne of humiliation." Katherine Angel, *Tomorrow
Sex Will Be Good Again: Woman and Desire in the Age of Consent* (London: Verso, 2021).

Almost a year to the day later, #MeToo started trending on Twitter.

Though I'd once been harassed for months by a forty-year-old mentor/boss I'd refused to sleep with at eighteen; taken into a back room "for a job offer," only to be unconsensually kissed and groped by an old Hasidic man; propositioned by an internship supervisor alluding to the possibility of employment; grabbed violently by the pussy at a club for turning down a dance with someone; and plenty else . . . I was silent. Like whatever had happened with Adam that night and since, my stories didn't feel terrible enough to mention. I had internalized that they were the standard taxes any femme person could expect to pay, certainly one as sexually adventurous—as newly "reckless"—as me. If anything, I knew I'd gotten off easy. I wasn't *raped*. I wasn't *hit*. I wasn't *abused*. I was *lucky*. Every cis woman and trans or non-binary person I knew had stories just as problematic as mine. Most much worse.

Of course, that was precisely the point.

Some studies say 1 in 6 women are sexually assaulted or abused; others say 1 in 5. Risk goes up substantially if you're queer; 44 percent of lesbians and 61 percent of bisexual women experience rape, physical violence, or stalking by an intimate partner, compared to 35 percent of straight women.* If you're trans, your likelihood of experiencing sexual assault is 1 in 2. For people of color, racism is also a significant (and systemic) increased risk factor.†

In researching this book, I was already familiar with the higher rate of sexual assault among folks who are trans and/or people of color. But

---

* Bisexual men are also at a higher risk than other cis men; 37 percent of bisexual men experience rape, physical violence, or stalking by an intimate partner, compared to 29 percent of straight men and 26 percent of gay men. "NVIS: An Overview of 2010 Findings on Victimization by Sexual Orientation," CDC, https://www.cdc.gov/violenceprevention/pdf/cdc_nisvs_victimization_final-a.pdf.

† Devonae Robinson, "Ethnic Differences in the Experiences of Sexual Assault Victims," Applied Psychology Opus, https://wp.nyu.edu/steinhardt-appsych_opus/ethnic-differences-in-the-experiences-of-sexual-assault-victims/.

I was very surprised to learn that bisexual cisgender people experience a higher rate of both sexual assault and mental illness than both gay and straight cisgender populations.* One potential reason? Because they don't "fit" into group expectations and dynamics, they're not trusted fully in gay or straight circles because they can "pass" in either identity. Potential abusers might also rationalize that bisexual/pansexual people are "oversexed" already, more "open to whatever" . . . including being assaulted. And by "abusers" I mean, often, partners. An extensive report by the US government found that 64 percent of the women who reported being raped, physically assaulted, and/or stalked were victimized by an intimate partner, not a stranger.†

I officially lost my virginity with a woman, and exactly a week later, I lost another sort of innocence in my own home. It's not a matter of direct cause and effect, though the chain of events was certainly linked. I'm struck by how quickly my lived experiences mirrored these statistics. And how immediately I rationalized that this is just what happens to femmes audacious enough to be pansexual, kinky, or non-monogamous.‡ *And you're all three at once! What did you expect, you greedy slut?*

---

* "Bisexual Health Awareness Month: Mental Health in the Bisexual Community," Human Rights Campaign, Mar. 24, 2017; CDC, "Findings on Victimization by Sexual Orientation."

† Patricia Tjaden and Nancy Thoennes, "Full Report of the Prevalence, Incidence, and Consequences of Violence Against Women," November 2000, NCJ, 183781.

‡ I haven't been able to find numbers on the overall rate of sexual assault among consensually non-monogamous (CNM) people. But in a survey of 1,582 CNM adults Dr. Ryan Witherspoon conducted, 5.1% reported having one or more experiences of sexual assault victimization they felt were *due* to their CNM practices/identity. In a separate sample he conducted of 1,220 polyamorous adults, 8.5% reported the same. Both samples included all genders, but skewed about two-thirds women. Of course, this doesn't capture rates of sexual assault *not* perceived as being "due" to CNM/polyamory. Ryan Witherspoon, "Stigmatization of Polyamory: Perceptions, Predictors, and Clinical Implications," 2016, 10.13140/RG.2.2.15901.61922.

Fuck the Pain Away

I found myself telling Miranda what had happened. I hadn't planned
to. I felt a confusing and deep shame, like I was stupid for feeling weird
about it at all, let alone betraying Adam by talking about it. But something about Miranda, the way I knew she'd never judge me or my relationship, made me spill whatever was on my mind. *Plus, who else could
I tell?* I'd long since dumped my therapist.

I'd been with that therapist for five years before I met Adam.
When I first moved in, he'd ask me what we talked about in our sessions. He made small comments that, for reasons I couldn't pinpoint, made me stop respecting her judgment as much, made me
worry she was biased against non-monogamy, against Adam. She
was one of the smartest people I'd met, certainly the best therapist
I'd ever had. But now, I suddenly felt I couldn't trust her. I'd stopped
seeing her abruptly soon after. And my best friend Robin, or Ayesha?
They might hate Adam and push me to leave if I told them what had
happened.

"Yeah, that kind of thing is tricky." Miranda sighed, sympathetic to
my story but hardly scandalized. We sat in an empty playroom at the
dungeon she worked at, atop a dog kennel. "Something like that happened to me, too, where a boyfriend didn't stop when I was crying and

not okay, but I didn't say no. I don't know, honey. Power play can get confusing like that sometimes."*

"Should we maybe pick a safe word?" I didn't know why I even asked. It just felt like something to say.

"Couldn't hurt to pick a safe word, sure," Miranda said gently, implying that was really only going to address a small part of the problem. "Being clearer on your boundaries is important, too."

But I was still afraid that having a direct conversation about our power dynamic might somehow kill its "authenticity," or annoy Adam, who continued to make clear he was actively averse to the idea of BDSM and role play. "If by talking about their dynamic people lose their charge around it, then the relationship isn't a match," BDSM coach Emily Anne said when I told her the story years later. "What happened to you that night was not BDSM. It was abuse, and the scenario was a recipe for disaster. You didn't have negotiated boundaries, you didn't have a safe word, and you had no self-consent, knowing where your own lines were. Yes, you provoked a response that night. But he's the one who didn't stop when you were clearly not okay." Emily added that Adam's behavior was "not at all what a real dom should act like."† She said someone who protects his sub knows to look

---

* But even "people with forced sex fantasies don't actually want to be sexually assaulted," Dr. Lehmiller later told me. "What turns them on about the fantasy isn't the reality of sexual assault itself—it's about playing with power, but only within one's comfort zone and personal limits. Some people do want to act on these fantasies, but that's something that would require having a trusted partner with excellent communication who knows and respects rules and boundaries." And Adam and I had no contracted rules or boundaries, no communication around BDSM.

† If you find yourself in a Dom/sub power dynamic, it's important to have a conversation about it, to look up resources and BDSM community standards around healthy Dom/sub relationships, and to discuss your boundaries and safe words—at a minimum. Emily suggests searching for the "Sex Exploration Questionnaire" online and using each of your answers as a jumping-off point for talking about your desires and boundaries. Dr. Witherspoon adds that it's also a good idea to connect with the BDSM community, either locally or online, to understand BDSM community standards. That way you'll have allies who can help if you aren't sure whether what you're experiencing is an abuse of power or not.

out for situations where they're so distressed, intoxicated, and/or dissociated they've lost the ability to consent. Or, in my case, to even reply to a question.

Miranda and I stared into the empty cages surrounding us. "Just keep listening to your instincts," she finally said.

"But Adam keeps telling me my negative instincts are 'just fear talking.' And I can see he's at least partially right—ever since he started dating other women, I *do* feel irrationally jealous and afraid," I said. But I hadn't asked him to pause dating for longer than a week. I didn't feel I could "say no" to non-monogamy for much longer. And I wanted to "rise above" this instinct to stop.

"Yeah, I know. It's really confusing." Miranda seemed at a reluctant loss for what else to tell me. Perhaps she too felt there was no way for me to go but through. She showed me around the dungeon and told me the stories of men on leashes, men used as footstools, men who wanted to be kidnapped with a bag over their head and flogged. Sometimes couples came. More than a few Orthodox Jewish women seeking femdoms, too. "Their dumpy husbands drop them off," Miranda said, laughing. "Unfortunately, I haven't had one of those women yet. But I did date a Hasidic guy for a year. A client, on the DL. So yeah, it gets *real* quiet here around the High Holy Days," she explained of the dungeon's emptiness. There was a throne and a few cages, ropes suspended from the ceiling. "Performance art with a very small audience," she called it.

The song "Fuck the Pain Away" was playing over the speakers and I thought it a little obvious until I realized the irony. No fucking happened at the dungeon. Those were the rules: no sex allowed, supposedly,

---

If you feel afraid to set boundaries or have these conversations with your partner, it could be a sign you're in an abusive or otherwise unhealthy dynamic. The Network/La Red particularly serves queer, polyam, and kink/BDSM populations; you can call their hotline at 617-742-4911. (If you're more comfortable texting, you can reach the National Domestic Violence hotline by texting LOVEIS.) You don't have to have physical bruises or "proof" to simply ask some questions. And you don't have to identify with terms like "abuse," "victim," or anything else.

not even pegging or happy endings. This was a legal operation, where you flogged the pain toward you instead. That impulse I could now relate to. I'd never identified as a masochist, but really, wasn't I becoming one in practice? *And an orgy-going hotwife, Adam's little girl, a queer polyamorist . . .* I felt like so many things now that no one label would quite fit again. Despite what had happened, I sensed a freedom in this.

———

Adam and I moved to LA a few days later, on Halloween. I worked up the nerve to ask for a temporary moratorium on dating other people, just until we got settled. He agreed that my jealousy had become exhausting for him, too. "I wasn't planning on dating now anyway. It makes sense for us to get settled first," he said. *First*—the expiration date was again implicit, undefined yet fair. I knew he would still talk to Leah and see her when he went to New York on business. But that I could live with. She would be far away now.

When we landed in LA and taxied, I saw a string of messages from Leah on his phone. I looked away, set my jaw, and tried not to care. *I might be a pain in the ass, but at least I'm still his workout of choice.* I gave myself an internal deadline of a few months' rest from dating other people, tops. Didn't I want to be a brave protagonist? This non-monogamous odyssey had led me to so many interesting places already. I'd be a coward and a fool to turn back now. *I don't want my fears or insecurities to sabotage my future happiness. I want to choose love. Miranda has to be a sign I'm on the right path. I'm being granted access to whole new worlds.*

In a very writerly adaptive fantasy, I'd begun to think of myself as on a self-authored hero's journey.* The familiar structure of this arche-

———

* The first steps on the traditional hero's journey: 1) Ordinary World (my pre-Adam pattern of serial monogamy); 2) Call to Adventure (to try non-monogamy and submission to "true love"); 3) Refusal of Call (not wanting to deal with Adam dating other people/internal denial of his

typal narrative gave me a framework to view my increasingly unstable reality through. This way, there was a clear order to my atmosphere of cloudiness: I was on an adventure that would all make sense in retrospect! That the hero's journey was popularized by men was subconsciously part of what made it feel "legitimate."* At the same time, I also imagined I would be subverting the stereotypical odyssey in my unconventional quest for romantic liberation. *Why is a man climbing Everest considered award-winning immersion journalism,*[†] *but a reporter plumbing her most extreme psychosexual depths is confessional erotica? Fuck that. I have to keep going.*

————

I tried to have a conversation soon after with Adam about what had happened that night. "I'm not saying you raped me or anything, but it did feel like a serious violation that you didn't stop when I was obviously screaming and sobbing," I said tentatively. As soon as he heard the r-word, he became extremely defensive and started yelling. I apologized for using that word in any way, and tried to clarify I wasn't accusing him of rape. But he was very upset; betrayed, even. I ended up reassuring him, and felt guilty for having hurt his feelings. *Of course he's*

————

polyamory); 4) Meeting the Mentor and/or Goddess (Kathy, Ayesha, Miranda); 5) Crossing the Threshold (threesomes/jealousy/everything else we're up to at this point in the story) . . . Christopher Vogler, *The Writer's Journey: Mythic Structure for Writers* (Studio City, CA: Michael Wiese Productions, 2007).

*   The Western focus on the hero's journey "dismisses stories like the heroine's journey or other stories in which people do not set off to conquer and return with booty (knowledge and/or spirituality and/or riches and/or love objects)," Salesses writes in *Craft in the Real World*. "Why, when the protagonist faces the world, does she need to win, lose, or draw? . . . What if she understands herself as part of that world, that world as part of herself? What if she simply continues to live?"

†   Jon Krakauer, *Into Thin Air: A Personal Account of the Mount Everest Disaster* (New York: Anchor Books, 1997).

pissed and feels like you don't understand him. Just using that word implies
you think he's capable of being in the vicinity of terrible things.

I journaled from a cafe in LA a week later:

> The rape thing too
> I need to apologize for that
> I want a butternut rosemary muffin
> But i don't want to be fat
> What the fuck that's so fucked up maybe i should
> just buy it on principle

I didn't buy the muffin. And I never brought up that night again.

———

While writing this book, I've often felt seized by a sudden ravenous hunger. I'll emerge in a haze, confused as to why my heart is beating in my ears, why I'm dizzy. And then I'll remember the obvious, take a deep breath, and bake. I'll remember that not-so-long-ago-Rachel, this me and not-me, circuitously wondering into her journal if she was sexually assaulted by her partner; redirecting that forbidden question into whether she should allow herself a caloric muffin. And then this present-day-Rachel, this also-me and impermanent-me, will take today's batch of treats out of the oven. Make no mistake—she's not magically "all better now." But each moment is another chance to write the story in a direction she'd rather read.

So, in the new ending to this chapter, she does bring up that night again. And this time, she definitely eats the muffin.

PART 3

Age 29

ROBIN AND RACHEL DRUGGED DISNEY TRANSCRIPT

Drugs: Marijuana mixed with shroom comedown

Movie: Beauty and the Beast

Date: It's 4/20 Someyear

PROLOGUE NARRATOR:

"If he could learn to love another, and earn her
love in return, by the time the last petal fell,
then the spell would be broken. If not, he would be
doomed to remain a beast for all time.
As the years passed, he fell into despair, and lost
all hope. For who could ever learn to love a Beast?"
*[Camera pans to Belle, foreshadowing that she will be
the one to learn to love a Beast]*

RACHEL:

This is the part that always makes me cry, this
transition right here . . . Because it's
her . . . She can do it. And I'm like, "She's
the hero."

ROBIN:

. . . But you won't know it until chapter 3,* when
she fixes him . . . That's fucked up. That's a
horrible thing to show little girls, man.

RACHEL:

You're telling *me* . . .

---

* Robin is referencing Belle's foreshadowing lyric, "Here's where she meets Prince Charming /
But she won't discover that it's him till chapter 3."

BELLE:

[Singing epically, emphatically, directly into Rachel's soul]

"I want adventure in the great wide somewhere . . . I want so much more than they've got planned . . ."

RACHEL:

Oh this part is so . . . This was always my favorite part.

ROBIN:

But her plans get completely derailed. She doesn't get adventure in the great wide somewhere. I know that's allegedly what happened, but . . . she gets kidnapped.

RACHEL:

[An hour later, talking over ending]

. . . *Little Mermaid* and *Beauty and the Beast* had so much impact for me . . . One of you all is changing species. Nothing short of total transformation is going to work here.

ROBIN:

Right. You have to literally change the essence of who you are to be able to have love.

RACHEL:

That's how you *know* it's love.

. . . And then you think about it, *Aladdin* was roughly the same time period, came out two years after this I think. And also a very good movie. But it has a boy at the center. And it's not the same fucking story at all . . . He does want something

more, it's true. He finds Jasmine, but that's not what
it feels like is the thing that ends up being his
[main] adventure.

ROBIN:

Oh no. *His* adventure is overcoming his own sense of
feeling less-than. And then just being true to
himself, telling everyone who he is.

RACHEL:

. . . But in [*Beauty and the Beast*] and *Little
Mermaid*, both of [the heroines start out saying] "I
want adventure. I'm looking for something. I don't
know what it is—"

ROBIN:

[Nodding sadly, finishing Rachel's thought]
—And it's a man.

My Precious

———————

From: Rachel to [Adam]

Subject: this is my way back in

> can you tell i'm High?
> again. i know
> . . . we will never be always-monogamous
> that i agree with you on
> some triangulation helps the high
> it just has to be carefully calibrated
> tested and adjusted over periods for ideal dosage
> i'm well,
> butrin,
> thanks for asking.

12/23/16

LOS ANGELES, CA

"What about her?" I asked Adam.

"Who, the waitress?"

"She was totally flirting. Do you think she's cute? I do. Maybe we should leave our number . . ." It was three days after my twenty-ninth birthday, and he'd taken me out for a special dinner and "a surprise celebration." He wasn't much for surprises, so I knew this must be it—

he was going to give me the ring. Though I believed *logically* it was all antifeminist bullshit, another voice told me I was right on track. *I could figure out this whole not-ending-up-an-old-unwanted-spinster thing before age thirty!*

He shrugged, stabbed a fried oyster mushroom. "Sure, I guess she's cute."

Maybe if we had threesomes with women, too, that would be enough for him? Yeah, that could work . . . I wanted to show him that this monogamish pause was fleeting, that he could feel good about offering whatever it was he was about to offer. It had been less than two months, and he was still talking to Leah; I felt my inner countdown clock tick nonetheless. The sooner I was able to sincerely set him free again, the more evolved and loving I would be. In his eyes or my own, there was now little distinction.

"So, I want to tell you something." He smiled at me, put down his fork, took my hand. *Here it is, I knew it!* "You know, I've understood the people I've dated before. Like, Kelly?" He smirked. "I understood better than she understood *herself.* But even though I've understood people, in over twenty years of dating, I've never *felt* understood. It took me all this time, but I feel like I finally found that with you."

"I feel that way with you, too," I said, squeezing his hand back. *I am the specialist.*

"Do you remember when we were tripping on acid and we saw that old couple walking ahead of us? And I said, 'That could be us?'" It wasn't the first time he'd called upon this memory; it had become an integral part of our narrative. "I still feel like"—and here he choked up just perfectly—"that *will* be us. I want us to be two old people walking arm-in-arm through the park together." He slipped the velvet ring box toward me with a sly smile. "So, you've probably been wondering what the word I chose is . . ." I felt that out-of-body sensation you get when a moment you've been fantasizing about for a long time is living up to your dreams but feels somewhat anticlimactic nonetheless. I opened it eagerly. The tiny turquoise stones were small and blue, alive. The word he'd had inscribed was even better.

"It's perfect. I love it!" I smiled widely.

"Yeah? You get it?" I could tell he was proud, despite himself. There was always such satisfaction in getting him to play.

"Of course I get it. It's so good." I'd never have guessed he'd pick this secret magic word, and that made it all the better. And yet, as he slipped the ring on my finger, I shit you not: I was suddenly flooded by the sound of an iron gate locking, exactly like that of a jail cell. Despite my increasingly lubricated fucking with reality, vivid sounds in my head were not usually part of my repertoire. *You crazy bitch. This is exactly what you asked for! What the fuck is wrong with you? You get what you want, and then you feel trapped?*

"I love it, thank you." I beamed. I did, but it was feeling so . . . *tight*.

He'd planned a celebration of going to see jazz at Blue Whale. There was a rare heavy LA downpour and we got soaked. As I sat in my uncomfortably damp socks, I turned the circulation-inhibiting symbol of commitment. "Don't worry, it gets looser," Adam reassured me. "The same thing happened to me with my wedding ring." I watched the cellist pluck strings wearing a silver band. I knew I'd never see Adam tagged that way. I diverted any sadness over this into a misogynistic smugness. *I've found myself one of the real men. Untamable.*

After the set ended, we ran to the car in the still-pouring rain.

"Every romantic movie has a rain scene, right?" I said when we got in the car, dripping.

"I was just thinking that," he said, squeezing my left hand as he warmed up the car. "Guess the drought is over, huh?" Our unspoken understanding was now compounded. He kissed my finger like I was his princess. I was officially his. "I'll need both hands on the wheel tonight, my love." He drove us home with a focused and fierce concentration, bicep veins the only tension he let show. The water came down in dangerous sheets on the freeway. Our car swayed. I realized, not for the first time, that I trusted him with my life completely. Trusted him with it more than I trusted myself. *If that isn't devotion, what is?*

When he parked in front of the house, I breathed a sigh of relief. "Good job. You got us home alive. That was intense."

"Yeah, you like that?" He smiled. "You like how your man keeps you alive? Other dudes would have killed you in that." He was often doing this. Joking about what losers other guys were, untrustworthy and immature. A control tactic, though perhaps not a conscious one. Creating a culture in the relationship where we both believed I'd never do better. We got dry and warm. He put on his most romantic playlist and we danced until I curled up in his lap. I rubbed my nose into his chest like someone's new fiancée might. I felt newly minted, adopted. He held me like that a good long while.

———

I knew I wouldn't tell my family or friends the "news"—what was there to tell if it wasn't an actual marriage proposal? But I showed the ring proudly to a stranger at a Christmas party the next night, blurting out my glee.

"Cute. So, it's like, a promise ring?" the stranger asked.

"I mean, I guess, sort of . . ." That sounded so Evangelical-teen-purity-pledge, though. "We already got domestic partnered a month ago," I added for credibility.

"But did he actually even *promise* anything?" The woman was middle-aged and bug-eyed, definitely drunk and maybe high.

"Well, no . . . I guess he more . . . stated his intention to grow old with me?"

The woman grunted. "Let me guess—he's been married before?"

"Yeah, but only for a year when he was twenty-four—"

"—Then it doesn't mean anything. Watch, he'll get married again. Just later. He has more stock than you do. How old is he?"

"Forty."

"*Psh*," she said, waving her hand dismissively. "In his late forties he'll still be desirable and he'll marry someone else. He's just found someone younger to have fun with now, and that's you." I couldn't believe it. It was like she was saying my deepest paranoid thoughts aloud. I'd told her a few minutes before that we were non-monogamous—maybe that was why she was being so harsh? "Look, I work as a counselor and I see women in your situation all the time. They try to rationalize, but they aren't happy. It *always* ends badly. I'm telling you the truth. Have your fun but don't think this is real commitment. If it's commitment you don't need other people."

On the way home, I told Adam what she said.

"But she was obviously crazy. Did you see her eyes?" He bulged his out for emphasis and pointed. "Crazy eyes. Plus you know people just don't get non-monogamy. They assume because you're a woman I'm taking advantage of you. They think monogamy and commitment are the same thing. She's just projecting her own shit."

"But . . . Never mind."

"What? Tell me," he said gently.

"It's fine, you're right," I said.

"Tell me," he commanded. I loved how that always worked. Being forced to express my feelings. He never let me get away with saying "never mind."

"Well, I love the ring, really. But she's right, you . . . you didn't actually promise anything." My voice went little. I looked down, embarrassed.

"You can't promise anything in life is forever," he said. "The truth is everyone's only as loyal as their options."

"How am I supposed to feel secure when you keep saying that?"

"Doesn't it mean more that I'm *choosing* you without lying about that and having you live in some fantasy?" he countered. "I'm telling you my intention, and it's real and honest. It's a conscious intention to keep you as my partner, so long as we're both happy." I shrugged, looked out the passenger window. He still hadn't once seen me behind the wheel. This was how we both wanted it. "Come on, talk to me."

"I mean, I know we're domestic partners now, but that's so easy to dissolve. And it doesn't seem to mean as much to your family. I'm not trying to be ungrateful. And I know I asked for the ring in the first place, but . . ."

"But what?" he asked.

"Well, what should I think of this as really meaning?"

"It means I want to grow old with you," he answered, feeling misunderstood.

"Right, but what that lady was saying is that you didn't actually promise anything, so it doesn't actually mean anything." He let the implicit question hang in silence. He took my hand and placed it on the clutch, rubbing his thumb over the ring. In just one day, I'd already grown attached to the secure feeling of it on my finger.

"You know I would get married to you, if you really want to," he said. "I just think it's a bunch of unnecessary pain if you do break up with me." He always put it that way. That I would be the one to break up with him.

"Maybe it would be good for me, for it to be harder to run away," I offered. I knew this was one of the most compelling arguments to him. For some reason, I felt it ungrateful to remind him he'd promised we'd get engaged once we moved to LA. *Maybe he changed his mind after you had sex in the bed with Mo.*

"Of course we'll try to work through things, but if it's not working anymore, I don't want us to be unhappy or in more pain because of some legal promise," Adam said. "Doesn't the choice mean more? That we don't need some government contract? That you know I want to be with you until one of us dies, and that I rechoose that each day?" I knew what he meant. There's something that felt extra poignant about actively continuing to opt in when you're non-monogamous. The way you're constantly reminded not to take your partner's desirability and both your choices for granted.

I'd never really fantasized about getting married before I met Adam, and certainly never wished to marry anyone else I'd dated. But now that I couldn't have what he'd proposed so passionately so many times, I wanted to achieve it.

"I just find that he led you on this way so appalling," Ayesha later told me. "I know from personal experience how much time he spent beating his breast in public about how he hated marriage and procreation, even when no one was arguing with him. So was he talking about it with you because that's what he thought you wanted to hear? Was he saying it because he's ultimately more normative than he thinks he is? Either way, it's another part of how he fucked with your brain, and shouldn't have been allowed to."

———

Until I was ready to open the relationship back up, I decided I would also document the effects of temporary monogamish-ness on both of us. I started recording my high streams of consciousness, even. The rules: I would type my thoughts as quickly as I could right as I had them, not letting myself censor or consider or delete a single word. I wanted to have the purest record possible of my mind, unfiltered. I became captivated by the ineffability of my objective; "the reality of what was happening could never be precisely expressed," Sigrid Nunez writes of the feeling.* "Even before I began I knew that whatever I might manage to describe would turn out to be, at best, somewhere to the side of the thing, while the thing itself slipped past me, like the cat you never even see escape when you open the house door."

———

* Sigrid Nunez, *What Are You Going Through?* (New York: Riverhead Books, 2020).

1/11/17

High Stream of Consciousness

[Adam] was so sweet out of nowhere yesterday seeing me typing in the living room saying 'alexa, how is my girlfriend so hot?' and she said 'sorry i can't understand the question' and he said 'i bet you can't'.

. . . In that moment i was filled with a desire to [let him date other women again]. Could see how when i truly love i will be able to uncage him

Meanwhile, I wrote my mom an email asking her about the diamond she wore while she was with my stepdad. I already knew they were also "only" domestic partners the entire time they were together. But were there other parallels, too?

2/4/17

Reply: [Mom] to Rachel
Subject: Ring

I wanted a symbol of [your stepdad]'s commitment to me. Hence the ring. Whenever I mentioned marriage to him, which was difficult for me, he was neither negative nor enthusiastic. But even as a feminist, I still wanted a "traditional" acknowledgment of my worth as a partner.

. . . I always felt I was the creator of this arrangement. He "let" me satisfy that need in me [with the ring I'd chosen].

I'd also asked her to tell me more about her first husband, Tom. I knew he was a *goy* her parents had disowned her for marrying, but what about the non-monogamy she'd once alluded to?

. . . I craved attention. I flirted and usually got what I wanted. . . . The [two men I was cheating with] made me feel desired and also in control, where otherwise I didn't feel in control . . . At some point, I felt I needed to tell [Tom about them], and I was surprised and confused by the answer. Something like, 'I love u and as long as u stay it's ok.' I saw that as indifference and an untraditional answer I wasn't expecting. . . . Then one day I came home to [Tom] revealing he slept with our neighbor. I became a screaming uncontrollable person. I felt out of control. I even suggested we do a threesome; maybe for me to be in control there also.

. . . I still wasn't content and moved out. Looking back, I feel I was so damaged that I didn't feel I deserved love and pushed it away . . .

Sent from my iPhone

Reading my mom's email, I noted history's rather un-nuanced way of repeating itself. *I need to learn from her mistakes, and not push away the man who loves me and gives me freedom. I need to be rational about non-monogamy, not self-sabotaging.*

The psychoanalyst Carl Jung believed that a woman with a "mother complex" can't accept her mother's tendencies in herself and fears reliving her mom's mistakes. According to Jung, this may lead the daughter to reject certain stereotypically feminine aspects of herself entirely, in favor of stereotypically masculine ones. By this logic, Adam was my way of both trying to mend my mother's "mistakes" and rejecting her. His hyperdominant and "rational" nature—the archetypal masculine—had certainly become valued and trusted over the more emotional and intuitive sides of myself (the archetypal feminine). Adam also continued to remind me not to be like my mother.

If I had trouble with his behavior, it was because I was self-sabotaging based on embedded "irrational fears and insecurities." What we both didn't seem to realize is that the high value Adam placed on his "rationality" over my "irrationality" was also a result of *his* projections. In part because he was not "supposed" to feel strong negative emotions as a man (besides anger, with maybe a little side of depression), Adam was unconscious or avoidant of his own vulnerable feelings, anxieties, and insecure manipulations. He then tended to project those suppressed stereotypically feminine feelings and behaviors onto me and other women. Can a pattern be ironic if it's also quite predictable?

"[Adam] trying to discredit your feelings is a toxic element of patriarchy. It's not about blaming him or seeing you as the victim," Buddhist teacher Kaira Jewel Lingo later advised me. "It's about seeing that there's a wind that blows through our society, and it was blowing through your interactions. Two people trying to figure out how to love and not be caught up in the stories that they've inherited. But maybe not knowing how to."

True strength lies in a willingness to do the work of disentangling. And it is often spotted in the gentlest of gestures. Leaning in to listen, taking a deep breath, rolling up one's sleeves.

If These Walls Could Talk

---

*"A house is never apolitical. It is conceived, constructed,
occupied, and policed by people with power, needs, and fears."*
—Carmen Maria Machado, *In the Dream House: A Memoir*

2/13/17

LOS ANGELES

Miranda was in town to see family and sissies. I'd told Adam earlier
that day about a comment she'd made, that she had a fantasy of us
tying him up and making him watch, powerless, as we had sex. Since
Miranda could take him in a fight, she wasn't his type. Nor was he into
being dominated. "Maybe I'd get into a normal threesome, though,"
he'd said before she arrived for dinner, shrugging. "You should do
whatever you want," he added.

I loved having people over to the house we rented in Atwater
Village—though if I was honest, it still felt more his than mine. I'd
dared ask to hang only a few "un-Adam-style" offerings, presented as
gifts: the dried flowers from our second date I'd had framed for our anniversary. A card I'd found depicting two rolls of toilet paper, one put
on "backwards," the other correctly. "There are two types of people,"
the caption read. "Those who get it, and those who don't." I was aware
that I'd only ever occupied the lower shelves of our three large book-
cases, in New York or LA. I'd gotten rid of most of my books in my

rush to move in with him in Brooklyn, and what was left—mostly vegan cookbooks, feminist texts, and memoirs—were implicitly not worth more prominent display. It took another six months of living in LA for me to work up the nerve to ask to move to a middle shelf. When I did, he seemed perplexed, inconvenienced. Like I was just creating more meaning where there needn't be any.

"What are some of the most interesting things you've seen in your job?" Adam asked Miranda now, passing her one of his perfectly rolled joints.

"Hm, well, there's a guy who's into Bible play." Miranda smiled, taking a drag.

"Like, playing Moses?" I asked.

"No, like literally shoving the Bible up his ass as he curses God," she said, smiling. "Or maybe the guys that like rods in their urethras. Filling up their ball sack with saline using a needle." Adam cringed, crossed his leg in a square, that way I still loved. "Mostly it's heartbreaking things. An elderly Vietnam vet saying, 'I love you, Mommy. Do you love me?' And I'd say, 'Well, I care about you very much, Robert.' And then he'd say, 'But do you *love* me?'" Miranda shuddered at the memory. "I don't want to be someone's mommy."

I felt embarrassed that hearing those words stung a little. But the organic, now-legal weed Miranda had brought from her dad's grow-op (#California) was making me feel mischievous. "I have a question: Where do you think Adam falls on the Dom/sub spectrum? Because he doesn't like role play or causing physical pain. He likes to be in control, to share me, and to give."

Miranda assessed him like she was guessing his inseam. "I think he's a service top," she said conclusively. "They want to take care of you, but only on their own terms. I don't like to work with them. Too bossy." She smiled at him. "No offense."

"Sounds about right." Adam nodded, amused.

"Do you think that everyone could benefit from exploring both sides of themselves, though, or that some people are really just dom or sub?" I asked.

"Honestly, I'm not even sure what's real or authentic for *me* anymore because I've played with so many sides of my sexuality." She sighed. "It's harder to suspend disbelief. I try to find someone who I can believe is topping me, but it's like I know all the tricks."

"In my experience, every woman I've been with likes at least some degree of pain,"* Adam added. The reasons why felt too obvious to speak aloud. Dating Adam elicited masochistic tendencies—or perhaps, they were a prerequisite to finding him attractive. Adam made a point of excusing himself to the bathroom. By now, I knew this was a sort of offering, a chance for me to initiate a threesome. By the time he came back to the living room, I'd already begun kissing Miranda. He drew our curtains.

"Is this okay with Adam?" She asked me as if he weren't there, staring at us.

"Of course," he said with a chuckle, as if it were silly to think my being with a woman could provoke jealousy. It didn't even turn him on that much, the idea. He said it lacked that feeling of real competition. But he did at least look mildly entertained now. I felt excited by my genuine hope he'd want to participate after all. I wanted to confront my fear of seeing him look up from another bush, watching his tongue in another mouth—and with the safest person I could imagine.

We relocated to the bed, and Adam grew hard as Miranda and I undressed each other. I suggested he go down on her; I kissed and fondled her as he did. I felt a deep pride when I could see she would

---

* According to Dr. Lehmiller's study of more than 4,000 North Americans, 65 percent of people reported fantasizing about receiving physical pain during sex. Women were more likely than men to have fantasized about both giving and receiving pain. Lehmiller, *Tell Me What You Want*.

quickly come, a choking mix of compersion and letting go. It was as if she were my surrogate, releasing on his face the cunnilingual orgasm I still could not. The pain of it turned quickly into an intense pleasure. I now understood: During sex, the prick of jealousy could feel fluid, fleeting, fantastic, fetishistic. Like being in total mastery of yourself at the same time you feel blissfully out of control.

When Miranda left much later that night, we both tasted like her vagina. To my great pride and relief, that turned me on. I could tell he was proud of me.

————

After that night, I officially lifted our monogamish moratorium. *I have to find a way to have long-term commitment and my freedom, too. I don't want cheating or serial monogamy. And I don't want to end up muting my true desires with one person only and forever. Figuring out some form of sustainable non-monogamy is the only viable path forward for me.* After all, during our monogamish pause I'd felt calm, happier . . . but less sexually excited. *Why can't I just feel safe and wild with lust at once? Is anxiety always tied to attraction?*

Or was I simply eager to give Adam what he wanted quickly, and to be desired again more intensely? It was impossible to separate my motivations fully. I wanted Adam's hunger for me to appear wild again, as

————

* Indeed, it often is, chemically speaking. This is why people on SSRIs usually experience a drop in sex drive. High serotonin levels—which usually mean less anxiety—also tend to result in less arousal. When we fall in love, dopamine levels rise as serotonin drops. But the body and mind are simply not meant to sustain that obsessive state of arousal long term (homeostasis, remember?). Chemically, psychiatrist Dr. Julie Holland writes, falling in love is the equivalent of a speedball, a combination of cocaine and heroin. And it can certainly be addictive. My pattern throughout my twenties—going off SSRIs when I fell in love, then back on them as I began the breakup process—is apparently not at all uncommon. There are many junkies whose drug of choice is the high of falling in love. Julie Holland, *Moody Bitches* (New York: Penguin Books, 2015).

it hadn't since our first MFMs. To give him what he wanted and to let him see me from afar, anew. I wanted passion with him, and I wanted infatuation with new people. I wanted all of the toppings at once.

I immediately booked a flurry of self-protective dates.

2/19/17

Journal Entry

[My date's] apartment is the basest form of bachelor . . . A toilet seat that fell off that day, cans of old spice, a bathtub i will not be taking a bath in . . . i grab his hair and ride his face and eventually tell him you must be tired and he stops and then we talk for a while, a good long while.

. . . i have a fantasy of how i'd like to celebrate our anniversary, which is to say [new guy] coming over and [Adam] watching us fuck. I am in heat . . . I get so excited by newness. But newness alone is not enough.

Within a week of that journal entry, whatever fantasy I had of that new guy cracked, and I lost interest in him. Soon after, the same thing happened with another man. It was officially a new pattern: Fantasize out of proportion about Adam's new competition (and it had to be a man for Adam to consider it exciting competition, which meant my blossoming queerness was deprioritized). Have sex with new guy hoping he might rescue me (from Adam or jealousy, I wasn't sure). Immediately lose interest when Adam was obviously superior (just like he'd said he would be).

Liam, who I'd been chatting with frequently ever since our threesome nearly two years before, remained a notable exception.

The Accidental Poetry
of Everyday Life

3/13/17
Kik Chat

> **Rachel:**
> I finally googled you and found your essay . . . i quite enjoyed it. The whole thing was touching . . .

> **Liam:**
> . . . Maybe you should get naked and have a photo shoot instead

[In a rare show of dignity, Rachel doesn't answer. This is rewarded the next day.]

3/14/17

> **Liam:**
> I'm glad you read that essay. Was from a time when I really felt like a writer. Maybe I'll write another. Welcome to my brain

> **Rachel:**
> You are a writer. You certainly can't fake what I read, and being a writer is as much chronic condition as it is verb, though I know that form of self-doubt/loathing well. I hope you do write another. I like your brain.

[Subconsciously punishing her unattractive sincerity, Liam doesn't answer. Rachel will cave soon enough, anyway.]

3/18/17

> **Rachel:**
> you know what's funny about my fantasies with you lately?

> **Liam:**
> What?

> **Rachel:**
> Lately my bush has been gone
> My bush is usually never gone
> . . . I think it has something to do with being fully exposed

[Liam responds to this admission ten days later with one line.]

3/28/17

> **Liam:**
> I hope you appreciate your perky titties

I knew my consistently engaging with Liam was a way I confirmed my sense of unworthiness, my suspicions of my fundamental unlovability and needy repulsiveness, even. Chatting with him was like snapping a rubber band on my wrist. He took too long to respond, obviously considered me much less, perhaps hardly at all. I was one of several women, I assumed. Yes, our entire dynamic was increasingly humiliating. But increasingly humiliating was my new normal.

I used to replay one video he sent in particular: his big hands a little grease-stained from fixing his boat, stroking his mast of a dick. *Up down, up down* his smooth foreskin went, pumping slowly to nothing less holy than the rhythm of the waves. He told me he wanted to fuck me on the deck under the sun, afterward in the ocean. The fantasy was as close as he got to romance, and I'd think about that as I replayed the video over and over, as well as the fact that Adam's hands were never dirty. *Up down, up down*, hypnotized by a vertical pendulum.

One day in April Liam was visiting California and asked me—day-of; I'm guessing his first choice canceled—if I wanted to go camping with him in Joshua Tree National Park. I could think of almost nothing I wanted more. But I'd committed to giving a talk for UCLA's animal rights club. I'd already promised myself (anticipating the crosstown traffic) that I wouldn't bail no matter what. I asked Adam what he thought I should do. He said it might be "bad karma" to flake on my commitment. "But do whatever you want," he added, his judgmental tone arguing otherwise. I very hesitantly told Liam I couldn't make it *and did the right thing, blah blah blah.*

After the talk, an enthusiastic student came up to me—a Liam in training, judging by the way the other young women stared at him and how contentedly oblivious he seemed to it. The student gave me his email: the same first and last name as Liam's. The accidental poetry of everyday life was frequently anything but nuanced. Each day was now a vignette I appreciated on a sort of meta-artistic plane, especially as my immediate reality felt increasingly cloudy.

I was also stoned much of the time now, which certainly helped lend the sense that everything was poignant, *beshert.** Now that I was writing a cannabis sex column, I was getting sent sample after free sample of high-quality product. I was also being invited to some truly fascinating brand launch parties, which handed out newly legally recreational cannabis like candy. I had more THC than I knew what to do with, even giving plenty away to Adam's parents and friends. It was a green rush in California, and I was rich.†

In an effort not to smoke every day, I'd placed Adam in the (even for us) highly paternalistic position of hiding all the freebies away in a literal lockbox only he knew the code to. The idea was he couldn't refuse me if I asked, but that I'd have to feel judged if I wanted to smoke too often.

"My little addict. You're like a raccoon. We have to lock it away or you'll sniff it out of the trash," he'd joke lovingly, nuzzling my neck and rolling his eyes. "But seriously. I just want your brain to still work when we're old, okay?" I was touched by his sentiment, but apparently willing to chance it. I found I wanted weed more often than I wanted to ask for it. I started hiding certain samples from Adam. In a relationship where nothing was supposed to be secret, my affair with Mary Jane was becoming my biggest, if most obvious, concealment. I told Adam I felt I might be forming a problem, but he didn't seem concerned so much as reassuring, like I was a hypochondriac making up an imaginary disease.

---

*   Yiddish for meant to be/destined (often in reference to a marriage).

†   Meanwhile, as I told myself I was elevating my consciousness, thousands of other Californians—mostly, Black and Latinx people—were still in cages for nonviolent marijuana "offenses." A 2020 analysis by the ACLU found that Black people are 3.64 times more likely than white people to be arrested for marijuana possession, though they use the drug at a comparable rate. Latinx people make up the overwhelming majority of those incarcerated for marijuana in California. There is a particular injustice to people still being in prison for something that is now legal in their state, as (mostly white) businesses profit off the drug, legally. To help change this, go to lastprisonerproject.org and get involved. And to learn more about why prison abolition—another supposedly unrealistic yet actually possible societal shift—is necessary, read *Are Prisons Obsolete?* and *The New Jim Crow* and watch the documentary *13th*.

4/23/17

High Stream

> *I chose to be alone [while Adam is on a date all day]*
> *To almost sit with discomfort but not really exactly*
> *To numb medicate it with weed and coconut oil*
> *weed on my pussy*
> *. . . anti-anxiety meds and now a grape soda vodka*
> *too*
> *But im sipping slowly and breathing and trying to*
> *not take it as a rejection . . .*
> *Don't i want him to be happy? The way i'm happy?*
> *Look at me i'm so happy . . .*

What's most striking to me reading these old journal entries is how consistently either *Meh* or *F*sdfkjhf;hef%*!* I seem—though I didn't think of myself as feeling either way *most* of the time. The pleasant details—the small moments that kept me in love—are mentioned far less often than negative events and anecdotes, the jealousy. A reflection of how I was feeling in the relationship, sure—but also indicative of how the brain works. Humans have a hardwired negativity bias. When we have a negative experience, it often immediately gets stored in our working memory in order to help protect us from potential future harm. A positive experience, on the other hand, only tends to leave a lasting impression if you linger on it.* Ordinary little moments, which

---

*   It's good to aim for at least fifteen to thirty seconds to let a positive moment really sink in—and to enjoy the feeling as deeply as possible. "The key is a matter of degree: the longer, the more intense, and the more felt in the body an experience is the more it will be encoded in neural structure," Dr. Rick Hanson, author of *Hardwiring Happiness,* writes. "It's also known that negative experiences have an advantage: they get encoded more readily. So we are trying to do two things: steepen the learning curve from useful, beneficial experiences, and compensate for the negativity bias of the brain." Rick Hanson, *Hardwiring Happiness* (New York: Harmony Books, 2016).

are often the happiest ones, simply aren't as dramatic. We don't remember them as "events" unless they're unusual, or we really savor them.

And there are only two positive phrases I notice as examples of consistent "savoring" in these 2015–18 journals: "Daddy," of course. And, more surprisingly, "little boy." Of all the dominant things I found compelling about Adam, it was also his unguarded moments of vulnerability—his head on my chest, finally admitting the desire to also be taken care of—that were so precious my memory reliably savored and stored them. These brief "reversals" of our roles, they never ceased to touch me. The contrast to his normal persona was stark, attractive to me in its rarity and transience. He had peeled away his many macho layers to expose the little boy inside. I clung to these glimpses because they were windows into his basic goodness, the goodness we are born with, but grow varying calluses around. When Adam's behavior was hurtful, it was so increasingly transparent it came from a place of repressed fear that it was hard for my inner mother to reject him for it. I wanted to nurture him, suddenly my little boy no matter what.*

He doesn't trust anyone else to see him like this, I'd think, stroking his hair as he finally let himself rest. *He's still the Russian doll I saw that first night he reached his arms out to me. The sweet little boy nestled deep inside. He deserves to feel fully understood and accepted. And he really does love me. He just has fucked up ways of showing it sometimes. But so do I, right?*

---

* "One of the great unnoticed psychological forces in the world is this: Whoever is on the feminine side of the equation has a profound impulse to protect the disowned fragility of whoever is on the masculine side of the equation, even while being hurt by that person," couples therapist Terry Real said on the podcast *Lovelink*. "[Women] form a deeper empathic bond to the little boy inside the man than the man does. The man has disowned that little boy and the man thinks, 'Ugh, if I could just love up that little boy, then I could get to the heart and all ›uld be well.'"

My Metamour, Myself

---

*"Rachel was always destined to share her lover [with her sister Leah] . . .
Rachel embodied sacrifice; she was unfulfilled till the end."*
—Miki Raver, Listen to Her Voice: Women of the Hebrew Bible
(read by Rachel hundreds of times 1998–2002)

Spring 2017

LOS ANGELES

When Adam asked what I thought of Leah coming out to visit for his birthday, I pragmatically decided to view it as the next step on my path. I'd read in *The Smart Girl's Guide to Polyamory* that one of the best ways to combat jealousy was to meet your metamour.* Since she would be coming to visit for a week in August (*a whole week straight, fuck!*), I decided to reach out. And thus began the most texting-intensive relationship of my life.

5/8/17

Text Messages

> **Leah:**
> Hey Rachel, it's [Leah]. I really appreciated your instagram message. I would really like to get to know you as a friend, and I'm very much

---

* The polyamorous term for "your lover's lover."

looking forward to meeting you when I visit in
August.
. . . I wanted to reach out but really had no idea
how to go about it. "Hey, we're both involved
with the same man so maybe we'd get along
but maybe we've accidentally already decided
to hate one another?"
God, I am bad at this, sorry.

Indeed it was actually a huge relief to text with Leah. Our exchanges were overtly kind; we were both going out of our way to signal politeness. It reminded me of how some femmes will reflexively compliment something about your outfit when they meet you at a party, as if to say, "I come in peace." *Or is it a keep your friends close, enemies closer kind of thing?*

Leah was deferential to my "primacy" in a way that made me feel like she had no interest in stealing my place. She did this by sometimes saying so directly, but also demonstrated it by rarely referencing her relationship with Adam at all. The same unspoken code didn't apply to me, with her making generous references to admiring our "primary relationship." But I tried not to talk about Adam in any way that might come off as bragging. On the rare occasion she did mention Adam with romantic undertones, I'd feel a twinge of jealousy, a feeling that it was somehow a passive-aggressive power play. And then I'd consciously try to shut the thought down, because it was unfair. When it came to everything but the man we "shared," we were almost compulsively forthcoming. We dished about sex (except sex with Adam) in the kind of detail I'd seen on *Sex and the City.* Was it because we shared the same man? Were we backhand bragging? Bonding? All of the above, I'd suspect.*

---

* When I couldn't find any research to answer these questions, one prominent human evolutionary biologist who studies female competition told me, "I think your guesses are probably right (i.e. submission is shown through continual self-deprecation). I don't think there are any

Soon, we could even commiserate over Adam's newer romantic prospects like more senior sister wives.

6/1/17

Text Messages

> **Rachel:**
> And she's like an adorable British actress

> **Leah:**
> Oh GOD, of course she is . . .
> Let's bear in mind that's her headshot, of course
> . . . God, she IS cute

I'm not including Leah's more vulnerable messages here, but I soon became very protective of her well-being, a sort of on-call counselor. I found she was sometimes even more anxious, insecure, and neurotic than I was, which was really rather impressive/a little disturbing. *Is this Adam's type?* No matter. Now that she was a real person instead of an abstract threat, what was important was Leah was no longer she-who-must-not-be-named in my mind. I was even able to talk with Adam about her like a mutual friend. Sometimes, I knew things that were going on with her before he did. That felt good, too, like I was less excluded and more in control. Leah and I congratulated ourselves often on our friendship. It was a choice we were making, and not an easy one, not to cast the other as the enemy. It felt not just evolved, but laced with real sisterhood.

---

empirical studies that can answer your thoughtful queries, however. You are ahead of the academic literature."

6/9/17

Text Messages

Leah:
I'm really glad we're talking, too—I really appreciate that you reached out to me, especially because I WAS really jealous of you and your relationship with [Adam]
And now, instead, we have this growing friendship, and I'm really looking forward to meeting you when I visit

Rachel:
Totally. Me too. It will be its own challenge for both of us I'm sure, but at least now we're facing it as allies.

6/10/17

Rachel:
Ughhhhh
So I went to see the [new] guy today
Get there rub up on him in my underwear and he says he didn't get tested [like I'd asked him to] and I'm like awesome
Asks me if I can touch him
I take off his underwear and there's straight up sores on it
And I'm like what is this? And he's like, "oh you think it's something?" And I'm like yeah
And proceed to give him a handjob anyway which makes me sick because I'm sort of in denial shock please a man mode
And then it hits me and I'm like when were you going to tell me this?

> **Leah:**
> . . . Oh FUCK
> Can I call you or are you busy?

Though Leah and I were texting daily now, that was the first time we actually spoke on the phone. She understood what was at stake in a way no one else could. This new guy, who I thought really cared about me, who I was getting legitimately attached to after being friends for months first, didn't even consider me enough to get tested like he'd promised before I traveled hours to see him. Or warn me about what turned out to be genital warts. This was now the second time that a guy hadn't disclosed an STI until after I'd been grinding on his underwear, taken it off, and inquired. I'd never encountered something like this before being in an open relationship. But now that I was an openly non-monogamous woman, the men I would date (only one of whom actually identified as non-monogamous rather than "just dating") treated me in ways I had been lucky enough to mostly avoid before: coming on my body without asking. Violating boundaries around condoms. Not disclosing STIs until the heat of the moment, even attempting to hide outbreaks.

But for me, the worst insult would prove emotional. The way in which I was now considered "already spoken for" and therefore somehow immune to attachment. The way it was assumed I wouldn't catch feelings, or want to be loved and treated with the usual care. After a decade of being considered girlfriend material, I was now experiencing what it is to be treated by men as if I was little more than an amusing pit stop on the highway to arriving at Respectable Womantown. That it was assumed casual sex was all I was available for, or wanted? It was frustrating and hurtful, to put it mildly.

It remained easy for me to find dates or sex as a woman in an open relationship. But when it came to finding people who offered actual intimacy, it seemed Adam had the upper hand. For one, he wasn't constantly anxious, projecting rescue fantasies onto everyone. But these other women he dated also seemed far less likely to see him as just an amusing sexual romp. If anything, I suspected that his being with me increased his market value, even if women were initially more cautious. That he was already with someone perhaps proved he was worth keeping.* It seemed that my already having a partner made men see me as more sexually loose and fun, but less potentially valuable. I was already "owned" and therefore used goods—nicely broken in to borrow and return. That I myself had increasingly begun to devalue sex and my body perpetuated this cycle. By this point, sex was mostly just another drug; either it was strong enough to ignite Adam's lust and distract me from jealousy—or it was insufficient. Given this consumerist mentality, it's no surprise I had trouble attaching to people, or attracting the types of people I might want to attach to me.

Whatever the reasons for getting the short end of the dick, I felt my dynamic with Adam needed to be more "even"—a rookie polyamorous mistake, since this is pretty much always an impossibility. Now that I'd set him free again, he was going on at least one, sometimes two, other dates a week. Everything felt like it was moving too fast, but I didn't want to pull the emergency brake again and end up ejected.

"Two dates a week feels like too many," I'd tell Adam, trying not to whine. "It feels like this is becoming too big a part of our lives. Like it's cutting into our own quality time. Like I'm always bracing myself for your dates or recovering from one."

---

* Indeed, 16 out of 18 studies on what's called "mate choice copying" had the same result: Adding a girlfriend or wife to a man's photo made other women score him as more attractive than when they were shown his photo alone. The effect has been consistently proven among women choosing men, but results are mixed among men choosing women. But there are also far fewer studies about how mate copying affects men's attraction to women, and why it might be so much less pronounced. It's *almost* as if there's an implicit bias to focus on what might make women more attracted to men! A. Gouda-Vossos, S. Nakagawa, B. J. W. Dixson, et al., "Mate Choice Copying in Humans: A Systematic Review and Meta-Analysis," *Adaptive Human Behavior and Physiology* 4 (2018): 364–86. https://doi.org/10.1007/s40750-018-0099-y.

"But you went on three dates last week," he said as patiently as he could muster.

"I know, because I'm trying to keep up with you." This was only partially true. "I'm trying to find someone I want to date long term so I can sustain this. But I can't seem to find anyone who doesn't end up disappointing me."

"Yeah, well, most dudes are losers, it's true. That's why you should make sure to keep me." He smiled, pulling me toward him with a condescending kiss upon the head. *God, I still love that. Why do I love that?* "Don't try to make it even. Just relax. You've dated way more people than I have, and certainly *slept* with more. It's just been a busy few weeks. And I'm not even having sex with any of them yet."

"Well, you've gone down on them . . ." I muttered.

"It'll fluctuate. You'll see. It's not going to be like this all the time," he said.

Even though Adam was now across the country from Leah, I learned their relationship seemed to be affecting the perception men had of her, too. When a guy she'd been dating for months had unprotected sex behind her back, he threw Adam in her face. (Like most men I've met who sleep with multiple people at once, he didn't identify as non-monogamous.)

7/12/17

Text Messages

> **Leah:**
> He used [Adam] against me like a weapon, and he always does this. . . . And he asked why I trusted [Adam] more than I trusted him
> And I explained [Adam] was the most mature, even-keeled partner I've ever had, and that I've known him for much longer

> . . . He's SO insecure about [Adam]. But he
> claims not to be

How awful and scary, that this fuckboy had unprotected sex without telling her. At least Adam would never do that. I stayed on the phone texting with her for an hour, deciding I'd ask her to get tested again before the trip at a later time. Sure, she and Adam were using condoms per our agreement, but you couldn't be too careful.

But sometimes, when I was really overwhelmed and jealous of his dating in LA, I'd have dark fantasies. That we'd contract an STI, or that I'd get pregnant despite my IUD. Then, at least, Adam would *have* to slow down. He'd be even more bound to me. I didn't want these things in reality. It was like the "fantasy" overworked mothers sometimes report having—that they'll be hospitalized. Then, at least, they'd have to rest.

Ah, yes, rest.

See, I told you not to get too comfortable.

Reverse Pretty Woman

Rachel:
I sort of have a sugar daddy now?
And I'm kind of digging it

Leah:
Whoa whaaaaaaaaaaaaaaaaaat
????????

Rachel:
But we haven't had sex or anything yet

Leah:
OMG you should see my face right now

Rachel:
. . . Now that I'm allowing myself to explore it
I'm like, why didn't I always do this?
. . . It's kind of empowering
. . . It's like a reverse pretty woman

Summer 2017

LOS ANGELES

I met Silas on OkCupid. His profile made it clear he was non-monogamous, with a primary partner. At forty-six, he was older than anyone I'd ever gone out with, but I liked the fact that we were in similar relationships. (I hadn't had much luck with being interested in anyone else who identified as non-monogamous besides Miranda.) I felt a little starstruck and flattered when I realized who he was. He wasn't famous, but his businesses were.

"I don't have time to play games, and I'm not looking for someone to see more than once a week." He smiled over our fifteen-dollar rice bowls. He was so forthcoming for a first date that it was actually refreshing. "My current girlfriend was my secondary partner for many years, until my wife and I got divorced. She's not possessive and really likes to share me. She's the one who actually encouraged me to get back on OkCupid. She thinks it'll keep things healthy between us. But I don't have much time, and I'm not into sleeping around casually. I'd like someone steady, no drama."

"I'm looking for something similar," I replied.

"Wonderful," he said, and smiled conclusively. "I have to get back to work, but I enjoyed meeting you. Can I take you to dinner next week?" I felt like I'd passed the first round of a job interview.

After our second date, Silas revealed more clearly that he was also into Daddy/little girl dynamics, with a financial component. I appreciated the fact that non-monogamy was helping me be more open to different types of relationships, less judgmental. Having a sugar daddy was something I'd never allowed myself to consider while auditioning "the One." Weren't those guys just buying the girlfriend experience and calling it something else? But it turned out even the *idea* of being kept that way turned me on, and now I felt free to explore that. I'd never even gone out with a man who regularly paid for dinner. (Adam always threw down the card, but it was our joint account.) How had I never considered that the Interesting Conversation in a Tight Package Services I offered could be compensated beyond bike repair and furniture assembly? I felt duped by my conditioning, like realizing thick brows are in after a lifetime of over-tweezing. *I'm already almost thirty—my best years and brow hairs are behind me! Like Liam advised, I will appreciate my still-perky(ish) titties and get wise.*

Silas asked for my shoe, bra, and clothing sizes; my favorite brands and foods, vacation destinations I'd like to explore. He told me that whether I replied or not, I would begin receiving things that week. He signed his email "Daddy." As promised, bags of gourmet groceries showed up at our door, along with the second air conditioner Adam had said we could do without. Ethically made lingerie and shoes. An adult-sized baby onesie that read "I [Heart] Daddy." Adam and I had a good laugh over that one—and then he threw me on the bed. Was it my imagination, or was he suddenly treating me with a little more respect, too?

When I eventually went over to Silas's house, I felt like I was in a movie. I'd never touched this level of privileged-white-male wealth so intimately. There was a big, long mirror across from us in bed, and as I looked at us having sex I enjoyed the distinct satisfaction of an overachiever. I was desired. So desired that someone not unattractive might even indirectly pay to do this with me.

7/29/17

Journal Entry

I've been rehearsing for this role my whole life.
[Silas] choking me [but] didn't want to send me back
first time with marks
* 'are you my little fuck hole?' and I farted and*
tried to pass it off as a queef am I a whore now?

. . . [Adam] proposed sort of 'I've been thinking about this I would marry you' and I looked him in the eyes and I couldn't say yes

These kinds of half-proposals from Adam were common whenever new sperm competition was in the mix. I didn't really take them seriously by this point; I didn't feel they "counted" as sincere, though looking back I'm not exactly sure why. Mostly, I just felt smug instead—and annoyed the stigma around sex work had made me miss this potential revenue-and-confidence stream until now. No more. *I have to stop giving away my time and body for free unless the person really deserves it. Adam is lucky,* I thought, briefly regaining my male-validation-dependent "self-esteem." *Yeah, that's right, I said it. Lucky motherfucker, to be with me.*

Considering I'd also started dating a German filmmaker I was waiting to sleep with, I felt I was in excellent shape ahead of Leah's impending visit. Silas and I talked about getting me a hotel room close to where he'd be vacationing with his kids that week. But as Leah's visit drew closer, Silas still hadn't booked the room. And was it just me, or was he being a little less doting ever since we slept together? I began to spiral. To believe I'd been used and that my value was now diminished for having entwined sex with materialism.

My increasing nervousness over Leah's visit morphed into a growing compulsion to test Silas. I knew I was being bratty, but I needed him to come through and *distract me, faster, harder.* For the high he provided to be as heightened as possible. I needed this now-constant cloud of generalized anxiety hovering over me to be *worth* it. I knew naming my feelings would likely provoke him to the point of rejecting me. That part of what Silas was "compensating" was an implicit promise to ask of him no emotional labor. Yes, I saw what I was doing as I hit send on the email. I was confirming my fear that I was like my mother, provoking rejection as a form of self-sabotage. And in so doing, I was also reaffirming that Adam was right to try to change me.

8/7/17

From: Rachel to [Silas]
Subject: Dear Daddy

. . . I felt a bit like a call girl to sleep with you and not hear anything
sweet from you for a few days . . . but I somehow felt I owed it to you
after everything you've given me. Don't get me wrong—I wanted to
give it to you—but . . . [m]y coming back with an ask for something
concrete [the hotel room] was an attempt to regain some power, to
assert my value, to say I will not be taken for granted.

Silas wrote back that he was "horrified" by my implication he would
ever pay for sex. He never wanted to see me again.

Non-Attachment

August 2017

LOS ANGELES

My first thought when I saw Leah: *She's even prettier in person than her pictures.* Leah is half-Jewish, half-Irish, and the end result seems to be that she got none of the less-lauded traits of either heritage. Big brown eyes, porcelain skin, a cute little nose—something intriguingly anxious, bookish, and horny underneath the only Jewish I could smell. Dozens of long gray streaks in Zooey Deschanel hair. Arms covered in esoteric yet somehow mostly unpretentious tattoos, mismatched delicate hoops creeping up tiny ears. Her clothes fit the perfect amount of imperfect, like invisible makeup, but it all came off as plausibly thrown together. *Touché, Leah. Touché.*

I was a little attracted to her, but knew she was straight. Before we became friends, this had been one of the things that most annoyed me about her. As if there could really be no such thing as a fully straight woman. Like she was only trying to hog him. You'll notice none of these memories of our first meeting particularly revolve around Leah's personality. As if all that really mattered was her appearance. I do remember that I liked her in person, too. She remained polite, kind, smart, deferential, and even more obviously anxious than me. We went to lunch just the two of us (as I'd requested and she'd agreed was best), where we continued to talk about any and all men but Adam. I dropped her off at the Airbnb where he would be staying with her.

Despite imploding things with Silas, I still had my own sleepover planned with the German filmmaker. Hopefully, I could ride that attraction out at least this one week. But that night, the same thing as usual happened: I felt my attraction almost immediately dissipate once we had sex. I saw Adam smirk in the corner of my mind at something he'd deem "lame" and lost my attraction in one swift poof. *Can't even fuck you properly,* Adam judged in my head when the filmmaker came sooner than he meant to. *Don't worry, I'll give it to you later. When I'm done taking care of Leah.*

———

I woke up early and left the filmmaker sleeping, walking to the Malibu beach. Adam and Leah had spent the night together, and they would again tonight. I felt cracked open, as if I'd been meditating for hours; the heightened sense of poignancy that comes with grief. Just when I thought I'd mourned all the little losses, the ways I no longer felt special, there were new layers of pain to sit with, new attachments to try to let go of. I kept thinking of how Adam explained he felt upon seeing me with other men: "torn open, ravaged, and raw." I spent an hour picking out a special rock for Leah on the beach. It looked like a black heart, her favorite emoji. I wanted her to know I loved her. I felt like a child whose parents forgot to pick her up from school. I saw an abandoned Bible blown open on a rock-face pulpit. A man caught a stingray and threw her back. *The accidental poetry of everyday life,* I mumbled. I bought a paper for the first time in years, so retro in my fragility was I. The main headline read "Countdown to Doomsday, Mutually-Assured Destruction." I was lucky. I was fine. None of my discomfort mattered.* Other people had real problems.

———

* This attitude is sometimes called "spiritual bypassing," in which you avoid feeling uncomfortable emotions by prematurely "rising above" them.

————

Later that day, I met up with Leah, Adam, and his best friend Christopher for afternoon drinks in Venice. When Leah found me sneaking a cry in the bathroom, we hugged for a good long time. How could my supposed source of pain also be such a comfort? It didn't make sense. "It's okay," I said into her shoulder. "I'm just feeling a lot, but I think it's good. Like, maybe after this it won't feel so intense anymore."

"This must be so hard for you. I can't imagine," Leah said into my hair. "If there's anything I can do to make it easier just let me know and I'll do it." *Why can't Adam just say that and offer the same?*

As I watched them walk off together that night without me I felt so . . . left out. Not-new. Unpretty. Strong and defenseless at once. The fear was not that I'd be permanently replaced by Leah, no. Rather that a life with Adam would mean watching him walk off into epic LA sunsets with an endless string of more attractive women. Women he might not *love* as much as me, but whose novelty and inevitably comparative youth he couldn't help but be more excited by. To mourn this reality—that I would never be new to him again, as sexually desired as I was in the beginning—was to mourn nothing less than my own decay and death. This was why I had to keep going. I sensed a sort of liberation waiting on the other end.

I asked Christopher to drive me to Adam's parents' house, since it was close to where he lived. I didn't want to spend the night alone in our bed, and I didn't want to see the German filmmaker. His parents didn't ask questions. I think they knew. Our open relationship was no secret.

"This is bullshit," Christopher said. Christopher was never one to mince words or actions. Once, he'd sent me photos of Adam flirting with another woman without a caption, like a cruel private eye. "I felt like *I* was cheating on you just going to meet Leah," he said.

"No, I'm really okay," I said meekly.

"You're deluding yourself! You're being taken advantage of," he said. I wondered why he was still Adam's friend if he found him so evil, but didn't say anything. "I've seen this movie with his other girlfriends a million times before. I'm sick of watching this fucking movie."

"No, that was different. I actually *like* dating other people . . ."

"If you were really polyam you wouldn't need to make yourself feel not-sad about this. You'd just like it," he said.

"No, that's not true," I tried to convince us both. "There's an adjustment period for a lot of people, the polyamory books say . . ."

"Bullshit. I'm sick of watching this fucking movie," he repeated. *You know Christopher's just dramatic and crazy,* Adam reassured in my head. *He just doesn't get non-monogamy. He's never even been in a real relationship.*

"But monogamy doesn't work for me, either," I whined in exasperation. "When we hit pause on dating other people, *I'm* the one who lifts it first. So what do you suggest I do?" Christopher didn't have an answer to that. He parked in front of Adam's parents' house.

"You gonna be all right?" he asked, softening.

"Yeah, don't worry about me. Thanks for the ride." He shook his head in pity and drove off. (About a year later, Christopher stopped talking to Adam. Cut him off completely after over twenty years of friendship, cold. When I asked what had happened, Adam said Christopher was mostly sick of all the "drama" in Adam's romantic life. I felt this too was my fault. If I didn't have trouble with jealousy, there would be no drama.)

I greeted Adam's parents with our usual warm hugs and excused myself to the guest room. I loved this clean and cozy house, these dream in-laws. If this was the price to pay for being a part of his family, for being the only partner who got to sleep in this bed, for continuing to have new romantic experiences to write about and look forward to, for unearthing more childhood trauma I might still dismantle yet—I could handle other, less serious girlfriends, right? *I've grown so much already, this feeling has to get easier at some point.* I sucked my thumb and murmured quietly to myself, like a toddler too overtired to cry.

I was sure that if I could come through the other side of this jealousy, I might just shed everything holding me back: my many insecurities, the belief other women were my competition and that I was fundamentally unlovable, the hope that *anything* could be held on to. I felt as if I might cease to fear death itself, like this was one of the most effective practices for letting go of one's ego possible. When I was able to withstand Adam going on a longer date, or developing a more regular relationship, I felt a sort of solid-self-purging I can only compare to tripping solo on psychedelics in a dark cave. Like I was working something out that needed layers and layers of subconscious, perhaps even intergenerational, expunging.

What if this is my path to a certain kind of enlightenment? A crash course in the concept of non-attachment—a concept I barely understood, but which sounded noble? If I can let go of my deep-seated belief that Adam being with other people is a rejection of me, what else might I be able to let go of?

———

Non-attachment, as it's been explained to me by Buddhist teachers, simply means that there is absolutely nothing that can be clung to as "I or mine." What we call our "self" is ultimately an illusory concept. Yes, we have a body, but that body is made up of countless other shared molecules and elements, and will morph into new life when we die. Our personal existence is like a wave in an ocean—inevitably changing and impermanent, part of a larger life force. Suffering occurs when we try to hold on to that which is not solid or separate—which is to say, everything. Non-attachment is the practice of accepting the reality of impermanence fully.

"The circumstances under which you were exploring were really quite extraordinary. I can imagine how you could sense that if you could live into that truth of non-attachment, how liberating that would be," Jonathan Foust, who teaches in the Buddhist tradition, later told me. But you can also become too attached to any concept, even if it's a wholesome one—including non-attachment. Non-attachment also has a lot of near-enemies, like indifference and dissociation. "When you are questioning everything, it can lead you to a certain kind of groundlessness. And then that groundlessness, while it sort of smacks of liberation, is also really borderline on psychosis," Foust said. "It's like that saying: 'A mystic swims in the same water in which a psychotic person drowns.'"*

I felt myself sinking at the same time I felt myself increasingly able to swim. But I could recognize that it was hardly spiritually evolved to have spent the last forty-eight waking hours stoned. Not Zen that I was now taking an Ambien I'd been doled out for this special occasion. Hardly enlightened that the list of drugs I couldn't trust myself not to abuse, that I asked my supposed protector to guard, was mounting.

---

* "The psychotic drowns in the same waters in which the mystic swims with delight." —Joseph Campbell. Stanislav Grof, *Psychology of the Future: Lessons from Modern Consciousness Research* (Albany: SUNY Press, 1931).

A Danger to Ourselves

August–September 2017

LOS ANGELES & SAN FRANCISCO, CA

After six days in a row of Adam and Leah seeing each other, I thought I could rest. But back at our house, Adam told me he wanted to see her again, just one last, unplanned time. He was also going to stay with Leah during a business trip to New York the following week, but wanted to make the most of her time in LA. It was not an unreasonable request, but I asked if he could reassure me of his love and my primacy first, something Kathy had suggested I do if I felt insecure.

"I've said it a million times." He sighed, exasperated. I didn't recall him overtly reassuring me more than once or twice that week. *But even if he did, why is it such an inconvenience?* "Like, how much more reassurance do you need? You should know how I feel by now."

I felt something in me snap. The thread I'd been hanging on by was far thinner than I'd admitted to myself. *Can't he see how hard both Leah and I have been trying? He asks me to sit with egoic discomfort unlike I've ever known, but what does he have to do? He can't even be bothered to placate me for a minute?* I lost my shit. I started yelling. I stood on a stool to reach my suitcase off the top shelf of the closet and leave. "I'm fucking done!" I screamed. And I really almost meant it. I was exhausted. If I still hadn't been good enough this week, I didn't know I could do better.

"Stop, you're going to fall! You're going to hurt yourself!" *The stool is only a foot tall, what is he talking about?* "What are you doing? Stop!"

"I'm getting my suitcase to leave your spoiled, entitled, ungrateful selfish ass!" I screamed back. I'd never been in a romantic relationship with yelling before (only parental)—but by now it felt almost natural.

"Stop it! Calm down!" He grabbed me by the waist before I could get the suitcase. I kicked my legs in the air like a child as he pinned me to the bed by my wrists. "Stop it. *Now.* You're going to hurt yourself. You're being crazy!"

"What the fuck are you doing? Let me go!" Here it was. It was really happening. He was using his force against my body in order to prevent me from leaving. I was sprawled, pinned, and wriggling. But now that it was here, I felt nothing like arousal or safety. I felt scared and dissociative. Like a small animal who, failing to flee, resorts to freezing. "What are you doing?" I croaked, wrists hurting as I pushed against his grip.

"I'm not letting you go until you promise to calm down," he said, neck bulging.

"Please, let me go," I whispered. I was floating on the ceiling once again, looking down at both of us, shaking my head. *This feels like the night when he didn't stop fucking you while you were sobbing.* But another part of me was already making rationalizations for his behavior, why I deserved to be immobilized in my "irrational" state. *Haven't I wanted to know he'd never let me run away? Why does this feel so fucked up?* I looked at him confused, whispered, "Please . . ."

"Do you promise to calm down?" A certain instinct arose to agree to whatever he demanded. I nodded, promised. Adam let me up. As I looked at the red fading from my wrists, I thought of something Miranda had told me about her stepdad: "He used to throw things at my head and push me. And I sometimes wished he would just hit me. Then maybe I'd have proof. There'd be a reason for someone to intervene."

I shook as I threw my clothes into the bag, silent, quick. Flight mode had truly kicked in, and it was guiding me.

"Stop it!" he yelled. "What are you doing? Stop! Look at me!" He was getting panicky. "You were going to fall off that stool," he kept insisting, his voice increasingly desperate. "Why do you always run away? Talk to me. Please. Don't do this. Don't sabotage yourself with your fear." I moved swiftly out the door and he yelled out after me. "Where are you even going to go? *Fine, get the fuck out then! And don't fucking come back!*"

I still remember the feeling of his large backpack bouncing against my body as I ran down the street. Tears blurred the Seussian succulents on Garden Avenue; I hated myself for squandering this idyllic life. I was dizzy, my vision narrowing. I called my cousin, and booked a one-way ticket to stay with her in San Francisco.

———

Yet I still wanted dibs on him, somehow. Adam had his business trip to New York the next day. The plan was to stay with Leah. I told him I didn't want him to, not when we were barely holding on. He refused to promise, said I was being ridiculous and that he didn't have anywhere else to stay. (Of course, he had many friends' futons to sleep on.) When I called Kathy, she agreed Leah should know I was no longer okay with our agreement. "She has the right to consider your feelings and needs, and to make an informed decision about what to do," Kathy said. "If you don't tell her, you'd be complicit in deception."

I messaged Leah to tell her his staying over with her was no longer consensual. I told her I wasn't angry with her, but that my primary relationship with Adam was in danger. I felt like an asshole, and I felt like I wanted to exercise veto power anyway. *It would be proof he really was sorry, that he loves me more.* When she finally texted me back, Leah told me she was "confused." She was getting his side of the story—absurdly, that the fight was about him sitting next to her on the couch instead of me. She got so little time with him as it was, and here I was, pulling rank? I felt sick with myself for testing both their loyalties, betrayed when they both refused to prioritize me. Leah and I stopped talking to each other that night.

But on his second day in New York, Adam told me he'd found another place to sleep after all. I knew he'd still see Leah, but that he wasn't staying with her felt manageable. *He's not the type to lie about it at least, even if it's more convenient. That's the whole point of this open shit.* But I still hadn't agreed to come home.

"Come back to me my little girl," he'd text, over and over. He called and wrote emails every day, many times a day, until I answered. He apologized profusely for his temper and impatience, though he maintained he'd pinned me to the bed because I was "a danger to myself." We argued for hours every night. "I'll do whatever you want," Adam promised sweetly into the phone. "I'll be monogamous even if you want, okay? I just want my girl to come home. Nothing else matters. Nothing."

I know he has no intention of being monogamous long term—not that I even want total monogamy! I just want to feel . . . safer. Prioritized. Respected. For him to at least apologize for holding me down.

But then Adam persisted so surely with his narrative that soon, I began to wonder: <u>Had</u> *I been a danger to myself on that one-foot stool?* I felt certain I wasn't, but the more we spoke, the more it seemed reasonable to believe he could have been trying to protect me. *I was angry . . . maybe I did seem crazy. Fuck, what if I really am crazy?**

I rationalized his harmful behavior by further blaming myself. *I mean, hasn't he seen me hit myself and knock my head against the wall during a couple of jealousy "tantrums" by now? Maybe I've traumatized*

---

*   I was no longer certain what I wanted or believed, whether I should trust any of my "fearful interpretations" of reality. If you've been waiting for me to call this repeated pattern by its name—"gaslighting"—the moment has arrived! Gaslighting is defined succinctly by the *Oxford*

him. I'd never self-harmed this way before in my life. But with Adam, the behavior sometimes arose when I could no longer tolerate his failure to acknowledge my emotions. If I could make the hurt external, maybe he'd take it seriously. *Plus, haven't I shoved him once or twice before during a fight? It's not like I'm so fucking innocent.*

––––––––

Let me be clear: It was not acceptable behavior for me to have pushed him. Even if he'd laughed at me when I did it—it was still abusive. I'd never gotten physical during a fight before Adam. But I had shoved him twice now in frustration over his refusal to admit my feelings were valid or real. So I felt equally culpable. "If you lie down with dogs, you get up with fleas," Amy Marlow-Macoy, LCSW and author of *The Gaslighting Recovery Workbook,* later told me. "Nothing against dogs, but I think it's a good way of acknowledging that when you are in a relationship that is characterized by toxic and unhealthy relationship patterns, the longer you're in it, the more likely you are to absorb some of those patterns and start to demonstrate them on your own."

And the truth is, sometimes, when I gestured in anger, Adam now flinched. His nails, like mine, were also now bitten to nubs.

––––––––

English Dictionary as "manipulating someone by psychological means into questioning their own sanity."

How/Why I Stayed

September–October 2017

LOS ANGELES

> *Beast: If you hadn't run away, this wouldn't have happened.*
> *Belle: If you hadn't frightened me I wouldn't have run away.*
> *Beast:* [hesitates a bit] *Well, you shouldn't have been in the West Wing.*
> *Belle: Well, you should learn to control your temper!*
> —Dialogue from *Beauty and the Beast*
> Rachel used to perform over and over with her dad
> as a little girl as their signature special *shtick**

Beauty and the Beast was the first movie I saw in theaters. I watched it on my dad's lap because I was too small to see otherwise, barely three years old. I remember my friend Emily sitting next to me, perched just the same. When the wolves came on-screen and attacked Belle's hapless father, we both burrowed our little faces into our respective dads' chests, tiny hands cupping even itty-bittier eyes. I remember feeling afraid but mostly performative, already knowing that the daughters and fathers were each doing exactly what they were supposed to do. That this was part of the fun. That we were just adorable. And the wolves *were* scary, sure. But mostly what was chilling was the idea that a father could be so pathetic and old as this bumbling roly-poly on-screen; that a daughter might have to one day grow up and protect *him*.

---

*   Yiddish for comedy routine, often an overused one.

The lesson imparted by the end of the film: For the truly heroic daughter, ensuring your father's future doesn't have to stop at taking his place in prison. It could *also* include seducing and transforming his wealthy captor, thus marrying the family into royalty.

"I know he looks vicious, but he's really kind and gentle," Belle tells the mob that wants to kill the Beast. Then, later, as the Beast is bleeding out, she cries: *"Of course I came back . . . Oh, this is all my fault! . . . Please, please, please, don't leave me. I love you!"*—thus breaking the curse and healing his wound with those three magic words. Beast turns back into Prince, externally and internally transformed. Lessons learned, he won't be so unkind anymore. Thanks to the very power of her love, he has been saved.

"Nobody understands him like I do. There's something sweet, and almost kind . . ." Rachel sings to herself again and again. *"Of course I came back. I love him!"*

———

One of my only confidants in LA told me she couldn't be friends with me anymore if I went back to him. "It's too toxic," she texted. I pretended not to see her at Kaldi Coffee and my dance studio Heartbeat House from then on. I'd made my choice, and I was ashamed. I'd agreed to come back to LA on the condition we start couples counseling and take a break from dating other people . . . again. Adam was amenable, certainly relieved. But he still refused to apologize for holding me down.

"I missed my girl. My girl," Adam kept saying when I returned. He squeezed me so hard. It felt so much better than what I'd been feeling, so much easier to just give in to his version of reality. He had grateful tears in his eyes, like he'd been returned a fortune. "We should just get married already. Admit we're going to be together forever. It's just the

way it is." I journaled that night that I was thinking then, over and over: *I missed you, Daddy. Why'd you hurt me, Daddy?*

"Should we go to Costco?" he asked, smiling. An inside joke of an offering. Costco had become the place where we re-upped our relationship for at least one more month. The place we shopped now that we were Real Americans with a car and space for bulk goods. On the outside, we seemed normal. Domestic. Just a man walking briskly ahead of a woman trying to keep up. I nodded softly at his offer, went into the kitchen to get some water. As I stood in front of the fridge, he suddenly grabbed me by the waist, turned me around, pushed me up against the counter. He kissed me deep, pressing his stiffness between my legs.

"I need to eat your pussy first," he growled. "*Now.*" He carried me to the bed. All these offerings—the spontaneity, the force, the feeling swept away—were just how I liked it. A special treat. In the same spot where he'd held me down, his tongue now delved entirely into my hole. I emitted a sound like a cry mixed with pleasure mixed with defeat. I saw how this moment was both real and performance at once: how we were working together to make our reconciliation what we both needed. How we were trying to create a new memory, to make good on the fantasy of being overtaken I'd once confided.

When there was hardly any semen, I knew he must have come inside Leah the night before. He'd just returned from New York. *But at least she only got it through a condom. At least he chose to sleep on a couch instead of with her. And he did it for me. I'm still primary.*

I got high in celebration. I was home.

9/1/17

High Stream of Consciousness

I think he would do almost anything to keep me. I think he means that.

After we rinse off and catch up on mutual friend gossip, go to costco

He keeps holding and kissing me in the aisles and i love it all the affection, i need it

'I never want to be without you that long again' he says

Ok, i say

. . . passing an old man [Adam] slapped me on the ass and the man looked and i looked at [Adam] smiling and that made me feel i was doing well

. . . 'You're an impetuous little thing. I'm glad you didn't move' [he said]

And why do i love to be made smaller when i am already so small?

A part of me, a very sorry part, felt all the more kept and cherished for being cornered. I knew I was being lured back into a trap. *But can I be truly manipulated if I seem more conscious of his manipulations than he is?* As if to prove to myself that I was onto everything, I even made a list of things I knew *were not okay,* nearly a hundred items long. And then I put the long list away, reassuring myself that at least I would have a log of the circles my mind did laps in. How a person could see so astutely in some ways, and yet still feel she was, for the first time in her life, losing all trust in her own reality and judgment.

———

My escalating pattern with Adam made more sense when I later learned more about how gaslighting works. Though people of all genders can gaslight, therapists tell me that in relationships composed of a woman and a man, women appear to be on the receiving end much more frequently. Interestingly, psychologist Dr. Robin Stern, author of *The Gaslight Effect*, observes that high-achieving, ambitious women like me are particularly prone to being in relationships with people who gaslight them.* They are determined to impress the one person they can't seem to fully convince of their aptitude. To be perfect for them.

When it comes to romance, gaslighters usually follow a predictable (if frequently unconscious and not necessarily intentionally malicious) pattern: They are incredibly romantic in the beginning, promising to protect you and making you feel like you've stepped into a fairy tale. This initial phase is so common that it's been termed "lovebombing." Lovebombing makes you feel chosen and adored. There's ample talk about rescuing you from lesser fates, and protecting you in the future. The experience tends to be extremely intense and rewarding. "This serves to hook the victim and pull them into the fantasy. Once they are committed, the narcissist can then slowly withdraw affection or increase control to maintain a sense of importance," Marlow-Macoy told me. "The victim tries to regain the lovebomb stage by appeasing the narcissist, reinforcing and increasing the power differential. The cycle goes on and on, getting more extreme over time."

Implicitly binary or fixed labels like "narcissist" and "victim" still don't sit well with me, even though different psychologists used these terms frequently when they reviewed my verbatim transcripts with Adam. My initial instinct was to censor quotes using these terms altogether, until I decided that was probably more in service of myself than

---

* The book does not mention/differentiate trans and non-binary people, just names "women" and "men." Robin Stern, *The Gaslight Effect* (New York: Harmony Books, 2007).

the reader. Regardless, how the next stages play out is rather predictable: The gaslighter introduces increasing rules and criticisms, and you begin to doubt your own self-sufficiency. You start to have quickly escalating fights, and might even try to leave. That's when they begin to apologize profusely, desperate you reconcile quickly. (*Rachel, look, I lost my temper, okay? I don't want to lose you. I'll do whatever you want, all right? I'll be monogamous even . . .*")

"The more upsetting the [gaslighter's] bad behavior becomes, the more welcome is the good behavior that seems to erase it and return you to those early magical days," Dr. Stern writes. "Some women spend months, years, a lifetime hoping for that trip back into the past." Indeed, I did. And there were enough respites—enough reassurances along the way that I was succeeding, thousands of small kindnesses and happy, loving moments—that this goal felt intriguingly *just* out of my permanent reach. (Having lived in New York City for ten years also made this sort of exhausting cycle feel almost familiar.)

Over time, this never-ending effort toward his advancing definitions of perfection was maddening. Eventually, as you'll see, things went as the books predict they would: The gaslighter might begin to punish your "bad behavior" by doing things like withholding sex and affection, and/or constantly upping the ante and changing the rules of the relationship. Your resulting low self-esteem and high anxiety fuel their argument that you're behaving irrationally and are controlled by your fears. Your need for validation and newfound belief you're fundamentally unstable, unlovable, and incompetent keep you locked in. Add to this dynamic that I was also trying to adapt to my first non-monogamous and ridiculously (uncommunicated) Dom/sub relationship, and it's easy to see how things got even more confusing. I wasn't sure what was the discomfort necessary for "growth," and what pushed me beyond healthy limits.

It sometimes felt like the dramatic quest for true love I'd been conditioned to believe *had* to be filled with obstacles. According to attachment theorists, people with more insecure attachment styles often do this, confusing the extreme highs and lows of an ill-matched relationship, or even mistreatment, with signs of "passion" and "true love."* When they meet a partner who doesn't play games, who is fully available and loving, they often mistake a secure relationship for boredom, thinking, *"But this can't be my soul mate. It's too . . . easy and calm. Where's the dramatic tension?"*

You can love someone deeply, and they can really love you, but if you were to make a physical list of the *symptoms* and *conditions* said love is creating and/or sustaining, what would it look like? For me, around this time, it might have read:

- Compulsively using drugs to cope; can't abstain for first time in life
- Overexercising to feel semblance of control
- Can't trust instincts or thoughts or judgments or maybe even reality; what is true and what is just irrational fear?
- Losing friends over relationship; increasingly self-isolating and quiet
- Missing period for many months
- Worried any food outside Adam's cooking is unhealthy/ "dangerous"

But I *did* make lists like this. And I was stuck anyway. I have a lot of compassion for that now—self-compassion is usually easier in retrospect—but I didn't have much then. And that was also an essential part of what kept the cycle going. I no longer respected myself. So of course I was less likely to trust that true love shouldn't look like someone pulling a Pygmalion on me.

---

* That said, attachment styles are not fixed, and can be healed or exacerbated depending on the individuals and relationship. Levine and Heller, *Attached.*

Plus, he was being so *sweet* now that I had come home. He was, of course, talking about marriage again. But I wasn't going to put my ring back on yet, let alone accept another half-proposal.

9/9/17

High Stream of Consciousness

I said no, baby
When he asked the second time,
Let's get married—next week
And held his head to my chest
Well maybe you could at least wear your ring
again?
He said in a small voice, like a little boy, mumbling
And it was the first time he ever acknowledged it
being gone
And missing it
And i knew how i knew this would be how it was
all along
You only want what you can't have

10/7/17

Journal Entry

Told me over dinner he's buying a house and i can
come with him or not
Rephrased it after dinner saying he wants me to
[move with him]. That this could be for our future
. . . I cry a quiet, very tired cry
. . . Must. keep. Moving. Forward?

Adam's late grandfather had recently left him enough money for a down payment. I had a choice, he said: I could move with him and "be his woman," or I could stay in the neighborhood I loved but couldn't afford to rent in alone, presumably single or demoted. I'd threatened to move out one too many times, and he wanted to protect himself. He'd upped the ante again.*

When #MeToo started trending on Twitter only a few days after Adam gave me this ultimatum, I felt disgusted by my place in history. So ashamed, so guilty for the choice I'd made. Instead of speaking out against my old teacher's and bosses' sexual harassment and leaving a man I'd been violated by twice now, I froze. *I'm choosing silence, the illusion of financial stability and safety. We're not married, so it's not like I'll even have any right to the property. I'll just be helping him pay down the mortgage. And Adam still won't even apologize for holding me down. And I'm staying anyway? And letting him corner me into doubling down? This is fucked up and embarrassing and weak.*

––––––

I never told my mom about Adam holding me down or anything else I knew might alarm her. But the following year, she would press a *New York Times* clipping into my palm. "I think you might find this interesting," she said in a hushed whisper Adam couldn't hear. The headline read "Men, #MeToo, and Therapy." I resented the implication, was embarrassed by her intuition, and stuffed it away. But I carried that newspaper clipping with me wherever I moved in the years to come nonetheless, a sort of talisman. I couldn't bring myself to read it any more than I could throw it out. In fact, I'm only looking at it now, as I write this.

––––––

* Whether or not this was a conscious control tactic on Adam's part, it was a move that created a sense of dislocation. I'd already mostly self-isolated from my friends, but I was extremely attached to my neighborhood dance studio and coffee shop for some sense of independence and stability. The place we ended up moving was up a very steep hill and very isolated by comparison—though tellingly, I helped choose it.

"I have found that for many men, underneath the anxiety that is always humming along are layers of shame. Shame at having feelings at all, shame because they believe that there is something fundamentally wrong with them, shame that they are not men, they are just boys," therapist Avi Klein, LCSW, writes in the op-ed. "Shame is the emotional weapon that allows patriarchal behaviors to flourish. The fear of being emasculated leads men to rationalize awful behavior."

Sustained shame and guilt require a lot of energy to suppress—energy one could be using to change, correct the harm done (to you or by you), and make sure it doesn't happen again. Like, if you realize your kid just ate a Tide pod, you shouldn't waste time feeling ashamed and guilty about leaving the container out. You regret it and immediately try to *fix* the situation. Regret can drive you to seek correction and change a behavior. But prolonged guilt and shame? They usually move you to hide and stall reparative action, thus perpetuating the cycle.

Though I can remember Adam groveling, I never recall hearing him say this simple phrase even once: "I was wrong." No one who is truly secure or self-aware lacks the ability to check themselves with humility, to fully own their mistakes. Adam knows this—he's smart. That he acts this way in relationships anyway, and so often gets away with it, creates a deep shame that fuels a further desire to feel safe again by exerting more "rightness." Tragically, this keeps him from experiencing the true intimacy and vulnerability he really craves—but deeply fears.

I lay us both bare in this book not to further shame Adam, but to understand and help dismantle this pattern. It is tough love, to say the least.

Young Swingers Week

10/21/17–10/25/17

NEGRIL, JAMAICA, HEDONISM II

I'd first gone to Hedonism II (there is no Hedonism I) on a press trip the year before. I'd felt profoundly liberated by my first nudist experience.

It was like a return to Eden, a total rejection of rape culture. I could walk naked and be left alone, feel the sun and water on my skin without anything between us. I realized viscerally then that my naked body itself was on no level "asking for" assault, even were I to walk nude down Eastern Parkway. Here I was accepted and secure, admired but not leered at. Everyone's body was "flawed" and yet somehow beautiful. The other guests at Hedo respected my personal space as if by unspoken contract, but were open and friendly if I engaged. There was a small hidden pool and I swam laps in it stoned all day, blissfully alone and free. *Back and forth, back and forth.* Like a goldfish who could leave her bowl for the river anytime she'd like.

And now, I'd been invited back to write an article about Young Swingers Week (YSW). Monogamish pause with Adam or not, there was no way we were missing this trip. YSW is held at Hedonism three times a year, and this October, 180 people were attending. A group called the Playful Pussycats (women who like women, and their husbands who like to watch and/or join), a pole dancing group, some older swingers, and some nudists who are not swingers were also going to be at the resort. Leading YSW were Michael and Holli, a celebrity lifestyle couple famous for their escapades on Playboy TV's show *Swing*.

When we arrived, Adam and I were led to the sign-in table, where we could choose between three necklace colors to wear as subculture shorthand: green for "open-minded but inexperienced," red for more experienced but "depends on the situation" (does it ever not depend?), and blue for what seemed to mean "pretty much always DTF." There was also an option to add a white bead that meant you were "allowed" to do things without your partner. In order to get one, you had to take an oath together saying you consented to solo play and sign a contract with a witness. I knew Adam would have preferred a blue necklace with a white bead. I asked for a plain red one instead.

We headed over to the pool—which at lifestyle resorts serves as the main socializing area, and is kept at refreshingly warm body temperature—and got naked. Despite being a newbie, Adam disrobed easily; these and many other fucks he did not give. It was much more crowded at the resort than during my previous visit, filled with people who seemed more on the prowl. Almost immediately, two couples came over to us and started flirting. One of them, a sexy woman with a beautifully round Russian face, sidled up to Adam. She was named Leah. *Of course. And she's just his type.*

As they flirted naked, another good-looking couple waded over to me. They'd bought a day pass, and meant business. Soon the woman and I were kissing, her boyfriend watching. She moaned and I began to touch her mostly bare pussy.* She clenched around my fingers, and I

---

* Almost all swingers I've seen wax off most or all of their pubic hair—including the men, who think it makes their dick look bigger. While this might make catching crabs less likely and looks more sterile, the micro-abrasions from waxing and shaving actually leave you vulnerable to a

had the same thought as with Miranda: *We are so fucking strong.* The couple asked if I wanted to go back to my room. I was tempted, but this was all too quick. I was more cautious now, in this post-scabies era. I politely declined, and they excused themselves to find someone·else.

"They were cute," Adam said into my ear.

"Yeah, I know, but people are moving so fast. I want to warm up some more," I said. I felt a little like a boxer getting ready to enter the ring, fingering pussies instead of punching air. *I want to fight, though, right? I didn't come all this way to be afraid of STIs or Adam fucking other women!* But this suddenly felt like a lot of pressure, a stark contrast to my first Hedonism experience. I was still safe, but feeling more like the usual object for appraisal. I couldn't indulge my loner tendencies; the pools were packed this week. I would be expected (by Adam? by myself?) to play well with others this time.

That night, Adam walked around like a kid in an XXX store. It was Lingerie Night (swingers love costume theme parties) and he wanted to go into the playroom, "just to see."

"I'm not ready yet," I said, thinking about *Leah Strikes Back: Return of the Novel Pussy.* Adam and I hadn't had sex in over a week, and I resented how immediately horny he was now.

"You know I can't go in without you, right?" he asked. As is the case with most lifestyle scenes, women are allowed into playrooms alone, but men are not. "We're only here a few days, and you're *supposed* to be

---

wider array of infections. Pubic hair is also beneficial in itself; it traps bacteria, among other cool perks you can read about in an article I wrote called "Reasons to Rock a Full Bush."
E. C. Osterberg, T. W. Gaither, M. A. Awad, et al., "Correlation Between Pubic Hair Grooming and STIs: Results from a Nationally Representative Probability Sample," *Sexually Transmitted Infections* 93 (2017): 162–66.

reporting. What is the point if you're going to act all scared?" He sounded whiny, an unattractive reversal.

"I just don't feel like I won't feel pressured to do something," I mumbled.

"*I'm not going to pressure you!* But fine, if you want to be all closed-off..." He was pissed. We went back to the hotel room and fought our same fight: I wanted to feel safe and privileged, that he would let me set the pace. He thought it should be obvious that's what he was doing without having to promise something that was "logically absurd," like the "manipulative" veto power I'd proven I'd abuse. "You want to live in a fucking fairy tale," I remember him hissing. "You want someone to give you a promise of security that's an illusion. And then you're mad when I want to give you reality, which is even better. Because it's *true*." He got much meaner from there. Eventually, he turned over and slept as I fumed.

I know he's right about my fairy-tale delusions, don't I? But if it gets him what he wants, why can't he just let me live in the illusion of assured primacy? Why is his being "logically right" more important than my feeling secure? By the morning my eyes were bloodshot, and I was convinced I was really going to leave this time.

10/22/17

Journal Entry

He called me weak says he doesn't respect i'm weak*
  Called me a bitch

---

*   Wikipedia defines verbal abuse well as "the act of forcefully criticizing, insulting, or denouncing another person. Characterized by underlying anger and hostility, it is a destructive form of communication intended to harm the self-concept of the other person and produce negative emotions. Verbal abuse is a maladaptive mechanism that anyone can display occasionally, such as during times of high stress or physical discomfort. For some people, it is a pattern of behaviors used intentionally to control or manipulate others or to get revenge."

Held me as i sobbed and told me sternly to stop
stop to lo[w]er my voice
    I'm grieving i said
    Stop he said
    And i froze again
    . . . "What's your work? To write down your
feelings about your relationship?" He says
dismissively, with disdain and a total lack of
respect . . . *
    . . . This is not ethical nonmonogamy
    . . . I need to not let him suck me back in.
    . . . I must be stronger than the strongest
personality i have ever fallen under the spell of

The next afternoon, still angry, we attended a talk called "Swinging Etiquette 101," led by YSW's host Michael. Sitting apart from Adam, I scribbled notes furiously as I recorded.

"Cheating is based on what? Lies, deceit, BS," Michael said. "But lifestyle is built on *trust* and *honesty*. If Holli said last night, 'Oh, baby my head hurts'—it doesn't matter who talks to me, who might proposition me. Nothing is going to happen. *That's* the trust." *Must be nice,* I thought.

Conventional swingers (and no, that's not actually an oxymoron) believe in prioritizing the primary relationship above the individual's whim. It's a "team sport," and from what I've observed, one of the emo-

---

* "When you write personally as a woman," Roxane Gay said, "people focus on the personal, and they completely ignore the professional. . . . That it's not a therapy session, or a diary entry. . . . You have to organize things, and you have to make decisions, and you have to think about voice and style and it's a lot of work." Lindy West, "Roxane Gay: 'If I Was Conventionally Hot and Had a Slammin' Body, I Would Be President,'" *Guardian*, Jul. 3, 2017.

tionally safest ways to practice mutual non-monogamy. Every couple I met that week at Hedo only had experiences together, and kept things *extremely* casual. Swinging was about sexual novelty and "strengthening the relationship"—aka the *only* relationship. If there was any ongoing communication with a third party, they kept it to group text in order to avoid confusing attachments from forming. I knew this model wouldn't fulfill me or Adam in the long run—we just didn't like casual sex enough. The emotional intensity, as well as the freedom to have experiences apart, was too much of what interested us about non-monogamy. But right then, swinging sure did sound nice; a safer way to avoid the potential trappings of long-term commitment. I heard a saying on some polyamory podcast: *If you'd rather deal with jealousy than boredom, choose non-monogamy. If you'd rather deal with boredom than jealousy, choose monogamy.* Of course, it's a reductive dichotomy—and it seemed to me that some swingers had found a way to minimize both undesirable feelings.

Michael laid out more codes of swinging conduct, emphasizing that everything you do as a swinger should be in the interest of your relationship. "Negotiate, don't compromise. Negotiation is a *win-win*. Compromise is a *win-lose*. Don't say, 'Okay, I'll do this for you, if you do that for me.' It's a *we*, not a *me*. Don't push your partner, don't pull your partner, don't drag your partner. Do this together. *Go as fast as the slowest person*," he repeated several times. "And if today you are just exhibitionists together, but tomorrow you talk and decide on a full swap,* and then you decide to just be voyeurs, and then to be exhibitionists again . . . *go as fast as the slowest person.*"

I glared across the room at Adam, who looked mildly amused and superior, also known as his resting face. He'd never be converted. To him, these rules were too fear based, built on a shared illusion of per-

---

* In hetero-male-centric lifestyle lingo, "full swap" = penis-in-vagina sex, while "soft swap" = oral sex/hand jobs.

manence. To think you could ultimately control other people that way was not only a delusion, but unloving, in his eyes.

Adam had recently given me Zen Master Thich Nhat Hanh's book *How to Love** to underscore this element of his romantic philosophy. "If we want to be with someone so that we can feel safe, that is understandable, but it's not true love. True love doesn't foster suffering or attachment," I'd underlined on the plane a few days before. I knew this was what Adam thought of swinging's many rules and restrictions on emotions—just more clinging. But then there was also this teaching: "In a good relationship we are like two fingers of the same hand. The little finger doesn't suffer from an inferiority complex and say, 'I'm so small. I wish I were as big as the thumb.' The thumb doesn't have a superiority complex, saying, 'I'm more important. . . . You have to obey me.' Instead, there's a perfect collaboration between them."

"I think I want to be like two fingers on the same hand," I told Adam that afternoon, as he attempted to reconcile. "But if you want to switch and get a blue necklace with a white bead, you can do stuff without me. I don't care anymore."

"Look, if you're not having fun, I'm not having fun," he said, an expert at calling my bluff by now. "You have control, okay? You're my priority. I'm not going to push you to do anything." Immediately, I felt myself relax. It was amazing how quickly having explicit primacy did that for me. I wanted to incentivize him to keep giving it to me. I wanted to enjoy my vacation. I decided to try, but I hadn't forgiven our fight.

————

That night, we went to another mixer. There was a game: Men were handed tickets, and the women had to collect as many as possible by inventing ways to ingratiate themselves. The woman with the most

————

* Thich Nhat Hanh, *How To Love* (Berkeley: Parallax Press, 2015).

tickets won. I found the premise insulting, an extension of the competition we're always made to be contestants in. I rebelled by approaching other women instead and conducting speed-date-length interviews. Most of the women I spoke to had been married for at least five years and wore the rocks to prove it. Several mentioned having children. There were no gay couples.

This is partly because being gay is actually illegal in Jamaica (if not discouraged at the resort itself). But it's also because swinger spaces in general tend to be incredibly heteronormative. "Historically these really have been spaces designed by straight men, with an eye towards straight men's sexual gratification—and one that, well, queer people haven't 'needed.' Gay men have a long history of spaces devoted to sexual exploration and freedom. And lesbians likely aren't interested in being subjected to the male gaze," journalist Lux Alptraum later told me. "There are a bunch of queer sex parties in New York City I know of and, yeah, I feel like queer couples seek out and create these spaces for themselves." Hedonism is no such queer space—with the ubiquitous exception that all women are encouraged to "play" with other women. I took full advantage of this, and credit these lifestyle spaces with helping me come into my queerness. And yet, I also knew that some women might ultimately be kissing me back in service of the heterosexual male gaze.

"Do you ever catch feelings for other people?" I asked over and over of the different women I approached during the game.

"No, it's just sex," the women always replied, a wink in their eyes. They agreed the premise of the game was fucked. But when the whistle blew, they each approached a new man and diligently worked to earn their ticket.

———

Determined in my own way to also prove myself a good sport, I suggested to Adam we go check out the playroom. There were a dozen mattresses with soon-to-be-soiled sheets, chains hanging from the ceiling, and a vinyl bench I wiped down as if at the gym. Adam pressed his immediate hardness against me. I was liking this already. I was being watched, and I was on a relatively sterile surface. Russian Leah from the pool came over to us. Now that I was aroused, I realized (once again) that beneath my envy for these Leahs was an attraction. I began to kiss her, and after a while, I surprised myself by asking if Leah and her husband wanted to come back to our room. I wanted Adam to see how open I would be if he let me drive. I also wanted to confront my fear of seeing him inside someone else (he hadn't penetrated Miranda). This seemed like an easier way to do it; her husband also fucking me, no chance of emotional attachment. Plus, though I felt neutral toward her husband, I very much wanted to keep touching Leah.

And just like that, I was having my first "full swap"—sex with Leah's husband while Adam fucked her beside me. Again, the prick of jealousy I felt seeing him with another woman almost immediately turned into a deep, only slightly painful, pleasure. I saw how handsome he was, how attentive, how reliably hard, even wearing the condoms he hated. She got on top of Adam. "You'll like that, he's really good at that," I said proudly, attending to her lips and breasts as she came, her husband inside me. Afterward, they left in an almost businesslike manner, as if they'd closed the deal and wanted to leave no space for renegotiation. We nearly felt used, and laughed as our camaraderie quickly turned to a reignited lust. Adam and I fucked furiously, clinging to each other all night with a newfound sense of mutually assured pleasure-destruction. Now I really saw the appeal of swinging. It was so . . . *even.*

The next day, somehow, it was as if we were on honeymoon. I went to the gym, and switched from Shania Twain's "That Don't Impress Me

Much"* to Beyoncé's "Countdown," my favorite anthem for high-intensity interval training/reinforcing my commitment to Adam.† I repeated egoic pep talks/imaginary scenarios that might make staying feel sustainable.

Maybe we can stay together but live apart, like Frida Kahlo and Diego Rivera.‡ Yeah, that would probably help him desire me more and make me feel less jealous . . . And then I might have the space I need to turn these experiences into art, and he'll prove his love by letting me tell our story always. Even when it makes him look like an asshole. Jay-Z does it for Beyoncé, and look at them. That's true love. Adam might be problematic sometimes, but who else would have his confidence? Let alone pay such

---

* Top 15 Songs I Used to Convince Myself I Was onto His Bullshit/Would Get Mine Anyway (Playlist on my Spotify)
　1. "That Don't Impress Me Much"—Shania Twain
　2. "Be Careful"—Cardi B
　3. "Needed Me"—Rihanna
　4. "Sorry"—Beyoncé
　5. "Tymps (The Sick in the Head Song)"—Fiona Apple
　6. "No More Room"—Emily King
　7. "She Wants to Move"—N.E.R.D.
　8. "Dancing on My Own"—Robyn
　9. "Kitty Kat"—Beyoncé
　10. "Freakum Dress"—Beyoncé
　11. "Love Song"—Sarah Bareilles
　12. "You Don't Own Me"—Lesley Gore
　13. "Better Version of Me"—Fiona Apple
　14. "Single Ladies"—Beyoncé
　15. "I Did It All"—Tracy Chapman

† Top 10 Songs I Used to Reinforce the Myth We Were Destined/I Had No Choice Anyway (Playlist on my Spotify)
　1. "Countdown"—Beyoncé
　2. "Unstoppable"—Lianne La Havas
　3. "Ever After"—Emily King
　4. "A Theory"—Tracy Chapman
　5. "Nakamarra"—Hiatus Kaiyote feat. Q-Tip
　6. "What You Don't Do"—Lianne La Havas
　7. "Ego"—Beyoncé
　8. "The Worst"—Jhene Aiko
　9. "Cranes in the Sky"—Solange
　10. "Drink You Away"—Justin Timberlake

‡ The couple was famously non-monogamous, passionate, and fraught—and Kahlo was bisexual.

eerily accurate attention to all the fluctuating subtleties of my mind? It's impressive he keeps getting me to come back, I have to admit. I know he can be manipulative, but he's so good at it. What if other people's more normal attention can't impress me anymore?

Any relationship is like a dance. I kept tangoing in part because it reaffirmed both my inflated self-worth (*"No one but Adam will keep up with me"*) *and* my increasingly low self-esteem (*"No one but Adam will want to deal with me"*). I've come to think of Inflated Ego/Low Self-Esteem as two sides of the same Vanity Coin. Too much of either and I believe I'm on some level "better than" the people who love me without trying to change me. The people who are treating me like I'm lesser-than, I'll start to think, *Well, they must be good enough for me. They see all the ways I could be so much better. Maybe they'll help me change.*

––––––––––

When we got home from Hedo, I told Adam we could fully open the relationship again. Either I had to adapt to his way of being for real this time, or admit that I could not. Shift or get off the dick, so to speak. *I just need to be sure I tried everything I could, or I'll regret it. Like he said, I don't even really know what it is to be polyamorous yet. I need to know I've tried as hard as I can . . .* At the same time, yet another adaptive fantasy had begun to form as well: that one day leaving Adam might create a sort of magic. I knew that several of Adam's exes had settled down in what appeared to be happy long-term relationships directly after breaking up with him. *Maybe it takes so much self-assuredness to grow beyond him that you can forever-after only accept and invite the treatment you now trust you deserve. Or just become exhausted enough that you never want love to feel like a test again and learn to settle . . . Or what if being with Adam is actually like kissing the last toad before you find your frog prince?*

Against all reason and evidence to the contrary, I continued to hope that Liam might be interested in the position.

Taming Dragons

_____

High Stream

I want my stomach to be impossibly beautiful for [Liam]. Everything beautiful.
   . . . You see how much i trust you, future imaginary reader?
   I let you into my stupid smart flawed ugly beautiful unedited . . .
   And god please let [Liam] come fuck me.

11/7/17

SANTA BARBARA, CA

Driving up the coast to see Liam for the first time since our threesome in 2015, I felt exhilarated, like a teenager whose parents just left town. Conveniently enough for me, Liam lived in California now, and was heartbroken. What he'd asked me to do would require my boldest improvisation yet. I viewed it as the next step in my romantic odyssey. _Why do I have to fight literal monsters to be a brave hero?_ A new refrain had begun to echo in my mind: _Taming my escape fantasies like dragons, one by one._*

---

* "She will be tempted by games of sex and manipulation disguised as requirements for power, achievement, and love. She will be flattered into thinking she has arrived in the land of power

Liam was of the clean-shaven yet bereft variety this time, and of course very much pulling it off. His long-term on/off girlfriend Sarah had finally left him for having an affair. Or rather, for having an affair again. "From the very beginning of our being together, I had this feeling. Something was off," he said, shaking his head over a craft beer at a bar. *Yeah, your attention with other women,* I thought. "It was never quite right, but I couldn't figure out why."

"And she was never open to maybe having a more open . . . ?"

"We talked about it, but not really, no," he answered.

Well, she forgave you cheating several times anyway, which is sort of a form of non-monogamy, when you think about it . . . "Do you think you'll try to ask for non-monogamy in your next relationship?" I asked instead. "I mean, I don't think anything good will come of continuing to cheat, right?"

"No, it won't, of course not." He deflected back. "But for you and Adam it's the ability to go on a date, not just to go to bed together, right?" I liked the way he said that, *go to bed together.* So quaint it felt nasty.

"Yeah, I think we both like the possibility to go it alone sometimes, to have feelings for other people," I answered, hoping he'd bother to read between the lines. "But what keeps happening is I become temporarily infatuated by someone, sleep with them once or twice, and then I lose interest." Did he realize I hoped he'd prove the most remarkable exception? "But knowing I have the possibility of experiencing falling in love again, it does make—when things are good—it makes me feel like I could commit to Adam in a way I've never been able to with someone else."

He nodded. "That's something that I said to Sarah, in this period

---

and independence when all she has received are the talismans of success. . . . The dragons that jealously guard the myth of dependency, the myth of female inferiority, and the myth of romantic love are fearsome opponents." Maureen Murdock, *The Heroine's Journey* (Boston: Shambhala Publications, 1990).

leading to breaking up. 'I'm not sure I'm done falling in love yet.' " I knew he was referring to the woman he'd cheated with. She was twenty-three to his thirty-seven, and he was smitten. She'd left for Argentina for the foreseeable future, and that was a lot of why he was actually sad. He wasn't done falling in love, and he wasn't done having his heart broken. He'd fallen for this younger woman largely because of how unusually immune to him she'd been, how she remained unattainable. Even the Liams yearned to be Liamed.

———

His apartment was humble. Neither clean nor dirty, nice nor repellent. No art or color. Emptied out by a woman. As if Adam sensed we were about to kiss on the couch, he called me and said it was urgent we speak. *Now.* I excused myself immediately. Adam said he had to decide whether to make an offer on a condo we'd seen the week before. I knew what he was doing—needing reassurance I wasn't leaving, applying pressure, upping the stakes again. I told him I could imagine living there a few years, maybe, but no more. "Then it's not worth it to me," Adam said firmly. "I'll just eat the money I put up for the inspection. I want you to be happy. It's going to be your home, too." *Jesus, I should really find a way to fuck Liam more often.*

When I came back inside, I told Liam to get in bed. I got an ice pack from the freezer and tied a blindfold around his eyes, mostly so I'd be less self-conscious. I felt nervous and playful at once, on a mission. I straddled him in my underwear and bound his wrists above his head. His penis at rest under me felt as thick as most guys' hard-ons. *Taming dragons one by one, Rachel. Taming dragons.*

"You have so much to apologize for. To so many women." I squeezed his thick throat. "You've been bad for a long time now."

"Yes. I know," he answered. I put the ice pack on his nipples and he sucked air in through his perfect lips, surprised by the cold.

"Then why are you like this?" He was silent. I used Adam's phrase, tightening my grip on his oxygen supply. "*Tell me.*" I felt I might just get away with mostly winging it after all. *This is like high school drama improv all over again!* Like the decent student I am, I'd also read *The Loving Dominant* and *The Mistress Manual* and listened to some podcasts and talked to Miranda in preparation for Liam's request. She'd said that what I imagined for Liam was called "character reform."

"I have such a hard time saying goodbye to women," Liam finally answered. "My dad was never there. I had my mom to myself, but then I gained a sister and a stepfather on the same day when I was four. I don't know if I ever got over losing my mom that way. I never want to let someone go." I looked over at his closet. His flannels and big workman boots took up only the long, left side. The right half was empty, a sort of backward shrine to his ex's departure.

"Was this the first relationship you cheated in?" I asked.

"No."

I slapped him on the side of his thick chest. "And what about sexting me all this time? Did you feel guilty for not being clear with me about where things stood with Sarah?"

"Sometimes . . . It's not what I want for a relationship, hiding things, lying by omission," he said.

"So no more lying. Do you hear me? *No more lying.*" Now that I had permission, I was actually getting pissed. Even his submission felt detached, unearned. I pulled his hair into a fist. "When you went silent for weeks at a time, did you even consider my feelings?"[*]

"I felt bad. I should have said something to you, that I was feeling guilty about Sarah, that we were back on. But I never want to be the one that pulls away."

---

[*] My experience of Liam was that he was a classic avoidant type. In attachment theory, the avoidant often pairs with the anxious type. It reinforces their self-image—that they are independent and their partners will be needy and demand more intimacy than they want to give. Jessica Fern, *Polysecure: Attachment, Trauma and Consensual Nonmonogamy* (Portland: Thorntree Press, 2020).

"But then you did anyway by disappearing." I slapped him again. We'd agreed on a safe word (the uninspired "red"), but he wasn't using it. My hand left another satisfying streak on his chest. I worked up the courage to ask what I'd wanted to for so long. "And what was I to you? What did I represent?" I was using the past tense, though my interest was of course still present.

". . . Sexual opportunity?" he ventured, invisibly hitting me back. I could tell he didn't even care enough to hurt me on purpose. *So he really considers me that little.* "Also, because you have ideas about sex, about relationships, that are different and that I've been curious about. And one can feel an intellectual undercurrent between us. That was something that was missing for me with Sarah."

He liked me for my brain more than my beauty, and this was apparently a bad thing. I began to feel the melancholy creep in. "You made me feel like garbage," I spat, again using a false past tense. "I felt made a fool by you. Yes, I have a boyfriend, but I'm a woman with feelings, too. I don't just represent 'sexual opportunity' or 'a different model' or something for you to keep on tap and 'learn from.' I'm a *person* with *feelings.*"

"I'm sorry." He didn't sound it. Not enough.

I took his pronounced jaw in my hand. His head was heavy, black-blue stubble pushing to come through after only the course of an afternoon. *Goddamn, this man.* "You're failing as usual, Liam."

"I'm sorry for the times I didn't sound like I cared. I hurt your feelings," he tried again. I slapped him.

"I don't get *what* you feel." By which I meant, *Why can't you just love me already?* "You sound so empty."

"I'm sorry." He licked his lips. "Maybe I liked that I knew I was being an asshole to you? To all the women."

"Or that you were doing something worth being punished over." I twisted his nipples, felt the weight of his crotch pushing against my underwear. *Must. Not. Let. Kryptonite. Distract* . . . It was no use. I began to grind up against him. I took both our underwear off, put a condom on him, and told him I was going to use him to come. "What are you thinking about?" I asked as he lay there, silent inside me but stiff, wrists locked above his head, still blinded. I knew it wouldn't be me, but I never would have guessed what he said next.

"I'm thinking about this guy I sometimes have sex with in New York," he replied.

Come again now?

The same as when he admitted a few weeks before that he wanted to be dominated: I was flooded by an image of life picking me up by the ankles, turning me upside down, and shaking all the loose change from my pockets. I had no idea he was even interested in men—but then again, I'd also never asked. He read so "hypermasculine" to me that I'd never even considered this possibility, let alone his potential submissiveness. I felt embarrassed to realize my prejudice.

Even the second time around.

When I was twenty-four, Basir had been my first brush with dominance. He flipped me over on my stomach and fucked me hard, almost with anger. "I think I might be gay," Basir said, months later, stoned and wide-eyed after I'd flown to Europe to visit him. "I've never told anyone. But I feel like I can tell you." I felt shocked then, too. I'd had a few past boyfriends admit to a lax bicuriosity; one even had his dick sucked by a man at the gym (before apparently immediately deciding he "just wasn't that into it"). But for some reason, I thought I'd see a fully closeted man coming. I'd made the same ignorant mistake: I'd equated a near absence of stereotypical femininity with heterosexual masculinity.

But learning a man also likes men while he's inside me? This is a first. I tried not to let my shock come through. *Also, I am very progressive and evolved and sex positive and queer myself! This is not supposed to shake me.* "That would be fun to fuck you with him," I told Liam, grinding on his wood. I realized only as I said it that I actually . . . meant it. I'd never before felt turned on by the idea of seeing a man have sex with another man. But imagining it with Liam felt . . . *quite hot, actually*.

"I had similar thoughts," Liam said. "But he's never been into bringing another woman in. He feels like—"

"—Like it's more like cheating?" I could intuit it immediately. Two guys on the DL. At least they used condoms, he later reassured me.

"Exactly. He has a woman already—his wife. She doesn't know. They have kids." *I'll ask more about that later.* I came on top a few times, suggested he get on his stomach. I put one finger inside his ass, then two, three, then four. He could take it much better than I could. Now *this* was what you call a teachable moment.

"Stop lying by omission. To me or to anyone else." I wiped my fingers on his back. I spanked him hard, over and over, until he cried silent crocodile tears. I made him apologize to me, to Sarah—to all of us, for all the Liams out there, really. For the ghosting and the cheating and the ambivalence and the refusing to love us back. It was a wonderful feeling, smashing my finest marble statue with a sledgehammer. It was also sad. "Look. You have a handsome face and a perfect dick. And you write poetry and you *seem* nice and you're smart enough. And that gives you power," I said, flipping him over and taking him firmly by the wide shoulders. "You need to be mindful of how you wield that. You have a responsibility to be honest about what you can and can't give, what you do and don't want. You don't owe anything else—your love, a relationship, your commitment, monogamy. You just owe people your *honesty*." I was pretty sure I meant it. Of course, I hoped he'd offer me more. He was silent. *Motherfucker. Oh wait, I am choking him.* I took my hand off his Adam's apple. *The way he swallows!* "Do you want to speak?"

"I need to recalibrate. I'm not entirely a sociopath," he answered. I hadn't used that word; I imagined other frustrated women had. "But my consideration really only went so far. I made a lot of half statements, I guess to absolve myself of responsibility or suffering."

"You're so fucking *lazy.*" I twisted his nipples again. I was starting to run out of moves. *Shit. How will I know when to end the scene? I forgot to research that . . .* "How is disappointing the people you sleep with something that keeps you safe?" I asked, channeling Adam's Socratic-therapist approach.

"I guess it keeps me from having to choose or commit. And it allows me to justify feeling poorly about myself," he answered.

"You seem mysterious but you're just withholding. You have more power than you want to over people because they fell for it. And you don't respect them for it because you know you don't deserve their admiration."

"Yes, I know," he said.

"Well then, change."

When I finally took the blindfold off and let him get on top, it was harder not to hope. *The way he fills me. The way he looks. The way he gives me his body but nothing more.* In the end, he pulled out and came on my stomach. *So he didn't even want to come inside me with a condom.* I wanted to curl up into my burnt rubble and weep, but felt I should stay at least somewhat in character. I examined his unearned privilege, flaccid but always full. "Have you ever felt insecure about it? Like, that women wouldn't be interested if you weren't packing this?" He nodded before I finished the thought, like a celebrity anticipating the end of a common press junket question.

"Yeah, definitely. When Sarah and I were breaking up, I felt she was almost more sad to say goodbye to my dick than she was to say goodbye to me." I had to laugh, but found myself petting his curls with sympathy, a fruit fly to a ripe plantain *siempre*. I wondered if I'd eventually come to feel the same way, grow similarly immune to all but his cock. I sensed I'd never be granted the access needed to reach that point.

He held me to his sturdy chest. *How can these Liams and Adams be so bad if they love to cuddle?* "Maybe I should write poetry like you," I said, instead of my feelings. "Must be nice not to have to explain every-thing so much, not to be limited by—"

"—Other people's understanding. I know," he finished. "But that was the best critique I ever got, from the poet Richard Howard. He said, 'It seems to me you haven't considered your reader at all.' I was like, '*Wow, that is a good observation, because I was not considering my reader.*'" He shrugged. "Then I said the same thing years later to a student and she started crying."

"She was probably in love with you," I said.

"Hm, I never thought of that," he murmured, falling into a long silence. "But this is nice with you. What we're doing." My stomach surged. *Maybe this is it! Maybe now that he saw I could hurt him, and he's brokenhearted, he'll have some feelings!* "It's so different with you."

"Oh yeah, how?" I tried to sound nonchalant.

"It doesn't feel like a love affair with you. It's always felt like some-thing else." I nodded, let the punch to my gut be absorbed so fully as to simply come out the other side. I swallowed and watched another part of me drift away. A private feeling, this increasingly skillful disso-ciation. I was tiny, nearly invisible. In the arms of these men who thought they held me, I was actually evaporating. Right before their eyes, and they couldn't even see it. *My quiet. My secret.*

Later that night, I worked up the courage to ask Liam why he'd come on my stomach (again, as if I didn't care). He said it was because coming inside me felt "too intimate." Also, he'd "always liked the pic-tures I'd sent with my stomach in them." Nothing uncommon, I sup-pose. A man eats his fill; a woman's increasingly concave belly makes a lovely porcelain bin. "I want my stomach to be impossibly beautiful for Liam," I'd literally written in my journal a few weeks before. *Diet it, and he will come.*

———

I drove home from Liam's the next day convincing myself that Adam remained my best chance at happiness, and I was going to be good at polyamory now. I did feel very inspired and alive, high off my performance and the thrill of novelty. I sang and sped into the night, feeling sharper than usual. I bought a big bag of reduced-fat popcorn I wanted to polish off but felt I must not. I stuffed fistfuls into my mouth like a paranoid chipmunk. I threw the bag onto the passenger seat floor so I couldn't get to the rest of it. I contemplated the odds of dying this way if I reached for it on the freeway. I called Adam instead and told him: *I get it now. I feel so clear. This freedom is worth it. Thank you for letting me have it. Thank you for being so patient with me. I'll get there, I will.* He was pleased.

I put my hand on my belly. *Ugh, too much popcorn. Why do you still want more? Because you're eating your feelings. Why are you eating your feelings if you're happy? Maybe because you feel you deserve pleasure. Well, why don't you just eat it all then? Because you already had dinner. So? Too many calories and you haven't even exercised.* Trauma and emotions are embodied; the stomach symbolic of what you stuff away. If I kept it flat, I had a feeling of control, as if I wasn't weighed down and was thriving. Emptied out for Liam, for Adam. For all the future lovers I might evaporate in the arms of next.

"Writing about my eating disorders is in a way a renunciation of empty," Susan Burton explains in her memoir, *Empty.** "Because I'll fill the blank white pages, I'll fill the emptiness in; and inevitably I will get it wrong, it will not be perfect, I'll feel somehow as if I've ruined it, as if I've wrecked it; and I will have to live with that . . . and that knowl-

---

* Susan Burton, *Empty: A Memoir* (New York: Random House, 2020).

edge is tormenting." This is how I feel, too, so often. As a writer who *does* consider her reader deeply, I often feel mortified by the ways I might let you down. My body and perspective are shifting in every single moment. By the time this book goes to print, I'll have hopefully matured far beyond what you read frozen here. This is an attempt to trust my own judgment again anyway.

And, in a way, to time-travel. I'm reaching out from the past—yet as you read, I enter your present. Look how I'm holding out my hand across time and space, and you are right now grabbing it. What a gift you've given an imperfect stranger. Can you feel how you were already pulling me through? How much you already mattered?

Yes, you. I am talking to you.

PART 4

Age 30

Never Been Healthier?

12/20/17

OAKLAND, CA

I took my mom out to lunch for my thirtieth birthday. She seemed in a nostalgic/possessive mood, an unfortunately classic combination. "I remember before your dad moved out, I stayed in the basement until he finally left," she mused.

"You did?" Why she was choosing my birthday to remind me of this, I didn't really wonder. I wished Adam were there to buffer, but he'd come down with the flu.

"Yeah, and it was so sad—you'd stand at the top of the stairs, and you'd say, 'Mommy, where are you? Mommy, please read me a story?'"

I'd recently taken to sleeping in the office instead of next to Adam. I told him it was my insomnia, which was also true. He'd ask me to come back to bed, then complain when I needed white noise to sleep. He reminded me that if I couldn't sleep next to him, he would have to eventually get this need met elsewhere. I knew this meant more sleepovers with other people, even a primary relationship with someone else. I'd compromise by waiting to creep into the other room until he was sound asleep.

As a child, I used to do this in reverse—tiptoeing into my mom's or dad's bed once they were snoring. My twelve-year-old cousin, the closest relationship I had to an older sibling, was killed by a drunk driver when I was nine. I wasn't afraid of monsters, but of death.

"What did you say to me about why you started sleeping in the basement?" I asked.

"I don't think I said anything. You were only two. Too little to understand." She shrugged.

"Hm, this is too salty, isn't it," I deflected, moving the green curry around on my plate.

My relationship with food had grown increasingly restrictive. Orthorexic compulsions I hadn't felt since before I met Adam had officially returned in a new form. It wasn't that I didn't eat. It was more like I'd grown so accustomed to Adam's cooking that everything outside it felt somehow deviant—too salty, too oily, too sweet. I usually allowed myself to eat as much of *his* cooking as I wanted. It felt clean and safe—pure nutritious fuel. But left to my own devices, food began to feel dangerous in a way it hadn't since my early twenties. Many things felt impossible when I imagined leaving Adam, but living alone with a fridge was one of the more humbling visualizations. *I can't trust myself not to binge without his presence blocking me. How pathetic. I know this mentality is bullshit. And I'm stuck anyway!?**

My mom pushed her plate out of the way. "Let's get the rest to go? My appetite isn't what it used to be," she said, I thought a little proudly. "Trying not to stuff myself, either, because neither is my metabolism. Not like you, so svelte!" I felt the desire to be stoned and exercising wash over me. To undo everything.†

---

*   "We rage at ourselves about why we can't seem to crack the clay of body shame. Across the landscape of our existence we see its ravages everywhere and feel acutely conscious of all the risks we have not taken because of it," Sonya Renne Taylor writes. "Splattered before us like bugs on the windshield of life are all the ways we have shrunk the full expression of ourselves because we have been convinced that our bodies and therefore our very beings are deficient. We can also see how our inability to get out of our shame story amplifies our feelings of inadequacy." Sonya Renne Taylor, *The Body Is Not an Apology* (Oakland: Berrett-Koehler Publishers, 2018).

†   Around half of the people with eating disorders also abuse drugs or alcohol. Cannabis is the most commonly abused substance. While this may seem counterintuitive, some people like me

We headed to the basement of the home we used to occupy. My mom couldn't afford the mortgage now that she wasn't with my stepdad, so another family rented it out while she stayed in the small in-law studio downstairs. She hated it. She hadn't made a house payment toward anything but interest in over a decade. Without savings, sufficient profit to be made from selling, or money for repairs, it was clear I'd eventually be paying for her life. I loved my new job working for the nonprofit Mercy For Animals, but how was that going to work? Thinking about it made the walls begin to close in.

Luckily, her friend Marta was coming over with my uncle Willie, which would help with my brewing panic attack. Around my mom's age, Marta's been a figure since I was a little girl, a Jewish Cuban ("Juban") aunt of sorts.

"Hey, honey!" Marta's nasal Queens accent welcomed me home. Her hair was flaming neon orange and she wore a leopard print jacket. Her prolonged, real hugs felt like being wrapped in a magic carpet that transports you back in time. "You look so tiny! You healthy?"

"I am," I said. "Never been healthier." And it was technically *true,* I reminded myself, if you looked at my blood work. But, according to the records I kept through an app, I got only three periods between May 1, 2017, and July 28, 2018. People were beginning to ask Adam if I wasn't too thin, as if I couldn't hear them. He'd shrug and reassure them I was healthy and eating plenty. I secretly cherished that feeling, too. Like I was being tucked in and having my temperature taken, rosy-cheeked and precious in my fragility.

---

experience marijuana as an energy booster and even appetite suppressant. Plus, both compulsive behaviors can be about attempting to feel at ease in your body and mind. National Center on Addiction and Substance Abuse (CASA) at Columbia University, "Food for Thought: Substance Abuse and Eating Disorders," 2003.

I knew that not getting my period meant something was not right. But I *was* eating three full meals a day—and so long as it was Adam's cooking, I didn't worry about calories. I didn't feel hungry, and suspected it had more to do with the stress of jealousy than anything else. Well, that and the increasingly compulsive exercising. *How could I be unhealthy when I've never felt stronger?* I could now bench squat more than my weight. I could bike like a boss for miles just to go to an intense dance class at Heartbeat House. There, I'd situate myself directly behind my favorite teacher and spend the hour fully embracing that I was most definitely not straight.* Back in our new Rapunzel-like dwelling atop the steep hill I'd climbed, a victorious lunch was waiting. On this wholefoods, plant-based diet of champions, I'd refuel and immediately feel filled with pent-up clean energy I was ready to spend again. I felt like a very efficient machine, if one performing a Sisyphean task: Eat and use the excess calories to work out, work out and cash in the deficit for more delicious food.† I was almost always in motion somewhere else.

Adam didn't explicitly encourage me to work out so hard. But he rarely missed a day of rather punishing yoga or biking himself, not even when he was sick. "Enough is as good as a feast," he'd remind himself (us?) aloud when we ate out, trying not to idly eat past when he was full. Afterward, he'd often complain of "feeling fat" and go to the gym

---

* In 1892, a neurologist recommended that people suffering from homosexual urges could ride their nervous energy/queerness away on a bicycle. Another un-fun fact: Queer women are twice as likely to suffer from an eating disorder as straight women. Graeme M. Hammond, "The Bicycle in the Treatment of Nervous Diseases," *Journal of Nervous and Mental Disease* 17, no. 1 (1892): 36–46. http://doi.org/10.1097/00005053-189201000-00007. J. L. Mensinger, J. L. Granche, S. A. Cox, and J. R. Henretty, "Sexual and Gender Minority Individuals Report Higher Rates of Abuse and More Severe Eating Disorder Symptoms Than Cisgender Heterosexual Individuals at Admission to Eating Disorder Treatment," *International Journal of Eating Disorders* 53 (2020): 541–54. https://doi.org/10.1002/eat.23257.

† Hardly anyone with an eating disorder stops eating entirely. Those who severely restrict calories—including more socially sanctioned "dieters"—also often still have normal blood work. For more on this, I recommend reading *Sick Enough* by Dr. Jennifer L. Gaudiani. If you see yourself or someone you care about in my story, you might also want to search terms like "orthorexia" and "exercise bulimia."

that same night to "sweat it out." Though I loved baking, I abstained; he didn't want sweets in the house, and I didn't want to eat them alone. When I was cold, which was most of the time now because I had so little body fat, he reminded me to toughen up. "Being cold burns calories," he'd say, as if to reassure me. When I'd occasionally ask him about his own body image and imply that maybe we had certain worries in common, he'd look at me like I was being ridiculous. *He was a man*, his amused eye roll seemed to imply. He wasn't *actually* worried. Sometimes, his frown in the mirror as he examined a rare bloat of his six-pack suggested otherwise.*

But the more I strived to make my body a reflection of his discipline, the less Adam seemed to notice me. He certainly didn't massage me, and initiated sex less and less. When I showered, he didn't hand me the towel anymore. I finally worked up the courage to ask him one day why he'd stopped. I knew the answer would hurt, no matter what it was.

"At the old place the towel rack was out of reach. I didn't want you dripping on the floor," he replied.

I blinked in shock. "It wasn't about making me feel loved and taken care of?"

"Well, that was obviously a bonus, too," he said, smiling wryly.

Now, instead, he reminded me hot showers would make me prematurely wrinkle. He began to complain my IUD strings were poking him, that his dick was sore. I trimmed the strings further, though the doctor warned me it was unnecessary and risky. It didn't make a difference.

"I think you place too much importance on sex for your validation,"

---

* Men and masc people are far less likely to seek treatment or report eating disorders, but account for as many as 25 percent of those who suffer from them. The number of men with eating disorders is also rising. Restrictive eating or compulsive exercise might look different in men, who are socialized to obsess over muscle mass at the gym. A quick online search will reveal lots of centers (and numbers to call) specializing in treating men and masc people. Eric Strother, Raymond Lemberg, Stevie Chariese Stanford, and Dayton Turbervillea, "Eating Disorders in Men: Underdiagnosed, Undertreated, and Misunderstood," *Eating Disorders* 20, no. 5 (2012): 346–55. https://doi.org/10.1080/10640266.2012.715512.

Adam said when I tried to talk about it. "It doesn't need to be such a big deal." When pressed, the only explanation he could point to for his lack of interest was that he didn't "feel free to be himself sexually with me." Sure, he was *allowed* to date other people, but he knew bringing up his experiences with them in bed might upset me. And this made him feel less amorous. So when I felt I could, I talked dirty about him having sex with other women. I experimented with acting unconcerned with sex for weeks at a time. Again, I didn't notice a difference.

"I feel more and more like a piece of comfortable furniture to you," I'd sometimes complain (because complaining is always an effective turn-on).

"This is just what happens after a few years," he'd say and shrug, resigned. "That's why having other people in the mix will help."

Indeed, non-monogamy seemed like brain-hacking. If the body wants to return to homeostasis by shifting from falling-in-love lust to calmer companionate feelings, perhaps dating other people was like jump-starting an old car. Could it be that when I fell in lust with someone else and got those same novelty-based chemicals flowing, I superimposed them onto Adam?* And didn't the threat of seeing him get ready for a date make me see him anew? Granted, I was often anxious when he was dating other people. But I'd also never felt attracted to someone for this long. *If I could just find another boyfriend, if I could just seem a little more unattainable, I know his desire will return.*

"Well if you're healthy, that's what matters," Marta *kvelled*† from my mom's sofa. "Tiny Rachel, *always tiny!*"

---

*   I asked every sex researcher I spoke to this question, but the science (and the funding for it) simply isn't there to know. All agreed it seemed plausible.

†   Yiddish for proud gushing/Jewish compersion, basically.

Who would I be if I wasn't? I often wondered. I'd gained a little weight in my early twenties and found I was not one of those women who simply ended up with a juicier ass and bigger breasts. Instead of going to only the socially sanctioned areas, I felt the effect was lovable toddler at best. As a five-foot, small-boned person with an aging metabolism, I had a very small margin of error if I wanted to stay within the short-girl-hip-to-waist-ratio Christina Aguilera and Shakira had exemplified throughout my adolescence. And for now, I was able to control at least this. Because without my girl-you'll-be-a-woman-soon tightrope of a figure, what did I have? *My eyes and personality?*

Yet no matter what I did, I knew I'd be deemed expired long before Adam. The task was to leverage what time I had left in the interest of securing a man's/men's future entrapment. I saw this for the fucked-up bullshit it was, and still couldn't escape it, which made me all the more ashamed. It turned out that non-monogamy had not allowed me to rise above these patriarchal and capitalist mentalities. What seemed to matter more than the relationship model was the power dynamic between Adam and me, and the broader societal system I was still living under.

Marta asked me what I was working on, this potential book my mom had told her about. "Ah, non-monogamy," she said, nodding. "I mean, we didn't call it that, but that's nothing new to me. My ex-husband, I'd just say to him, 'I don't want to know.' It had to be when he was far away, because I didn't want to *ever go anywhere* and run into *anybody* who was all excited about seeing him. I said, 'It has to be a total secret. It's yours. I respect that.' But that didn't work."

"Why not?" I asked.

"Because they're not thinking once that dick goes up!" Marta said, my mom and her cackling. "When they're old and they don't have dick anymore, they're wonderful people. They have to try to relate like an actual *human*." My uncle Willie, listening quietly in the corner as usual, laughed good-naturedly.

"Isn't that a little sexist?" I asked.

"No, it's *true*. You'll see, soon enough." My mom and Marta are prone to this kind of casual misandry, like it's a benefit you earn along with your AARP card. "I've had that kind of betrayal no matter what sort of relationship I was in with a man. And make no mistake, it's betrayal."

"But how is it betrayal if both people agree to the open relationship?" I countered.

"You show *me* the woman who's totally cool about her guy fucking around with a lot of other people." Marta paused for effect. *"She doesn't exist."* I thought of a few women I knew, but took her point that it was rare.* "What, you're not jealous with Adam?" she asked.

"No, I am, sometimes . . ."

"So why are you interested in the agreement?"

I gave my now-practiced explanation. "Well, grappling with the feeling of jealousy has been emotionally and spiritually interesting for me. It's forced me to sit with uncomfortable feelings over and over. Like I'm confronting perhaps the most vulnerable part of me and having to become stronger by unlearning certain beliefs about myself and love that aren't beneficial." Marta nodded, but seemed skeptical. I tried to add something she could relate to more. "And I like that I could commit to Adam without having to give up the chance of ever falling in love again. Because that's one of my favorite feelings."

---

* I asked Dedeker Winston, who both appears to usually be "totally cool" with her male partners being with other women and is a relationship coach, if she wanted to offer comment on this. "What I have noticed among my clients is that women in heterosexual relationships are much more likely to be concerned about whether or not her male partner is using his sexuality in a responsible and caring way," she said. "So many straight women have stories of being on the receiving end of a man being exploitative, coercive, disrespectful, or violent and abusive. The thought that her male partner might be wending a path of emotional destruction as he sleeps around is disturbing to many women, even if she's on board with a non-monogamous relationship. When a woman feels trusting of her male partner to not only respect and care for her, but to also respect and care for the other people that he's engaging with, there's a much higher likelihood of her being 'totally cool' with it."

"So you don't feel cornered when you imagine the future with him."
She nodded, now understanding.

"I mean, we both know I was raised by a mother who doesn't like
people telling her what to do. And I very much inherited that," I said.
"I have a lot of sensitivity around feeling like people are trying to restrict what I can do with my time or my body." I was aware of my hypocrisy and honesty coexisting, as usual.

"And how long have you guys been together?" Marta asked.

"Three years." It felt like so much longer. *It is longer in soul-time,*
Adam inwardly reminded me.

"Boy, little Rachel. *Still little!*" Marta said again, shaking her head
proudly. "Well, I guess our generation was only just figuring out how
to have sex and relationships now that there was the Pill. But let's hope
that something new will come of your generation, too. Here, you want
some?" Marta offered me a hit off her vape.

I took a puff and felt gratitude wash over me. I leaned back and
almost felt okay that I hadn't had time to create a big calorie deficit
before my thirtieth birthday dinner. *Sometimes being a Bay Area cliché—
getting stoned with my matriarchs while talking about non-monogamy—
makes me so proud.* There was a magnificent precipice I could increasingly
sense I was on the edge of. I wasn't sure what it was—a break with reality and/or more social constructs, a separation or real engagement? The
most precious idea of all: a gestating creative birth, this book. Or maybe
that was all adulthood was. A perpetual sense of epic vista ahead, followed by a sudden drop-off.

Relationship Anarchy

January 2018

LOS ANGELES

"You *have* to listen to the *Multiamory* podcast about relationship anarchy," Adam told me with a breathless smile when he came in the door, flushed from his post-yoga bike ride. "It sounds scary—but it's really not, don't worry. It's like . . . it's like how I want to *be* in a relationship."

By now, Adam had started seeing Mira, a married woman who actually identified as polyamorous and was in a happy primary/secondary model marriage. Thanks to my aerobic exorcisms, taking Zoloft to quiet my sex drive and anxiety, and getting stoned more days than not, I was *actually doing* all right! It was also reassuring that she was the first lover he'd had who wasn't single and had real experience with polyamory. "It's hard to explain. Just look it up," he said, with a tone like a salesman's wink. *"Relationship anarchy."*

Relationship anarchy (RA) is, by definition, not easy to define. Its values and the term itself were coined by the Swedish writer Andie Nordgren in their 2006 essay "The Short Instructional Manifesto for Relationship Anarchy." These are its core principles, with a very brief summary/translation of each added by me. My interpretations are in no way standard definitions of the ideas—that's kind of the whole point; there is no standard way to interpret RA's principles.

1. "Love is abundant, and every relationship is unique" (my unofficial summary: Avoid hierarchies and terms like primary secondary, or otherwise putting relationships in boxes)

2. "Love and respect instead of entitlement" (just because you have a history with someone doesn't mean you're entitled to their future actions or decisions—respect their freedom wherever possible)

3. "Find your core set of relationship values" (define your desires and boundaries for yourself; don't impose them as rules or let others dictate them for you)

4. "Heterosexism is rampant and out there, but don't let fear lead you" (larger systems of oppression at play will try to discredit this model and/or you—don't let them)

5. "Build for the lovely unexpected" (don't let duties or demands run relationships; allow for change)

6. "Fake it till you make it" (this model is not going to be easy)

7. "Trust is better" (trusting relationships are more loving than jealous ones that demand constant validation)

8. "Change through communication" (be explicit and get ready to talk through a lot)

9. "Customize your commitments" (you should design your own life, not society)

Sounds pretty enlightened to me. The issue is of course that anarchy in practice can sometimes be less loving utopia and more oddly dogmatic chaos. "I usually see one person who believes in relationship anarchy, surrounding themselves with non-RA partners—all of whom usually end up disappearing because they don't feel they're being treated well, or that RA provides them with enough stability or security to plan their lives around. Or even to plan their next weekend around," Kathy later told me. She says RA is on the rise among her younger clients, especially in the United Kingdom and among queer and politically radical people. She says it's also pretty common that one partner wants to switch from a more primary/secondary model to relationship anarchy, like Adam was suggesting. "In hetero dynamics, it's almost always the men saying they don't believe in the hierarchical model, saying, 'These relationships are all individual and each one is special. And I don't want to make a priority of anyone's feelings at the expense of someone else's.' "

Adam used that last phrase often. He didn't want my "irrational insecurities hurting other innocent people." He also said he liked the idea of relationship anarchy because it was less possessive and dictated by insecurity, a more pure way to love. If we went with the primary/secondary model—which he insisted we already basically *were*, in practice—my fears could be wielded to innocent people's detriment. What had happened with Leah was his proof that I couldn't "be trusted with veto power." Aka, that I might actually deign to use it.

––––––

Though we never explicitly agreed to it, it was clear that relationship anarchy was to be my new ideological goalpost. *If I can learn to embrace this way of loving fully, I'll have really evolved.* The carrot on the stick: The more open I could be, the more he'd want me again. That was a very strong incentive.

I'd later learn that this feeling of being tested is common in gaslit dynamics. As is the sense that the goalpost is always moving. The person-in-control's expectations never seem fully met, and continually shift. This keeps the other person unbalanced. Most often, the gaslighter simply believes they're "right" and have their partner's best interest in mind. *If Rachel could see things clearly and just trust me, she'd be so much happier.* And remember, rationality and paternalism are core values of white supremacy culture. If you're a white man, it's especially easy to internalize that your responsibility is to uphold these values for others' "benefit." You're supposed to know best. This is its own, albeit roomier, cage.

I now questioned myself endlessly. *I thought I was doing well and not being jealous, but it still isn't enough or making him want me, so maybe I need to do better.** I was almost as invested in proving the "rightness" of Adam's ideas about relationships as he was. His opinions had become the compass by which I made almost all my decisions, the clearest voice inside my head.† In defending him, I defended myself.

"JUST TRUST ME" TRANSCRIPT

1/7/18

Los Angeles

ADAM:

```
The irony is that you'll have a happier
relationship with me, and I'll be happier with you
and the relationship, if I am not manipulated into
trying to appease your insecurities. Like, just
trust me and trust my decisions.
```

---

*   "If our gaslighter's bad behavior is all our fault, then [we can believe] we've got complete control of the situation. All we have to do is try harder, and the relationship is sure to improve." Stern, *The Gaslight Effect.*

†   Top 10 Songs I Used to Help Normalize Feeling Gaslit/Stoned All the Time (Playlist on my Spotify)
   1. "The Wilhelm Scream"—The Bamboos feat. Megan Washington
   2. "I Can't See Nobody"—Nina Simone, Daniel Yaghoubi
   3. "What's Wrong with Groovin'"—Letta Mbulu
   4. "Love on the Brain"—Rihanna
   5. "Redbone"—Childish Gambino
   6. "Down"—Emily King
   7. "No Room for Doubt"—Lianne La Havas feat. Willy Mason
   8. "Trying My Best to Love You"—Jenny Lewis
   9. "Take the Night Off"—Laura Marling
   10. "Across the Universe"—Fiona Apple

RACHEL:

. . . But you just made a unilateral decision [to practice relationship anarchy].

ADAM:

[Growing frustrated]

. . . If three years of being with me isn't long enough to feel secure about the relationship or trust me, or understand who I am and know me and trust my decisions, then it's not going to happen. Or, you need to make a different kind of effort to trust me. If you just allowed me to be myself and make my decisions, you would be happier. It would be better for you.

[Softer]

Wouldn't it be nice to have an honest relationship without ego and control?

RACHEL:

It feels dishonest for me to pretend it doesn't hurt.

ADAM:

. . . I really think that's because you're not facing your trust issues* . . . You just have to trust life, really. But part of that trusting life is extending [it] to trust in me. Don't you want to be with someone who feels more alive and feels

---

* "Adam is demonstrating a common defensive tactic of people with narcissistic personality styles, in that they refuse to accommodate to the feelings or desires of others, while simultaneously expecting others to accommodate theirs, and if the person resists they point out that resistance as the problem," Dr. Witherspoon commented upon reviewing this transcript. "That way they get what they want and feel like they're actually being the 'patient' ones, or the 'honest' ones. But often they're really just being rigid and inconsiderate." (It's important to note that practitioners' comments here and throughout the book are solely intended to be educational in nature, and do not represent any formal diagnostic or clinical services.)

happier with you and doesn't feel trapped by the
relationship, or trapped in what I can express?

RACHEL:

[Confused, probably wanting to get high]
. . . I should take a walk.

ADAM:

I would just be very wary of how you're going to
represent this to other people on your walk, so
that you get a sounding board for what you want to
hear. If you frame this in a way that upsets other
people, then you're just going to make things even
harder for our future relationship.

Adam often did this, discouraging me from "poisoning" my friends and family against him by reaching out when I was upset. I didn't always listen, but I often did, leading me to further self-isolate. I'd *literally edited articles* teaching me this meant You're in a Controlling-or-Worse Relationship. But part of what made this dynamic so confusing is that I didn't (and still don't) believe Adam had harmful or even unloving intent. The idea that someone has to be *trying* to hurt you or can't love you in order to be manipulating you is part of what kept me in denial. I think Adam really believed this was the best way to love me. That if I just did what he wanted, aka "trusted" in him and life, I would be happy. His main delusion was that he thought he was above delusion.

――――

When the idea of abandoning rules I'd never managed to establish in the first place made me anxious, I tried to spin new escape plans. I decided I'd log on to the site SeekingArrangement and find another sugar daddy. That way, I'd have money to move out, if I ever needed to.

Despite his ongoing insistence I was "free to do whatever" I wanted, Adam wasn't pleased. He clearly felt this brand of freedom reflected poorly on him. Having a sugar daddy had been fine when I stumbled into the dynamic with Silas—but seeking it out was a different matter.

SUGAR DADDY TRANSCRIPT

1/21/18

Los Angeles

ADAM:

[Annoyed]

Just say it. Say, "I want to try out being a prostitute."

RACHEL:

. . . I think that our relationship would be stronger if I was on equal financial footing as you and if I had these other relationships that kept me feeling desired, that kept me feeling appreciated and valued, quite literally.

ADAM:

"Purchased" is different than "valued." . . . That's why I don't like BDSM. I don't like people having power over one another. I don't like the idea of trying to get someone to be my slave or need me or things like that. To me, all that shit is ugly as fuck.

RACHEL:

[Pausing to consider the irony with her future imaginary audience]

Well, I think that's a little judgmental.

ADAM:

No. It's not judgmental . . . Power games, to me,
are ugly.* Trying to manipulate someone into being
under your control, to me, that's just ugly. . . .
You'll feel a little bit sick with yourself. . . .
You're picky as hell . . . but now it has to take
money. It has to take someone dangling dollars in
front of your face.

I think sex work is legitimate labor that should be legalized, taxed, protected under the law, and respected. I'm also not sure having a sugar daddy actually was, for me, sex work. Either way, I knew I was being unfairly shamed by Adam. And yet after this conversation, I told him I wouldn't look for a sugar daddy again. Though I was technically "free to do whatever" I wanted, I continued to defer to what Adam wanted instead. And, ironically, to organize more free luxury vacations to take him on.

---

* "It completely makes sense to me, based on what I've read, that Adam would be so averse to BDSM and consciously eroticized power dynamics," Dr. Witherspoon commented. "This feels like classic projection, where we project onto other people or situations disavowed aspects of ourselves that we can't tolerate. Perhaps unconsciously he might fear, or even be aware, of his own misuse of power dynamics. To pretend that he can remain completely outside power dynamics in relationships helps him avoid consciously acknowledging that anxiety."

The Desire Crew

CANCUN, MEXICO, DESIRE RIVIERA MAYA RESORT

For our third anniversary, I arranged another comped press trip* to yet
another clothing-optional resort. Desire, which has two different loca-
tions in the Cancun area, prefers not to brand itself explicitly as a
"swingers resort" so much as "lifestyle-friendly." Considering there's a
playroom that's open every night for sex, I'd say it's a little more than
"friendly."

On our first day, we met a group in the pool who would become
friends. While all of them identified as "in the lifestyle" and were married, several of them were arguably more polyamorous than swingers in
practice, dating outside of play spaces as well. The group of roughly
fifteen stood out in the otherwise largely white and fifty-plus crowd;
many of them were very attractive, they were in their late thirties and
early forties, and at least half of them were Black. Multiple studies over
the past few decades have found swingers are actually more politically

---

* Many of the gift and vacation guides you read, even if they are not officially sponsored or af-
filiate content, are little more than quid pro quos between underpaid freelancers, burnt-out
editors, and PR agents offering "samples" and "media invitations" in implicit or explicit exchange for coverage. For more on this (and other aspects of this ecosystem), I recommend
Gabrielle Korn's memoir, *Everyone Else Is Perfect: How I Survived Hypocrisy, Beauty, Clicks, and
Likes* (Miami: Atria Books, 2021).

conservative* (making exceptions for LGBTQIA+ and abortion rights); this group, however, quickly made clear they were liberal on all issues. The group did fit the average swinger profile in other ways, however: The majority of swingers also have above-average incomes, higher-than-average levels of education, and work in professional and/or management positions.† As is typical in the lifestyle, the women were all some degree of fluid, none of the men were, and all were cis people in straight marriages. These couples in the Desire Crew, as I would come to think of them, have been together since their twenties. The women wear big diamonds, the men gold or black bands.‡

Rich and Pam came over to talk with us first. Pam's personality was immediately infectious; extroverted friendliness is her resting state. Rich was similarly outgoing; he told us he and Pam married in college, and had been loving each other ever since. As we spoke in the pool, it was clear Pam was not threatened in the slightest by her husband's flirting with me. Instead, they seemed to be constantly loving and complimentary toward each other, like newlyweds who were also each other's wingmen.

"Pam is even sexier to me now than when I first met her. I still have to drag myself out of the house some mornings when we're getting dressed for work." Rich smiled at Pam. I thought of my dwindling sex

---

*   Psychologist Dr. Ley explains this surprising trend with a theory that casual sex without love is a way to "resolve moral conflicts" for people with more conservative/normative values—people who would say "it's just sex." People who are more liberal, he says, tend to show less interest in sex without love. In my very anecdotal experience, my friends who identify as polyamorous tend to be far more radical, queer, and questioning of social constructs than any swinger I've met. But there's selection bias in that sample since all my friends are politically liberal. Justin Wilt, Marissa A. Harrison, and Cobi S. Michael, "Attitudes and Experiences of Swinging Couples," *Psychology & Sexuality* 9, no. 1 (2018): 38–53. https://doi.org/10.1080/19419899.2017.1419984.

†   A. S. Ruzansky and M. A. Harrison, "Swinging High or Low? Measuring Self-Esteem in Swingers," *Social Science Journal* 56, no. 1 (2019): 30–37. https://doi.org/10.1016/j.soscij.2018.10.006.

‡   A black wedding band can be a secret signal you're in the lifestyle (though it certainly isn't always, especially with the popularization of silicone fitness tracker rings).

life with Adam, and wondered how this could still be true more than twenty years in.

"I talk about this all the time with Amalia," Pam said, gesturing to a naked woman across the pool. Amalia was a Latinx woman with a beautiful face, large, high breasts, long brown hair, and an iconic hip-to-waist ratio. A crowd naturally formed around her. She was standing next to a pleasant-looking but unassuming white man, her husband, Rory. "Amalia reminds me, 'Pam, your husband is just worshipping you. *Bask* in it.'"

"She knows that if she wanted me to give it up tomorrow for her, I would," Rich added in that swinger way I now recognized. I envied how easily the men in the lifestyle seemed to mean this. They were grateful for any and all this gravy.

I looked at Adam, who was flirting across the pool with Liv, a petite, beautiful woman in the same group. *Doesn't he know if he could promise me the same sense of control I also might relax?* He still refused to grant me veto power in "normal" life, or to really promise anything about the future. But at least we'd learned from our huge fight at Hedonism: He promised he would let me lead the way at Desire. We would be swingers for the week, a team that went as fast as the slowest person. Again, this seemed to make me feel safe and open.

When we passed the group in a large circular cabana the next day, they invited us into their harem pile. The topless women cuddled and massaged each other, braided one another's hair. I offered some of the weed I'd procured on the beach. Being immediately naked around people stripped away barriers to vulnerability and friendship with a speed I hadn't seen since freshman orientation in college. Rich came over and touched the blond hairs at the small of my back, fascinated.

"Dude! You're supposed to ask to touch her first! *Consent!*" Nate, a tall man with huge muscles who was clearly the gregarious ringleader, called Rich out.

"Shit, you're right, I'm sorry," Rich said, retracting his hand like he'd burned it. He'd asked me the day before in the pool if he could touch my leg, kiss me. I was open to it, but my eyes seemed only able to fixate on one person: Amalia. Ever since I've met her, Amalia has elicited in me the awkwardness of a teenage boy. Looking stupefied for a prolonged period is no way to attract most women, and to Amalia, it is repellent. But there I am, trying not to gape at the outrageous balance of her form, like God's whipping my ass at Jenga.

Catching me staring, Amalia and her husband, Rory, approached me. I quickly found out their origin story. Rory was a virgin when they met in their early twenties, inexperienced with non-monogamy. "I remember she turned to me after the first time we had sex and said, 'At some point you may want to have sex with someone else and that's okay, we'll just talk about that,'" Rory told me.

"Well, I do come from a culture where it's expected men are going to cheat," Amalia said. She grew up in the Dominican Republic. "Maybe I establish trust by essentially positioning myself as someone who won't get mad about those things. But I *will* say that I've had four serious relationships in my life, and *I'm* the one who cheated in every one of them—except for this one. Rory's never cheated, and before me, he was totally monogamously inclined."[*]

"Plus, there's your kink," Rory added.

At fifteen, Amalia found out her first boyfriend was cheating on her with an eighth grader. At first, she was just pissed. "But then I started to obsess about her," she told me. "Soon, I was thinking about her with

---

[*] Research on diverse samples has found that women are just as likely as men to engage in consensually non-monogamous relationships. But more men actually *report* doing so, which the authors attribute to the greater stigma women face for non-normative sexual/relational behavior. J. D. Rubin, A. M. Y. C. Moors, J. E. S. L. Matsick, and T. D. Conley, "On the Margins: Considering Diversity Among Consensually Non-monogamous Relationships," *Journal Für Psychologie* 22 (2014): 1–23.

my ex-boyfriend all the time. From then on, I'd get off on the thought
of whatever boyfriend I had with other women."

"That's what happened to Adam—he realized the same kink when
he found out his girlfriend was cheating. But your boyfriends must
have thought they hit the double jackpot with you," I said, attempting
to flirt.

"At first, but then they'd get frustrated," she answered. "I remember
my college boyfriend complaining, 'It's been three weeks since we did
anything where we weren't pretending to be other people and where I
wasn't talking to you about other girls. Like, can't we just do us?'" I
guiltily thought of my own frustration with Adam and how he always
seemed to want to imagine some form of triangulation.

"So you're into hothusbanding." I nodded. "But you never hear that
term.* Among straight people, anyway."

"Exactly! I'm a hothusband," Rory said, winking in self-deprecation.
"And I'm *definitely* not complaining. But the most important thing to
me is that I make my wife happy."

"Hey, what y'all talking about?" Liv sidled up to us with Adam.
Though they'd been flirting heavily, I mostly felt sisterly toward her
already, even attracted. Liv's been blessed with a socially idolized figure
and an age-defying metabolism. But as a Black woman with an unusual
birthmark and a punk haircut, she certainly knows being marginalized,
too. She shines in all of herself, radiating sex and friendliness and wit at
four feet eleven. I had to give it to Adam, as usual. He had good taste.

"Rachel was asking us about how we became perverts," Rory said,
offering Liv a hit off the joint.

"Ah, well, Nate and I, we were never monogamous. When we met
he was a bouncer, and girls were always hitting on him," Liv recalled
fondly, inhaling. "Inevitably, there's some girl who tried to go down on

*   Psychologist Roy Baumeister suggested that women who practice this kink, aka "reverse cuck-
      oldry," are virtually nonexistent, likely due to core gender differences. Obviously, Amalia and
      other women I know would beg to differ. Ley, *Insatiable Wives*.

him, or he would be making out with a girl in the corner, or somebody's hand was in his pants. And I would wait up for the story about
it when he got home, and we would have sex the rest of the night, and
then we would fuck all day, and then he would go to work." *When did
they sleep?* Are non-monogamous people drawn to the lifestyle because
they're more sexual, extroverted, and ambitious, or do they continue to
be more that way because they get energy from being non-monogamous?
Knowing these couples better now, I'd say both causes appear to be at
work.*

But Liv's husband, Nate, is certainly unique. Like a male Samantha
from *Sex and the City,* only less discriminating. I've never witnessed a
woman he wasn't at least somewhat interested in. I already wondered
how Liv dealt with it, even if it was "just sex."

————

I invited the entire crew over to our hotel suite that night. I didn't
know if I'd have a comped suite with a ten-person jacuzzi and room
service ever again, and I was determined to carpe the hell out of this
diem. We ordered a few bottles of champagne, some fruit plates for
good measure. Adam looked extremely happy playing host, and I
knew I was "succeeding." We piled into the Jacuzzi bath naked and
started talking. The group knew I was working on an article about
Desire, potentially even a book one day. They agreed they were fascinating people, and assured of their anonymity, enjoyed being extremely
frank.

"I mean, as a white guy, Rory can get away with a lot more than I
can, when it comes to making his interest known to women. He can

————

*   From the studies that exist, we know that polyamorous-identified people tend to be, on aver-
    age, more sensation seeking, more extroverted, more open to new experiences and to uncom-
    mitted sex. "But the chicken-and-egg question can't be addressed via the research yet, in my
    opinion," Dr. Witherspoon told me. "As with most things, I imagine it's a bit of both."

escalate in a magnificent way that I just can't, you know what I mean?" Nate said. "I try not to inject race into every fucking interaction, but I'd be lying if I said it's not a factor."

"But being Black also helps you get girls sometimes," Liv added.

"Right," Nate conceded. "Whereas I think for Liv, a lot of the dudes are intimidated because she's a strong Black woman, even if she's small. Plus, she's with a Black dude. The assumptions that come with that, her expectations from a physical standpoint. The whole BBC thing," Nate said, referring to the stereotype of the "big Black cock," a popular fetish among many into hotwifing. "You see that on dating apps, people saying they want a Black dude for their wife."*

"Does that piss you off? Being objectified like that?" I asked.[†]

"I mean, I think race is a part of people's fantasies—I know it is for me, so I can't be upset if somebody found me attractive based on that." Nate shrugged. "But maybe you could also *finesse* that shit a little."

"It's like a Hobson's choice, right? It's like, good and bad, right?" Rich added. "I recognize that in the lifestyle there are women who are attracted to me cause I'm a bigger-than-average Black dude. So it benefits me, but it also makes me uncomfortable because I don't want to be just 'a thing.' I've played in situations where women say, '*Fuck me*

---

*   A Black history teacher who commented on Dan Savage's website under the username Satadru posits that the BBC fetish might also be a way for a white husband to vicariously get homoerotic pleasure from looking at a Black man. He also suggests that perhaps the desire is a subliminal one to relieve the "white man's burden" and guilt of being "superior" over both women and Black men in our society, that it may be a way for a white man to "hang up his racial and gendered boots and not be so dominant." It may also be that he simply wishes to imagine himself as the racist stereotype of the Black man—virile, well-endowed, and strong. Regardless, in the context of white couples that are into hotwifing, the BBC fetish generally harbors unexamined racism. https://www.thestranger.com/seattle/SavageLove?oid=133984; https://slog .thestranger.com/2007/01/cuckolding_confusion.

†   In Dr. David Ley's research into hotwifing and cuckolding message boards, he found that many non-Black couples described their encounters with Black men, or even having sex itself, as simply "BBC," both verb and noun. What in the objectifying fuck. For more on how objectification, fetishization, and tokenization of Black people and other people of color plays out in non-monogamous communities, I highly recommend reading *Love's Not Color Blind*.

*with your big Black cock.'** And that shit does not turn me on. I've also seen straight-up on dating profiles: *'Black dude need* Man, get out of here with that!"

"The difference between a preference and objectification is not seeing the whole person," Pam added. "When a guy is approaching me just because I'm a Black woman and he has a fantasy, you can just feel it. It feels bad."

"Asian women have it way worse than Black men do when it comes to this.[†] And I *like* Asian women, so I feel like I can't get too upset," Nate added. "What gets me more mad is, why do the Black dudes in pornos have to look like ex-convicts? Shit like that is offensive. That said, if you try some thug talk on me and you're cute enough, there's a chance I'm gonna let it slide. I just won't invite you to hang out with this group later. In this group, the sex is some bonus shit, right? These are people to hang out with.[‡] You can't be spewing that nonsense. At the same time, we do try to be really inclusive. We're way more millennial polyam relationship anarchists than most swingers in that way. We

---

* While it's somewhat well known that enslaved Black women were sexually exploited and raped by white slaveholders, there are records of slaveholders abusing enslaved Black men in a similar way. These men were often referred to as "bull dicks, a term that is almost certainly involved in the etymology of the term 'bull,' often used to describe Black men in [current iterations of] cuckolding and hotwifing," Dr. Ley writes in *Insatiable Wives*. White male obsession with Black penises also meant castration was a common punishment for enslaved people. Long after slavery was technically abolished, Black men have been assaulted and lynched for less than the suggestion that they engaged sexually with a white woman, or cuckolded a white man.

† For further reading on this and racial fetishization in general, check out Robin Zheng, "Why Yellow Fever Isn't Flattering: A Case Against Racial Fetishes," *Journal of the American Philosophical Association* 2, no. 3 (Fall 2016): 400–19.

‡ Indeed, community is a key reason many swingers cite for being drawn to the lifestyle. Research with swingers shows consistently that sexual variety, the excitement of the taboo, exhibitionism, and voyeurism are the main motivations, however. Interestingly, one study found that when swingers were asked to rank their personal values, having an "exciting life" came in tenth. Self-respect, family security, and inner harmony were ranked first through third, respectively. K. T. Vaillancourt and A. L. Few-Demo, "Relational Dynamics of Swinging Relationships: An Exploratory Study," *Family Journal* 22, no. 3 (2014): 311–20. https://doi.org/10.1177/1066480714529742.

don't want some exclusionary hierarchy or club. Our 'core group' is probably at least thirty deep now, and it's always changing."

"But there are certain social norms that must exist in the group, even if it's fluid, no?" I asked.

"Well, there's the importance of consent. And your boundaries are your boundaries," Rich said. "Do whatever makes you happy as long as you don't harm anyone. There are people in our group who do full swap and date outside of play parties, some only do soft swap, some only like to watch and do things together. And we're cool with all of it. No one is going to try to push you, and everyone is respected equally."

"But people think the lifestyle is some utopia, and it isn't," Nate added. "That everyone will be all welcoming, all accepting, and everybody's going to be a great person. And that's just stupid. The same jackasses you hate at work are going to be at these parties."

"But you guys do have a pretty special thing going here. I'm not sure I've seen such a large, diverse, and obviously closely knit set of friends," I added.

"No doubt," Nate answered proudly. The concern for friendship also means, among this group anyway, that sometimes you take one for the team. If you see a play situation is being cockblocked by there being too many people around, you might choose to recuse yourself. Eventually, people began to filter out. To my great disappointment, Amalia wanted to go back to her room and rest, but encouraged Rory to stay alone. Rich and Pam remained, and so did Liv. I lay on the bed with the women. I wasn't sure how a sixsome would work, but I felt ready to find out.

"I think these men should give us massages," I offered, turning the page.

"Oh, yes!" Pam and Liv agreed, giggling.

Rich, Adam, and Rory began to massage our feet and legs. I turned my head to one side and kissed Pam, then to the other to kiss Liv. The men began to go down on us this way. Liv moaned into my mouth under Adam's tongue. Once again, I felt more proud than jealous, turned on acutely. Things ended when they ended. Some of us came, others didn't, and it was 3 a.m. I was reminded how condoms make cleaning up easier. We went to eat tacos at the bar. And with that, our friendship was solidified.

So went the rest of our trip. Adam was nothing short of profoundly moved. "This is the first time I've really felt like I belonged in a group of people," I remember him saying, tears in his eyes. "Thank you." Though I'd taken him on many comped vacations, he'd never thanked me this sincerely for being my plus-one. I squeezed his hand, enjoyed the reward of hard-earned praise. *These couples—they're so happy and free, so smart, cool, and committed at once. Maybe there's hope for us after all.*

Only a few weeks later, Liv reached out to say she would be in LA on business.

That Deviant and Criminal Box

3/2/18

LOS ANGELES

A threesome with Liv was implicitly on the table, but there was no sense of pressure or plan. We went back to her hotel room after a few drinks, and Adam began to ask her probing questions, his sincere seduction method of choice.

"So you're asking me why I still sometimes get upset or jealous after all this time?" Liv asked us. "Like after Nate sleeping with so many other women? And why I don't date by myself outside of parties, if having feelings excites me more than just sex?"

Well . . . yeah. We both nodded.

"When we got married, I think something shifted. I met all these people who told us that what we were doing was called 'the lifestyle.' I didn't know there was a name for it," Liv remembered. "I'm like, *Oh, is that what we've been doing?*" These couples cautioned her that it took many more years of being married to be stable enough to swing. "I was like, 'Nate, I think we have to be married for a little bit more time before we can do this because that's what everyone is saying.'"

"Even though you'd already been non-monogamous the whole six years before?" I asked. That this was possible unnerved me. I was counting on things getting easier with time, not harder.

"It was something about the seriousness of like, *Oh, I just committed my life to this person.* Let me make sure that I do want to do this open shit." Marriage is proprietary, and really can change how people feel about non-monogamy—for better or worse. Liv told us that from there, her jealousy began to arise. Before, Nate had been choosing to come home to her, and knowing that she was special and winning in that way had been a lot of what turned her on. Now that they were married, she felt more like his default. "You go to work, you pay bills, you argue about the kid." Liv sighed. "I don't know if women are as willing to say that that monotony does something to the feeling of attraction. But it *does something to you.** I was no longer the new thing, everybody else was the new thing. And I was the thing that was just going to be there." I noticed she used the word "thing," not "woman." "And there's this pressure to prove you're perfect when you're in a non-monogamous relationship, even though it's just shades of gray, like any other relationship. And my flaws lead me to feel insecure sometimes, inadequate."

"What do you mean, insecure?" Adam asked.

"Like, this is honestly the most deviant thing I would ever do when I'm traveling for work," Liv said, referring to the fact we were in her hotel room, "because what I do is so emotionally draining."

"And not very sexy," I added sympathetically.

"*Never* is it sexy." (To say why would compromise her anonymity—which would put her job at risk.†) "If work found out, I'd be seen as deviant, I'm sure. Meanwhile, I don't even *know* what Nate's job is—

---

* Plenty of studies have proven that women are particularly affected by both a lack of novelty and living with a partner. A study of over 11,500 British people aged 16–74 found that lack of interest in sex was more common among women in a relationship over a year old. If they were living with their partner, they were even less likely to be sexually interested. Other studies have found women's desire drops drastically after ninety months—but men's actually tends to hold relatively steady. (Women who didn't live with their partners seemed to avoid as steep a decline.) C. A. Graham, C. H. Mercer, C. Tanton, et al., "What Factors Are Associated with Reporting Lacking Interest in Sex and How Do These Vary by Gender? Findings from the Third British National Survey of Sexual Attitudes and Lifestyles," *BMJ Open* 2017; 7:e016942. https://doi.org/10.1136/bmjopen-2017-016942; Wednesday Martin, "The Bored Sex," *Atlantic*, Feb. 14, 2019.

† "I have had a client who was fired for being non-monogamous," a lawyer to the non-monogamous, Jonathan D. Lane, later told me. "But there's not much you can do about it because the law just isn't there to protect against it."

that's how high his security clearance is. But I know he has to take lie detector tests. So for him, he can't hide being in the lifestyle. The government knows about all of it—Desire, the sex parties."

"I'd love to see *those* lie detector transcripts," I said, laughing.

"Yeah, it's ironic. I don't even know what his job is, but in every other way, Nate's life is an open book. Me, I have to worry about anyone finding out." It occurred to me that Liv having to be in the closet would maintain an understandable level of shame and fear—the main emotions jealousy needs to sustain itself. "I think that any type of sex that's outside of traditional monogamy is viewed as 'deviant, criminal, and bad.' And that 'deviant and criminal box' includes 'consenting adults' and '*actual* deviant criminal.' I just feel like it all gets funneled into the same thing."* Liv sighed. "Maybe I've internalized the shame."†

"Well, how couldn't you?" I asked. I lay next to Liv on the hotel bed and cuddled with her in that fluid and juicy space between sister and lover. She stroked my hair in her lap. We left Liv's room that night without having sex, though it didn't matter much to any of us. I thought we were all just tired.

A year later, Liv told me why she'd really called it a night. Outside the dreamy haze of Desire, something about Adam now rubbed her the wrong way. She still thought he was cute, and definitely smart, but . . . she couldn't put her finger on it. It was there, though. And something in her just didn't want to reward it.

---

*   Psychiatric and psychological fields have a long history of conflating "deviant" (for example, non-normative or statistically unusual) sexual behavior with criminal acts, although the most recent *DSM-5* makes a distinction between what they call "paraphilias," which are unusual sexual practices, and "paraphiliac disorders," in which those practices lead to significant distress, impairment, or infringement on the rights of others.

†   Preliminary research has indicated that non-monogamous people may experience an internalization of negative societal attitudes about non-monogamy. Dr. Witherspoon's research has also found that experienced non-monogamy stigma and discrimination is strongly related to increased depression and anxiety symptoms in polyamorous people. And we know from other studies that relationships that are societally marginalized (like queer, interracial, and/or age-gap) face worse relationship outcomes the higher the perceived marginalization is.

Trespassing

Spring 2018

LOS ANGELES

Ivan showed up on Tinder like manna from the gods. We were neighbors and he was handsome, a grown-up Peter Pan with an Irish accent. He brought his dog on our first walk: Sonia, a beautiful black mutt. She was off-leash and allowed to do whatever she wanted. I liked that for obvious reasons. "Where do you want to go next, Sonia?" he'd ask with all the respect you'd afford a person. Often, she walked us. Within a week, we'd already snuck into more than a few different condos' private hot tubs (and played fetch with Sonia in several pools, also against the rules). When we made out, it was wet, dirty, adolescent, and crusted in harmless trespassing.*

"So, what you're saying is he has no respect for property or rules." Adam smirked. "Sounds immature." Adam was still doing this. Mak-

---

* That we did this repeatedly without worrying about getting arrested or shot is a classic example of white privilege. Each month, at least thirty people in the United States are killed as a result of "Stand Your Ground" laws. In Stand Your Ground states, one analysis found these murders were ruled legally justified in 45% of cases involving a white shooter and Black victim, but just 11% of cases involving a Black shooter and white victim. Read the Giffords Law Center & SPLC Action's comprehensive report "'Stand Your Ground' Kills: How These NRA-Backed Laws Promote Racist Violence" to learn more about this and take action/donate to the above organizations. https://www.splcenter.org/sites/default/files/_stand_your_ground_kills_-_how _these_nra-backed_laws_promote_racist_violence_1.pdf; Chandler McClellan and Erdal Tekin, "Stand Your Ground Laws, Homicides, and Injuries," *Journal of Human Resources* 52, no. 3 (2017): 621–53.

ing undercutting comments about whomever I liked, only as if he couldn't care less either way.

"Aren't you glad I found someone I like who I can do stuff in the dirt with?" I asked. Adam had a mild phobia about getting dirty. Also, sand. He didn't like unexpected sand.

"I am," he said, and I could tell he did mean it. I was happier when I was distracted like this, far less prone to jealousy. On his end, there was still Mira, the married polyamorous woman. He'd also started going out with the lead writer of one of my favorite TV shows. I found myself actually hoping she'd stick. (When she didn't, I realized she'd caught on quickly to something I was still learning, and that only made me admire her more.) "Look at you—you're all in *love*," he teased.

"No, I'm not! We haven't even slept together yet." I was trying to take it slow. But I was horny as fuck. I'd been trying on this relation-ship anarchy mentality and hadn't had a bad jealousy attack in months. But it didn't seem to be making the difference Adam claimed it would. I knew having sperm competition would kick-start things. This idea, that I could biologically manipulate his desire in this way, was learned from Adam.

———

A few weeks later I was in Ivan's room, Sonia watching us from the corner.

"Um, is she going to stay in the room, or . . . ?"

"Aw, poor girl. She gets jealous," he cooed. "Sonia! Come here, girl!" He patted the bed and she leapt up next to him, right between us. As he petted her stomach, her leg splayed open, I thought rather sug-gestively. He kept rubbing down her belly in the direction of her groin. Lying down, Sonia's body was roughly the same length, width, and weight as mine. As he stroked her underside down, scraping past her erect nipples, this was suddenly feeling weird as hell. He kept kissing me intermittently.

Oh my God, am I in a threesome with a dog?! Fuck! Sonia can't consent to bestiality! Though she does look happy, even a little smug . . . "Ha, I guess maybe she was jealous," I said, that familiar out-of-body sensation creeping over me. *Okay, you're probably overreacting. Come on, you need this to work . . .* "Um, I think I might get allergic if she's up here much longer," I tried.

"Aw, okay, okay. Sonia! Down, girl," he said. She returned to the corner to watch her man fuck some *Homo sapien.* Ivan proceeded to hump me, to my great relief not ineffectively. For a moment he slipped in, and I let myself feel the smooth thickness before pushing him out.

"No, we can't," I repeated. "I told you, I have to use a condom."

"Okay," he said, pulling out and rubbing against the outside of my pussy.

"Get a condom," I insisted. He put one on, and lost his stiffness promptly. We took a break and made out some more until he was hard again. He slipped back in and began to pump. Now *this* was what I was talking about. He kept thrusting and I let myself get lost for several wonderful minutes. Until I realized this was feeling a little *too* good. "Wait, are you not wearing a condom again?!"

"No, I thought you knew . . ." he answered.

"No, I didn't know!" I said, pushing him out. "I thought you still had it on!"

"I thought you saw me take it off,"* he mumbled.

"No, I didn't! I told you so many times I have to use a condom! What the fuck." The fantasy I'd worked to build for weeks was crashing all around me now. Again.

---

* Though it is not a crime in the United States (yet; some bills propose changing this), what Ivan did is known as "stealthing," and can be prosecuted as sexual assault in the United Kingdom and Germany. Swiss and Canadian courts have also prosecuted cases of stealthing.

Ivan had violated our main rule, so I thought Adam might get angry when I told him, ideally want to defend my honor. But Adam seemed oddly undisturbed by the whole thing. *Maybe there's no honor left to defend.* When I burst out crying later that night, admitting I felt more violated than I'd let on, he comforted me a little. "Aw, my poor girl," he said, stroking my hair. "I told you that dude didn't respect boundaries. You should listen to me next time. It's probably for the best."

Here was more proof: Adam was morally superior to other men. *Everyone new I like, they end up being so disappointing. Even Adam undercutting other guys might be to protect me. To help me see reality instead of my projections. To help me stay with the person who's actually best for me.*

———

It was only over a year later, during an interview with my once-metamour Leah in December 2019, that I found out why Adam was so unmoved by Ivan's violation. Leah mentioned, offhand, that she and Adam had been having frequent unprotected sex when they were dating. While she was also having unprotected sex with another partner. Who, it turned out, was also having unprotected sex behind *her* back. Leah thought I had known the whole time. That I had of course consented to Adam having unprotected sex.

I most certainly did not.

Ladybird Is Nesting

4/24/18

MANHATTAN

The Desire Crew had invited me and Adam out to their annual play party, and we decided to travel to it. We stopped in New York first. Adam slept at Leah's apartment while I stayed elsewhere, alone. Though I didn't feel compersion, I was proud to find I was fine with the arrangement and even enjoyed the solitude. Leah and I still weren't speaking, but I was clearly evolving in the less jealous direction Adam wanted. I was learning to tolerate things that used to feel unbearable. Mira had slept over in our bed when I was out of town, and semi-regularly had sex with Adam in our home now, too. And though I didn't *love* it, I also wasn't freaking out about it. What if that was the best I could hope for?

Kathy told me that for most people, some degree of discomfort is inevitable in polyamorous relationships; that it's unrealistic to expect your partner being with other people to bring you joy or arousal. What mattered was that the arrangement was tolerable, healthy, and worth it for all people involved. I told her that in my case, I hoped it still was. That I still wanted Adam, and my freedom. I could sense that Kathy, too, sensed there was no way for me to go but through. Her job was to be nonjudgmental, supportive, and patient in the meantime. To occasionally ask questions that poked holes in Adam's internalized infallibility, but not so many that I stopped talking to her and further self-isolated.

———

I met Miranda at the vegan restaurant Ladybird. I'd pitched an article just so I could get the comp to take her to this extravagant dinner. Heads should have turned when she walked in, but because it was New York City, they didn't. I felt an urge to kiss her deeply, but wasn't sure I could.

"So, how's married life?" I'd found out the surprising news over FaceTime, and only because I'd asked about her ring: a plain, traditional gold wedding band. Though we talked every month or so, I hadn't even known she'd been dating someone.

"Oh, Rachel, I love it! It's so funny—who would have thought it? Maybe I wanted a man to take care of me this whole time!" She blushed and looked down like she was about to tell me a secret. "We're talking about trying to get pregnant in about six months. He can support me while I'm a mom. We want to live somewhere where it's calm and cheap, where we can have a big house with a lot of land. Like, maybe in the South."

"Wow! Um, so tell me the full story of how this even happened!" I was still in a sort of shock but I liked to see her so happy.

Miranda smiled in that way women do when asked to tell the creation myth. "*Well*, when my friend told me she knew a great guy who would pay to marry for papers, I was open to it. But I wanted to be sure he was someone I'd actually want to hang out with, who I'd want to do something like that for. When I first met him, he just seemed like a sort of nerdy Indian dude. I didn't think of him that way at all. But I liked him. So I decided to do it."

"But you weren't into him yet?" I clarified.

"No, not at all. We spent all this time being friends, getting to know each other for the interview, and then we passed and got married," she said, laughing. "To celebrate, we went to a meditation center for a long retreat. And I don't know . . . it was like one day, I looked to the left, I looked to the right, and I looked at him. And I realized, *Oh. He's actually cute.*"

"Oh my God, I love it!" And I did, I realized. I was downright *kvelling.* "That is such a great story." It really was. *And all of this happened since our threesome with Adam last year?*

"Um, you want another?" I asked, swallowing the rest of my drink in one gulp.

"She's trying to get me drunk," Miranda told our server.

"I am." I smiled.

"I'm trying to get you both drunk," the waitress replied with a grin. Was she flirting? Around Miranda, everyone seemed Sapphic.

"So anyway, at first, I told him, 'I'm non-monogamous,' " Miranda continued. "And he was like, 'Sure, whatever you want.' But then, I don't know, something changed. After so many years of being polyam, I realized I just wanted to focus all my emotional energy on him, at least for now. I just want to *nest.*" Sitting at the bar, our knees touched in that easy way of close female friends. I wondered if she still felt anything romantic toward me.

"So you don't miss it? Being open?" I asked.

"Not yet, anyway. With being polyam, I was spreading myself so thin that I didn't really feel like I was getting anything at all. And then, with my husband, it was just like an experiment. To see what working through that desire would feel like. Of not having all of my needs, all my desires—"

"—Which are potentially infinite anyway—"

"—met. Right," she said and smiled.

"Like how polyam people often say, 'Love isn't finite—but time is,' " I added.

"Yeah, and I guess I realized the things I wanted most were actually very mundane, you know? Just having one partner to build a life with. And sure, you can't expect one person to fill your every need. But does every need really need to be fulfilled?"

I saw her point. But at the same time, the non-monogamous people I knew (besides me and Adam) seemed *more* centered and happy than my monogamous friends. Being honest about their desires appeared to keep them grounded, satisfied, and able to give to their relationships.* They didn't seem spread thin so much as deep. *Which is why it sucks so much that if I write a book one day my story will probably end up reaffirming the fucked-up stereotype of an open relationship resulting in a hot mess, and all the monogamous people reading it will just feel vindicated and superior. But also, of course a hot mess is a potential outcome of any relationship! And why should polyam people have to prove they're only ever in happy relationships in order to be respected?*

I worked up the nerve to ask Miranda the question I'd wanted to all night. "But then I wonder when it comes to your queerness, how does that fit in? Like, in choosing to be with a man monogamously, does that mean never being with women again?"

"My frame of mind right now is so focused on having a baby that bringing other people into the mix isn't even in my thoughts. But I'm pretty confident that if I want to be with women again, he would be open to it."

"Well, that's good . . ." I smiled, feeling hope surge.

Miranda sighed, tipsy now. "Oh, Rachel—*he's just so wonderful.* I've always had partners who were annoyed by my emotions, you know? And he's just like . . . he's just really grounded. Not fazed by the tides at all." I felt a familiar resentment well up. *Why are we always seal-clapping for men who can weather our basic humanity? And why do I believe Adam when he says no one else would be able to deal with me?*

---

*   I'm talking about much of the Desire Crew, Ayesha, Dedeker, Kathy, and several happy poly-
       orous friends you unfortunately haven't met in this book, due to how important events in my
        unfolded/limited space/the fact that negativity bias means conflict = plot.

"So, how's work going?" I asked, pivoting. Miranda had started her first job as a social worker.

"It's so stressful. I see twenty clients a day, a lot of people with co-occurring issues, addiction and mental health disorders. And I'm making as much in a week as I would in an hour domming. But I was ready to let domming go. There was no *play* anymore, no sense of invention. Plus, hubby can cover the difference now, so salary doesn't matter as much." She winked, somewhat jokingly. "Well, I do still see *one* client, though. He brings me an apple and poorly done math homework and I punish him. It's so fun!"

When we left the restaurant, I was cold. She gave me her curly scarf, placing it around my neck like a regal wreath. She stopped to check on a man lying on the street, engaged with his eyes. She said I could keep her warmth and kissed me platonically on the mouth goodbye, the peck of an aunt. I ran through the rain for thirty blocks in my winter coat and boots, Miranda's remembrance trailing behind me. No matter how often I got high to slow time down, life only seemed to move faster. In the past year alone, Miranda had married a man, chosen monogamy, and was very much "trying to be someone's mommy." Ayesha had come out as non-binary, my best friend Robin as trans. Leah and I, once such close confidants, no longer spoke.

———

Shortly after that visit to New York, Leah broke up with Adam. When I asked what had happened, he said (as he often did when broken up with) "she was confused." That they'd never recovered from my trying to assert veto power the year before. That it had slowly poisoned the relationship. "Oh God, you didn't poison my relationship with him at all," Leah told me in 2020, rolling her eyes. "I just lost interest in him, the more time we spent together. But it was toxic from the start." Leah talks about their relationship like a war she was discharged early from. "I feel lucky I got out mostly unscathed. It was fucked up, but I didn't have to suffer the worst of it, like you." Classic Leah, still deferential. In the end, still an incredibly generous friend.

As for Miranda, these days, she tells her husband that I'm "her girlfriend," but it is half a joke. She reminds me I'm her "top girl," and that is serious. We tell each other we love each other, and it is romantic but also sisterly, fluid. She is still monogamous and happy with her husband. They live in a big house in the South now. As of this writing, they are still trying to conceive. If she does have a baby, I'd either move to be near them for at least the first year, or travel there all the time. I wouldn't want to miss worshipping at that altar, that's for sure.

When she read her chapters, Miranda wanted to know if there had been other women I fell for like her, or if she was special. I told her she would always be special. "So I'm your top girl, too?" she asked softly. The hopeful tone to her question, like music from the future I rewind and replay.

Not Either/Or

Adam and I traveled together from New York City to the big Desire Crew play party, and here I measured my "progress" again. I noticed I didn't have to stay attached to Adam in swinger spaces anymore. I was increasingly happy to lose track of him, to have sexual experiences apart and not mind if he did the same. I felt evolved to be able to do this. When I locked eyes across the patio with Adam, I couldn't deny I was still proud to be his. *Can you imagine anyone else being able to read your mind? Wouldn't you miss feeling your every move and thought anticipated and understood?*

I stripped down and climbed into the hot tub Amalia and Rory were also naked in.

"Left to my own devices, I probably would have a lot less sex with women than I do," Amalia told me as we got to talking. "I like women, I *enjoy* their bodies—but I need a man present." There's this way beautiful women twist the knife that's worse. Like their slip of the wrist is your new deformation, like, *Well, I guess this is how I look now.* Rory bit Amalia's ass as she emerged from the water to cool herself, and though I didn't begrudge him what made her smile, I certainly coveted my Jacuzzi neighbor's wife. I and another middle-aged man in the tub locked eyes and shook our heads in disbelief, widening our stare as if to ask: *Are you seeing her, too?*

My crush on Amalia had become an open joke by then within the Desire Crew. They weren't used to women like me, whatever I was. Women sometimes stupefied by other women.

"You know, Amalia has been encouraging me to date on my own now," Rory told me. "I must have saved a baby from a burning building in a past life. I married up, but this is beyond."

Amalia splashed him from the tub's rim. "I hate when you say stuff like that, devaluing yourself." She turned to me. "*I'm* the spoiled one. I don't have to do chores. If my water glass is half-empty, it will be filled. Like, we took acid recently, and all he kept repeating over and over was how making me happy was 'the only thing that mattered in the world.'"

"It makes sense that's part of what makes you feel secure enough to want to share him," I said, nodding.

"Definitely. I don't think I'm even a naturally unjealous person," Amalia said. "If he didn't make me feel so loved, I wouldn't feel safe enough to really enjoy my kink. But I know that the moment I feel uncomfortable, it will stop. The setup is one hundred percent designed around my ideal."

"So are you guys polyamorous now, would you say?" I asked.

"No," Rory said, and shook his head. "I talk with other women, but no one is like an emotionally attached relationship. Most of the women are recently single and want to try non-monogamy without so much threat of jealousy. But it's not *romantic* for me with anyone but Amalia. Even if I have a real friendship with other women." I thought of how Adam insisted on calling his other ongoing experiences (even with Leah) "romantic friendships" rather than "relationships" or "girlfriends." It made me feel gaslit and chosen at once. So, how I often felt.

"How do you even know where that line is, between romantic and friendship?" I asked Rory.

"I ask myself: 'Would I have a candlelit dinner with this person?'— and so far, that's only for Amalia," he replied easily.

"I'll be the first to admit I don't know how I'll feel if that changes," she added. "I'm open to it, but I'd need to continue feeling like the top priority, always." I envied that Rory would never hesitate to promise this or anything else Amalia desired. "But I'm more than happy for him to be acting like a pseudo-boyfriend to the other women he sleeps with. He might not call it emotional, but he's texting with them all the time, supporting them. But I don't mind that it's time he's paying attention to somebody else's problems."

"She likes that I can expend some extroverted energy without her having to participate," Rory added.

"That and I get to watch you having sex with someone else in our living room. Or hear it from the other room. Or see pictures later. Sometimes, I don't even need to hear or see anything to get off on it—I just like to know it happened." She smiled. It struck me that this arrangement must keep their power dynamic feeling more even than it might otherwise. When a man is continually overtaken with love for you, what better way to lessen your sense of control? Like Adam, Amalia got to enjoy the "challenge" of other people with her partner, while feeling confident there was no real chance she'd be replaced. In the same way that a CEO wants to pay Miranda to dominate him because he's tired of being in charge, he also knows he's the one paying, and is therefore still in a sort of meta-control.

"Is it a dominating feeling?" I asked her. "Having him do this for you?"

"No, I'm definitely not a *dom*." She seemed offended by the suggestion. "It's more like an act of submission. A submission in which I feel totally safe." This is indeed indicative of a healthy Dom/sub dynamic. Amalia knows she has the power to withdraw consent at any time; she has full (if unexercised) veto power. And this allows her to release control in the moment. "There's also a sort of market valuation to this. I know I find my partner attractive, but now I realize how desirable my partner is to other people. It sort of . . . *solidifies me*," she said, adding that she only gets annoyed when women play hard to get with her man. "I don't want Rory to win a war of attrition where he's somehow slowly eroded their objections." I noticed both Amalia and Rory frequently used the terminology of economics and battle when they talked about non-monogamy. There's certainly a power trip in "sharing your favorite toy," as Rory likes to put it. Because your wealth runneth over and shows no signs of running out, you toss spare change to the plebes.*

"You know, I bet it wouldn't be unusual for women to be into hothusbanding if more women felt as admired and safe in their relationships as you do," I said to Amalia. *Or were as hot as you.*

"I genuinely don't think my kink is that rare," Amalia agreed. "If other women were made to feel as desired and secure as me, I bet they'd be into sharing their husbands, for sure. There's even a lifestyle meme about it online: '*When the dick's so good you want to share it.*'"

"Ha, totally! I feel that way whenever Adam grants me temporary veto power, or lets me set the pace. Turned on by sharing him, watching him. We both know it, but he still refuses to grant me full primary privileges explicitly."

"Why?" Rory asked, genuinely puzzled why Adam would do such a thing.

"He doesn't believe in it . . . morally," I said, embarrassed. "He thinks it's sort of weak of me to demand." They didn't say anything, looked down. An awkward silence. "Anyway . . . ugh, it's hot in here, right? I'm too hot. I'm gonna take a break." I got out of the tub and felt Rory pay his polite respects to my naked body in the twinkling outdoor lights. From Amalia, I felt the usual indifference.

Liv glided up to me once I was inside the house, put her arms

---

*   As sex researcher Dr. Gilbert Bartell wrote in the 1970s, "In pursuing swinging sexual activity, the middle class were mimicking the lifestyles of the modern American royalty, the Hollywood star." Gilbert Bartell, *Group Sex: A Scientist's Eyewitness Report on the American Way of Swinging* (New York: Signet, 1971).

around my shoulders. I experienced the rare vertigo of looking into the eyes of someone even shorter than me. "Hey, girl . . . want a massage?"

Her body was slathered in coconut oil, and a room of roughly thirty people watched as she used her body instead of her hands in an S-shaped, surprisingly skillful rubdown. It was one of those moments where you realize you're actualizing a fantasy you didn't even know you had. She massaged her pointy, perfect nipples into my belly button, her sparse pubic hair into my own, and oh how I wanted her to kiss me then. She didn't. I wasn't surprised. It was why I held back. She'd told me plenty of times that she also needs "a dick in the bed" to really get into it with a woman. You go as fast as the slowest person.

After we got up, we quickly switched back to feeling like platonic girlfriends, gossiping. There was some drama going down between her and Nate, as I'd learn happens at just about every party. We found him in the hot tub and climbed in. She and Nate started bickering. They argue with all the confidence of a couple that's been together so damn long they don't care who might judge them. They are open books. Even in front of their friend who's openly working on a book that might include them.

"It's hard. Nate is always searching," Liv said to me.

"I don't know if I'm always *searching,* just open to whatever the universe brings," he corrected. He sounded just like Adam.

"And part of my work is recognizing that," Liv answered. "Loving the person I married, knowing that his base is so different from my base. The biggest challenge with having a non-monogamous marriage is that it is the most truthful relationship I've ever been in." *It's also one of the only relationships she's ever been in. If I already can't imagine life without Adam, imagine how it would feel if I had also met him at nineteen and was now forty.*

"Do you think there's anything sexy you guys get out of the tension between what you each want?" I asked.

"We don't, like, fuss and then fuck each other," Nate answered. "A lot of times it's like, *Oh God. We're NOT fucking after this.*"

"How much *are* you guys fucking at this point?" I asked.

"Worst-case scenario? Twice a week," Nate said. Liv nodded to corroborate, sipping with raised eyebrows a red Solo cup giving off steam.

"I would bet that's more often than most people who've been together twenty years,"* I offered.

"Here's the thing," Liv said to me. "His Tinder profile says, 'I am happily married, in a non-monogamous marriage, *blah blah blah.*' And I am super supportive of, 'Vagina, like, great! Do it.'" I noticed once again how Liv said "vagina" or "it" in place of "another woman." I wondered if reducing them to holes rather than whole beings was a coping mechanism. "And I love seeing him with other women, too, that sharing of joy. But if something *surrounding* the act isn't quite right, like tonight, *that's* what doesn't feel good." And this is the feeling Liv has quite often, no matter what rules they try to set up to avoid it. It's not that Nate exactly breaks them. It's more that Liv ends up taking issue with the way she feels he's trying to subtly resist her parameters.

"But she knows other women are no threat," Nate said. "Or I *hope* she does by now. I'm not *romantically* interested in them. It's just sex!"

"How do you make that distinction, between romance and sex?" I asked, repeating the question I'd posed to Rory.

"I'm very aware of the traps that people fall into, like the whole

---

* A 2017 study found the average person in the United States (factoring in both coupled and single people) has sex roughly once a week (I have to imagine many people round up). People in their twenties reported having sex an average of about 80 times per year, those in their sixties about 20 times a year. The average adult had sex 9 fewer times per year in the early 2010s compared to the late 1990s. *Thanks, Netflix!* J. M. Twenge, R. A. Sherman, and B. E. Wells, "Declines in Sexual Frequency Among American Adults, 1989–2014," *Archives of Sexual Behavior* 46 (2017): 2389–401. https://doi.org/10.1007/s10508-017-0953-1.

'new relationship energy'* thing. It's why people feel like they have a more intense connection with the person they have an affair with. And you just have to be smart enough to understand that's all it is." Nate shrugged. "I'm not delusional. *I am forty fucking years old.* The notion of trying to start from scratch with somebody is not appealing to me in the least." This was not a romantic answer as to why he'd never leave Liv, but it was certainly honest. "I just hate the perpetual-romance-novel idea of marriage. You don't expect that with your friends or children, so why is your marriage the only place you expect that? It is some for-better-or-worse shit. Despite the worst, you're still hanging out." He turned to Liv. "You've been gross, I've been gross. You've been annoying, I've been annoying. But despite that, I'm still very much down, I'm still very much invested."

I looked at Liv, who was wearing her perfected "what am I going to do with this man" resting eye roll. "Have you ever been tempted to go out with people on your own, too?" I asked her. "So he feels a little, I don't know . . ." That she didn't share my insecure compulsion to try to keep things more "even" was foreign to me, if impressive.

"No. Because if I did, I would feel like I'm going to leave him," she replied. I wondered if this was a threat.

Nate shook his head sadly. "See, you might not explore a lot of dudes, but that statement is so much more dangerous than anything I say or do. Like, your shit is terminal, right? My shit is like, '*I'm just checking this other store out here in this strip mall.*' Yours is like, '*I'm packing up, fuck your mall.*' Just because you haven't actually exercised it, the fact that's your mind-set is far more dangerous."

"I see what you mean, Nate. But I just want to say I also relate to what she's saying," I interjected into the ensuing silence. "With Adam,

---

* He's referring to the term polyamorous people use to describe the phenomenon of a new relationship's rosy sexual and emotional energy, often abbreviated as "NRE."

there's a part of me that's always thinking of other men as the competition who could steal me away. But that's how women are *socialized* to
think about it."

"Maybe there's something deep-seated in me I'm not willing to un-
lock by dating other people," Liv offered, to me more than Nate.

"It's reminding me of how you've talked to me about being alone
with a woman, kind of," I tossed back gently.

"Perhaps. I just don't want to go there," she replied. "But I just
haven't been willing to test it with another man because I've been feeling fulfilled in my marriage." Nate snickered caustically.

"Nate, why do you laugh at that?" I was feeling like a couple's therapist. But also one sitting with two people who would be having this
same argument into very old age, gesturing with their hologram canes,
still having at least biweekly orthopedic sex.

"Because when she makes those statements, the obvious conclusion
for me to draw is that she feels like when I am pursuing things with
other women, it's because I'm not feeling fulfilled with her." We all
knew that this must be a lot of what's at the root of Liv's jealousy. In the
same way, it was clear to me that so long as I viewed other men as Adam's potential replacements, I would continue to experience him dating other women as potentially trying to replace *me*. But I couldn't
seem to stop feeling that way anyway. I was simply getting better at
tolerating the discomfort of it.

Yet if I could continue to adapt, I couldn't deny the potential benefits before me. How *alive* Nate and Liv still seemed, how wedded and
attracted to each other they remained. And then there were Rory and
Amalia, Pam and Rich, and many of the other non-monogamous couples I'd met—so irrefutably, unusually, undramatically happy and hot
for each other. I didn't know any monogamous couples who seemed so
awake to each other so many years in, who still looked at each other in
that craving way. *But here I am, less than four years into an open relationship, and I already feel like Adam's becoming sexually inured to me.*

Perhaps romantic happiness had less to do with the relationship model itself than having a foundation of secure attachment and compatible desires. The couples who were able to negotiate just the right amount of danger, as a team, seemed able to maintain a both companionate *and* lustful bond. These couples were not anarchistic. But their relationships were unequally non-monogamous—and yet still egalitarian. Two people don't think or feel or want the same things, and don't have to. Navigating the trouble that can arise from that seemed part of these couples' deep attachment. It was a shared commitment to go through the thorniness of these freedoms, no matter how difficult, honestly and openly. *Maybe my "problem" this whole time hasn't been with non-monogamy, but with the lack of respect and teamwork from the person I'm practicing non-monogamy with. Sure, I'm adapting to what Adam wants, but I still don't feel like I'm allowed not to. I don't feel safe like Amalia does with Rory, like I really could say no . . .*

"Hey, you want to come upstairs?" Amalia asked from the hot tub's rim, snapping me back to the present moment. I was being summoned.

––––––––

I don't remember the details of going down on Amalia that night, of losing myself in her softness. I was blissfully mostly out of my head. I do remember that "having a dick in the room," as Rory's and eventually Adam's were, felt, as usual for me in these situations, both annoying and somehow reassuring. Not unlike being within the confines of the structure of the hero's journey. But increasingly, something was shifting. I was starting to believe I could write the story another way.

"Our attempts to make sense of sexuality are a wishful fiction. We're trying to come up with a narrative to explain things that are determined by a huge number of complex impactful factors," Dr. Ley later cautioned me. "And a nice story helps us put it away and simplify it." Like, is Liv trying to force herself to be the woman Nate needs—or is she a sexually fluid, non-monogamous woman who still gets jealous in part because it maintains her attraction to her untamable man? Is Amalia a sub who grants a freedom that only solidifies her confidence in Rory's loyalty and dominance? A wildly attractive woman looking to cast her doting husband in a more equalizing light? Someone with the early trauma of being cheated on who redirected pain into kink? Probably all of the above, and so much more. It's both/and+, not either/or.

What Evidence Do You Have?

6/18/18

LOS ANGELES

When I was upset, Adam often asked for the evidence that justified my feelings. But it is very hard to provide concrete evidence that proves the validity of an emotional experience. This was much of the reason I felt compelled to record us. I knew I could never out-argue Adam, and that without these kinds of records, it would be almost impossible to explain the intricate dance he led me in. That any of this had been real at all. As a woman in our culture and a reporter, I also knew having proof might one day protect me. That it might be the only way I'd be believed, or viewed as credible, should I ever write about this. And in the present? Recording allowed me to more easily dissociate.

One night, I requested we have a sort of State of the Union, to communicate in-depth about our relationship; why I continued to feel unsafe, why our sex life was stagnating. Adam agreed to let me record the whole thing, and I've spliced it together here as a reconstructed conversation.* I am the editor—don't underestimate that power and bias. But he is speaking almost entirely in his own words here; some phrases have been reworded or reordered slightly for clarity or space, this is otherwise both our words verbatim.

---

* This is my method for reconstructing much of the dialogue in the second half of this book.

Note to reader: This chapter has been the most emotionally difficult one for me to continually revisit. Amy Marlow-Macoy, LCSW and author of The Gaslighting Recovery Workbook, *and Dr. Witherspoon generously agreed to help me contextualize by reviewing this entire conversation and providing their insight throughout, which you can find in the footnotes.*

––––––––

"What does your fear tell you?" The conversation had just begun, but Adam had already switched into the Socratic mode.

"That you've been tricking me all along, that you're a potentially dangerous person to be with," I admitted. "That you're manipulative, but don't even really know it, which might be the most dangerous kind of manipulator. A feeling I should leave, but that I'll never find someone I'll love as much as you."

"What evidence do you have that any of your speculation is correct that I'm manipulating you?" he asked litigiously.

"The evidence is your lack of patience helping me navigate jealousy," I answered.

"But your jealousy is based on negative feelings that you have about yourself. I can't fix that," he said.*

"I know. And because I'm not allowing you to do whatever you want with other people without sometimes getting upset, of course you're going to be pushing me and testing more." I preemptively blamed myself. "But I feel like I lost your deep, concentrated attention, in certain ways. Also, sex. Sex made me feel taken care of. I want to be

––––––––

* "This statement indicates a lot. It takes a kernel of truth, that jealousy often relates to negative feelings about oneself, and then uses it to completely deny any sense of accountability for how his actions consistently affected you," Dr. Witherspoon commented. "This disconnect demonstrates, and helps perpetuate, his lack of empathy for your feelings."

able to help you share that burden* by dating someone else, too, but . . . I don't want to have to. I feel like you don't really want to protect me anymore. Like how you were going to help me and be my teacher, rather than just my challenger."

"This is all teaching," he replied.

"But I've felt like the lesson you're trying to teach me lately is that I need to be strong enough to leave you." A silence.

"Feeling strongly, whether it's a positive or a negative valence, for me, is really a positive thing," he eventually answered. "Unless it's all negative all the time."

"But when I'm upset, I think that if you could agree you'd put aside whatever's going on with other people to focus on getting me back to a place where I can consent, then I would feel so much more—"

"—You're already consenting. I'm never forcing anything on you," he corrected. He often got agitated when I used the word "consent."

"Well, you get the absence of a 'no.' I feel like, well, *I got myself into this situation,* but I don't feel like I'm allowed to express jealousy without you feeling it's a manipulation."†

"You can *always* express your feelings," he corrected. "It's just how they're expressed is what makes a difference."‡

---

* "Notice how you've internalized that sex with you is a burden, rather than a basic need," Marlow-Macoy commented.

† Even if you are in a 24/7 Dom/sub dynamic, there needs to be a way for the sub to express their true feelings, limits, and boundaries. "If they can't express those feelings, then they can't really meaningfully consent," Dr. Witherspoon said. In a healthy relationship, he added, a sub might feel happily "nervous," sure. But they would not feel constantly anxious, fearful, or coerced. That is a sign you've crossed over into abuse. To find a kink-friendly therapist, check out Kink Aware Professionals from the National Coalition for Sexual Freedom, https://www .kapprofessionals.org/. Dulcinea Pitagora, "Intimate Partner Violence in Sadomasochistic Relationships," *Sexual and Relationship Therapy* 31, no. 1 (2016): 95–108. https://doi.org/10.1080 /14681994.2015.1102219.

‡ "Because of comments like this, a person believes their partner will change or finally understand them if only they could find the right way to *express* the feeling," Marlow-Macoy commented. "This is a common fallacy among survivors of gaslighting and emotional abuse."

"There's this feeling that you're testing me, and I'm failing. So my failing just makes you resent me more and want to put in less effort," I said, again blaming myself.*

"What do you think I can do about your interpretation† that really, every time, seems to come back to how you feel about yourself?" Adam asked.

"I think verbal affirmations would be good for my self-esteem," I offered. "Maybe still initiate sex sometimes? Also, not treating doing the emotional labor of polyamory as stupid." He frowned at this, but I was just getting started. "And as much energy as you're giving to other people, that you're giving it to me, too? I know I've demanded all kinds of other energy that they're not demanding," I clarified, having internalized his deeming my basic needs "demands." "But if you're going on two dates that week, maybe we at least have one date? I know it's more exciting and interesting to go out with other people, because it's a new person to figure out. But I just feel like, there's a reason you're with me. I'm interesting. Aren't you interested?"

"Why do you think I haven't left you?" Adam asked the questions, I provided the "confused" answers, and he helped show me how my logic was flawed through more questions.

"Because you just haven't met the right person yet, or you're still waiting to see if I can be what you want me to be," I answered.

---

*   "One of the more insidious parts of being perpetually gaslit," Marlow-Macoy noted, "is that you begin to undermine yourself. You preemptively take on the gaslighter's arguments in order to prove you are also 'rational.'"

†   The emphasis Adam often put on my "misinterpreting reality" is a cornerstone of gaslighting. The rhetorical tactic might not always be consciously employed, but serves to cast doubt on another's lived experience nonetheless. Of course, our experiences *are* layered with interpretations, and some of them are mistaken. But Adam failed to acknowledge his own similar fallibility or subjectivity. He viewed his own interpretations to be the Truth; the rational counterpoint.

    It's good to examine your own initial thoughts and judgments. But the distinction is, someone *else* shouldn't be telling you what should and shouldn't be in your thoughts and feelings. "Feelings are real. Period. Regardless of whether the thoughts, fears, or conclusions underlying those feelings are demonstrably 'true,'" Dr. Witherspoon commented.

"Are you concerned that you can't be?" he asked, rather than reassuring me.

"Yes," I answered quickly. "Whenever I think I've met a new goal, it's like the goalpost moves. I feel like I have to keep leveling up," I said. "It feels like I finally found someone who's more ambitious than me, and I can't be with you without destroying other hopes I have for my life in the process. It takes too much of my psychic power to just maintain this relationship as something I can stay in. And you already seem so bored by me, and it's not even four years."

"If I were bored with you, why would I spend more time with you than I do with anybody else?" he countered.

"Because it's comfortable, and then it would be losing out on your investment in me, which is still worth more at this point than the people you've met so far," I answered easily, having thought about it plenty by now.*

"What would happen if you were to remind yourself that my being out with someone doesn't really mean anything about my feelings for you? I always come home," he said tenderly.

"Well, it's *your* home," I muttered. *He's even the owner now.*

"Yeah, but *you're* my home." He touched my knee, moved in closer. "Any situation you look at, you can find reasons to mistrust, right? You can always invent reasons. But there are also plenty of reasons to trust, right? Why do you choose mistrust? Why do you still think that that's more protective, somehow?"†

---

*   "When he dates others casually, they are also serving a very different internal need for him than being with you. He has no power over them," Dr. Witherspoon commented. "But his attachment to you is based on his experience of your emotional need for, and supplication to, him. This helps support his own need to feel powerful, in control, and valuable. Without you, those needs would be threatened."

†   "This is just textbook gaslighting," Dr. Witherspoon commented. "He is explicitly asking you to ignore your own perceptions and emotions, and reframing them as a weakness you indulge in."

The subtext we both knew well: *Why are you choosing to be like your mother? You know that ends up with you alone.*

"I just feel like I'm being thrown into the deep end to learn to swim," I said, my voice going little. "And sometimes I'm like, *But, I'm tired. I thought I was getting to rest today.*"

"How would you feel and react to a situation where you want to do something, and because I'm 'triggered' by that, then I'm going to impose that on you and restrict you?" The way he said "triggered" sounded like "rainbow unicorn." "I don't *want* my insecurities to ever be prioritized. My love wants you to never change what you want because of my insecurity. That's never what love is to me. I don't want those insecurities attended to, because I think that it actually just enables them," he said.*

"I disagree. I think it helps them heal," I countered. "The fear can be named, and then it can be unlearned through some exposure *and* reassurance. I don't have a problem putting you first."

"You say that, but I think you always put yourself first," he replied. *He means you're selfish.*

"I mean, putting you first over other people," I clarified. "I would rather sometimes compromise what I want to do in that moment to nurture the relationship."

"Unless I think you're in danger or I have a real concern about the situation, then I just don't see that I have any right to impose what I know is a manipulation," he said, getting annoyed now. "We know I have trouble with manipulation, right? That includes anything that is indirectly demanding rather than explicitly expressing a desire. If the way you actually just expressed your feeling was, 'Hey, I need a little

---

* "People often unconsciously act out, over time, aspects of themselves they hate, deny, or have disavowed. He likely despises his own insecurities, perhaps because they make him feel weak and vulnerable," Dr. Witherspoon noted. "So he tries to avoid 'indulging' those feelings by allowing himself to consciously ask for support, reassurance, or otherwise showing vulnerability. Then those same insecurities get acted out on you. However, this allows him to blame you, your actions, and your insecurities and therefore help him avoid feeling his own."

love right now,' that, to me, is not manipulation. That, to me, is a direct expression of a desire." *But that's almost exactly what I asked for the last day of Leah's visit, when you refused to reassure me and ended up holding me down on the bed,* I thought but didn't say. "What I do feel like I want to deny," he continued, "is when something is indirectly demanded or indirectly requested."

"But I don't feel like I can say anything about having trouble with non-monogamy without it being seen as my weakness or your perceiving it as manipulation," I said.

"No, that's not true," he replied.*

I tried to get through from a different angle. "It just feels like this constant rejection, even though I'm so supposedly free. Like my self-esteem has plummeted with you. That's my responsibility at the end of the day, I know," I preempted, "but I don't see even a fraction of the effort on your side to do the things that I need."

"I mean, I think you can get better," he said softly, referencing my now low self-esteem. "If you see that you're loved and not rejected."

"And if I basically resign myself to your low sex drive," I replied.

"No, that can change." *That's what he's been saying for almost a year now, but nothing is different.*

"Withholding sex just feels like a very passive way of controlling me. It keeps me feeling weak and low. And I know I should just try to get it from other people, but I want it from my *partner*. But he doesn't want it from me unless there's other people in the mix, and it's just fucking infuriating and humiliating. I just feel angry that triangulation is your only way of accessing desire for me."

"Yeah, but look what *you* need," he replied. "I mean, should I feel

---

* "This sequence clearly shows the trap: When you ask for things directly you get denied. Indirect requests get denied. And attempts to express your feelings or address the fact that he leaves you no ability to communicate feelings or needs in a way that will be heard also gets denied," Dr. Witherspoon commented. "This leaves you emotionally trapped, which raises pressure and anxiety over time, and when that results in you becoming emotional or demanding he then uses that as evidence of your irrationality."

rejected because you need a vibrator to come? Because a lot of guys would."* He knew this was another one of my insecurities. "You started relying on it." I had indeed become more dependent on the vibrator, my hand on my clit no longer reliable during sex. A toy helped me "keep up" with men, even with little foreplay; to still come now that I was back on Zoloft.

"I just don't really ever want sex to be difficult. I want it to be *easy.*" Adam sighed. "I never lose myself in it. I mean, I'm kind of detached from it—"

"—I think it's kind of ruined it for you, studying desire," I said.

"But I've *always* been detached," he replied. "At twenty-two, I thought I'd never be able to take sex seriously enough again to get it up, just because I was very detached.† I feel desire, I like sex, but I don't . . . I think it's a fascinating phenomenon, but I don't know how profound an actual experience it is."

"But it doesn't have to be profound for it to be worthwhile," I said. "What if it's just something you know makes me feel good? Even if you were like, 'Hey, I want you to go masturbate right now while I'm cooking.' Or just sucking on my tits while I use a vibrator, so that you basically have to do nothing." *Any of those things would be so much better than the way he sometimes catches me masturbating in bed, snickers, and shuts the door.* "Desires aren't being met on my end and then it's expected that I'm going to meet your needs."

"What do you mean 'it's expected'? It's not expected."

"Well, it's expected I be okay with you being with other people if I'm going to stay with you," I said. He didn't refute this, so I continued.

---

* Dr. Witherspoon commented, "He turns the conversation around on you, shames you for something he knows you are insecure about, and then somehow acts like the fact that he doesn't 'feel rejected' by your use of a vibrator is an act of maturity and grace on his part, as if somehow men should feel rejected by this in the first place."

† "It seems inconceivable to him that, perhaps, this is something he could (and should) seek to improve," Dr. Witherspoon noted. "His detachment is just an immutable fact about him, but your insecurities are a problem he needs to 'teach' you how to fix."

"The things I'm asking for are not that big. I just want to have date nights or feel safe communicating things and be considered when you're going out with other people. Desired by you." I was starting to get angry now. "And if I *do* need a fucking vibrator to come, and it feels really fucking good, like, why the fetishization of the 'natural' orgasm?"

"*Come on . . .*" He was using the gentle voice now.* I was starting to cry.

"You just used to be so different, and the contrast is so painful. Like it must be something I've done. I was so desired by you in the beginning, so given that feeling of being chosen, and you just really fucking turned it on with me," I said. "How am I not supposed to interpret it as this massive rejection, being forced to watch the parade of other women you desire more? It creates this terrible loop because I feel less and less secure, and so I'm less that person you want to fuck. I'm in a relationship where I feel ugly. I think I know on a certain level that I'm not ugly, and so why am I choosing to be with someone where I feel that way so much?" I tried to check my self-pity. "It's my own fault in the end. Unless I believe that I deserve more, I'm not going to get more."

"Come here," he said, holding out his arms. It was the same voice he'd used on our second date, reassuring a child afraid of monsters.* I shook my head. I wasn't responding to the command.

"It's fucking infuriating, dude, it's humiliating," I continued. "But I must believe I deserve to feel perpetually rejected. And *that's* what makes me feel desirous of you, *that's* what maintains my respect for you? That you basically don't make me feel worthy of love?"

"I want to give you what you want, okay? Don't you go away." He

---

*   "Your requests of him were specific, clearly articulated, and entirely reasonable. And perhaps he felt cornered, or saw that you were escalating into anger which could potentially give you the courage to leave. It makes sense then that he would suddenly soften his tone, so that you would calm down by seeing a glimpse of warmth from him," Dr. Witherspoon noted. "A lot of people who are highly narcissistically organized in their personality will do stuff like this, in which they keep the person emotionally 'not too close, but not too far away.'"

closed the space again, the way he always did. He began to speak even more softly, reassuringly. "Don't you think tonight was a lot of progress? You're not taking it personally, right?"

"What?! It's the most personal thing!" I said, exasperated.

"But it's not, it's not at all."

". . . 'It's not at all'?! Are you kidding?" *I feel crazy. Am I overreacting? Look how calm he is.*

"But you can talk to me about anything and I don't punish you for it," he said.

"No, you just lose respect and desire for me, and get annoyed and shut down," I replied.

"Okay, so what you just said made me feel very annoyed." He took his hand away, proving my point. "I want to go to sleep," Adam said, abruptly closing our hours-long conversation. I had pushed back too far and long and well, and withdrawing was a way to get me back in line, perhaps. As he turned away from me, I was suddenly terrified by the idea of life without him. Though once again I wasn't sure why, considering everything I'd just named.

"I don't want to end on this note," I pleaded. "I just want to know we tried to work on this."

"We are trying." He sighed, exhausted as I was. I shut the recorder off and resumed my regularly scheduled inner programming. *Who else would let me indulge this compulsion to record something so personal and probably pointless? He's right that I'm not ready to write a book anyway—I can't even focus when I read anymore! Yes, he's an asshole sometimes, but he's just trying to help me not sabotage my best shot at happiness. Like anyone else would want to deal with someone as crazy as me . . .*

Sometimes Saying No
Is the Experience

7/31/18

SAN FRANCISCO

I'd been up in the Bay for several weeks, helping my mom clear out her house so she could sell it. I invited Liam over to where I was staying alone. Now here he was, gently plucking rosemary sprigs for my cocktail. *What is it about big hands doing delicate things—licking a finger to turn a page, offering a pinky to a baby's fist, tracing your naked scars?*

"I'm not totally on board with the idea of non-attachment," Liam said. He knew I was recording. I wondered if this was him pontificating. "I *enjoy* attachment. I think there's a lot to be gained from it. Of course attachment causes suffering, but I'm not sure I'm down with a life in pursuit of the absence of suffering. I've had experiences where people are like, 'I'm just trying not to be attached.' " He rolled his eyes. "I'm like, 'Well, what are we doing? I *want* to be attached to you, that's why I'm *choosing* you. Otherwise I'm just accepting your presence in my life.' " I could tell he didn't even consider how hearing this might make me feel.

"Well, then how do you categorize what we're doing?" I asked, emboldened by the pretense of recording. It wasn't the first time we'd seen each other since I first dominated him. But he remained as emotionally inaccessible as ever.

"Interesting question." Silence. "I don't have an answer."

"Be honest with me." Another humiliating pause.

"Well, I haven't had anything quite like this. But I don't feel we're choosing each other. I feel we are experiencing some things together." He pivoted quickly. "But when somebody I'm in a *relationship* with has said to me, 'I'm just trying to practice non-attachment,' it makes me feel like . . . it hurts. You know?"

"Yes, I do know."

"Here you go." He handed me the cocktail, grains of salt and all.

"I am curious about having you explain more about your attraction to men," I said, pivoting away from my sadness.

"Well, I'm not *attracted* to men," he answered.* "It's purely sexual curiosity. I've never had a crush on a guy, for example. It's not necessarily about wanting to be with a man. It's about exploring what it is not to be the man, or not to be the dominant one."

"But if it's just about submission, why wouldn't you have just found a femdom first?" I asked. He fell into another long, semi-contemplative silence. "Is it that it's never fully convincing unless you believe the person could physically overpower you?" I finally offered. "Like, an internalized idea that men are always more powerful?" A rookie mistake, asking a leading question, filling a pregnant pause that might have birthed something truer.

"Yes, I think that's what it is." He nodded. "I just know it doesn't torment me the way it seems to the guy I see in New York, like what we

---

* There appear to be more people who in surveys call themselves "mostly straight" than there are people who identify themselves in surveys as lesbian, gay, or bisexual combined. But not much is known about them because they (cis men especially) usually keep it quiet, having occasional same-sex experiences and arousals. Their motivations are varied, although there's no question homophobia and biphobia play a role. Many "mostly straight" people would likely identify as bisexual or queer in a world free from stigma. That said, in the cuckold world, there are straight men who enjoy being "consensually forced" to be with men, not because they are bisexual, Dr. Ley says, but because they enjoy the utter submission of engaging in sex with men when it's not actually arousing to them. Ritch Savin Williams, *Mostly Straight: Sexual Fluidity Among Men* (Boston: Harvard University Press, 2017).

do means some redefinition of his identity. I feel like it's an experience I'm occasionally curious about, occasionally not at all. It comes and goes." Much like his interest in me.

"There's a fluidity to your sexuality," I said, nodding. "But there's an incredible double standard about men exploring that, even in progressive circles. Like, at these sex parties, the women play with each other, and none of the men do. After I came out as non-monogamous, not just you but several other male friends have admitted their bisexuality or fluidity to me.* Like they were given permission to be honest because I was also now 'sexually deviant.' I feel like if most women openly considered it 'hot,' you'd see *a lot* more male sexual fluidity. I think the play spaces and MFMs are a sort of compromise. A man gets to see another dick and be naked around another man without touching him. All while reaffirming his straightness."

"I'm sure you're right," Liam said. "But for me, the interest in MFMs is more about feeling like I'm being used as an instrument of the couple's pleasure."

"A submission." I nodded. "Speaking of which, should we go downstairs?" The plan was to dominate him again.

———

I kept the recorder on, slapped him some as a warm-up. "Were you told you had a lot of potential growing up?" I asked.

"Always. But I felt there was something wrong with me. How emo-

---

*   Bisexual men are the group most likely to be in consensually non-monogamous relationships. "And bi men very commonly report they are rejected by both [straight] women and gay men if they are open about their bisexuality. To avoid this, on Tinder they might present as straight, and on Grindr as gay," Dr. Ley said. E. C. Levine, D. Herbenick, O. Martinez, T. C. Fu, and B. Dodge, "Open Relationships, Nonconsensual Nonmonogamy, and Monogamy Among U.S. Adults: Findings from the 2012 National Survey of Sexual Health and Behavior," *Archives of Sexual Behavior* 47, no. 5 (2018): 1439–50. https://doi.org/10.1007/s10508-018-1178-7.

tional I was. Very sensitive, prone to tears in a way that didn't seem like how other people were." *Other boys, I think he means.*

"And you learned to push those emotions down?"* I asked.

"Maybe." He seemed to have nothing else to say. I spanked him harder. He didn't cry this time. That's how it went for a while. I asked interesting questions, he gave one-word answers.

"I'm *vastly underwhelmed,*" I eventually said, channeling the voice of Maleficent, even in syntax. "I keep feeling like there's hope for you yet, and then I remain so unimpressed by your progress. I see your desire for growth. But I also see the lack of follow-through." He never sent me the poems he'd promised after our session in Santa Barbara, continued to complain of not writing enough. *Is it always the muse's responsibility to strike on his behalf?* "I don't even know if you deserve to be spanked," I spat.

"You're right," he conceded.

I grunted. "Fine. I want you to tell me about the sex you have with that guy while I put the dildo inside you." He'd bought a new harness and dildo for me—he wanted me to fuck him with a strap-on. I'd never pegged someone, but he didn't need to know that. I'd be the only woman who'd done this for him, which felt almost like being chosen. (Plus, you know, *Broad City* goals.) But when I took the dildo out of the bag it looked like it was covered in . . . *shit? Well now I'm actually pissed.* "Can't even bother to wash your dildo," I said with slow menace. If it hadn't been so gross, I might have thumped it into my palm like a baton.

"What, really? It must be mud, from the rain. I've never even used it, I swear! It was in storage. It's brand-new. Shit." He sounded genuinely upset.

---

* Reporter Peggy Orenstein, who interviewed hundreds of teenage and college-aged boys for her book *Boys & Sex,* says that nearly all of them had a memory of a moment they learned they had to push their feelings down and stop crying. If you're close to someone who was raised as a boy, ask him about this memory sometime. The result, I've found, is heartbreaking.

"And you didn't even check what kind of state it was in before you brought it to me? Didn't even care enough to clean it first," I answered.

"I'm sorry. Fuck."

Life really isn't quitting with the perfect symbols. My once fantasy-rescuer brought me a shit-encrusted dildo to fuck him in the ass with. Happily ever after to me! I went into the bathroom and cleaned the dildo off. *It's mud after all, I'm pretty sure. It doesn't smell. But it looks so . . . shit-like.* I scrunched my nose to do what I had to do. *I can recover from this. I want to peg him, right? Maybe he'll appreciate me more after. Either way, it will definitely be an interesting new experience . . .* Mid-scrub, I looked up in the mirror. An inner voice, perhaps my future self, returned and asked:

So, Rachel, is this liberation?

I looked myself in the eyes and realized I had a choice. *I don't have to do this. Just because I'm curious about what would happen next, just because I hope it might make him feel something, and will definitely make me feel something, that doesn't mean I have to turn the page. Maybe I can channel my disappointment into giving him the railing he deserves. But that's also exactly what he wants. And now I want to punish him by not giving it to him. Yes, I think that feels right, actually. Why reward him? What am I trying to prove?*

Maybe the truth is I got scared that fucking him in the ass would snuff out my fantasy for good. Or maybe I wanted my first peg to be with someone who actually loved me. Maybe I knew I'd feel sad afterward when he still didn't, and I was finally getting tired of punishing myself by pretending to punish him. There's never just one way to tell a true story.

I reluctantly but firmly sent Liam to another bedroom to sleep. I almost lost my resolve when I saw his big man hand dwarfing a toothbrush, but returned to Rachel Cusk's *Outline* instead.* The next passage I read felt like another sign:

---

*   Rachel Cusk, *Outline* (New York: Farrar, Straus and Giroux, 2015).

One could make almost anything happen, if one tried hard enough, but the trying—it seemed to me—was almost always a sign that one was crossing the currents, was forcing events in a direction they did not naturally want to go, and though you might argue that nothing could ever be accomplished without going against nature to some extent, the artificiality of that vision and its consequences had become—to put it bluntly—anathema to me.

———

In the most memorable advice she doesn't remember giving me, my mom once put it a different way. I'd just asked her if I should potentially sleep with my forty-year-old boss/mentor, whom I'll call Kai. It was the summer before I left for college. I'd accidentally sent Kai a text meant for my friend, talking about my crush on said mentor. I was mortified when I realized my Freudian/first-cellphone slip. But then Kai wrote back that he liked me, too, that he was "flattered." I should come over, he said. When I hesitated in the face of my fantasy becoming what was beginning to feel like a creepy reality, I asked if we could go out to dinner instead. I'd just broken up with the high school boyfriend I'd recently lost my virginity to. My mentor/boss knew this, and persisted aggressively. "I just wouldn't want you to regret saying no to something you really want because you're afraid," I remember him trying to persuade me. "For you to deny yourself an interesting experience you would grow from either way. Wouldn't you rather know than always wonder?" He knew me so well.

I felt able to ask my mom for advice, to both our immense credit. Instead of freaking out, my mom told me I was eighteen; she wouldn't stop me. I was going off to university in a month, and there I would make many more choices. She told me she understood my impulse to try new things, even just to see what they were like. "I was the same way," she said. "~~And it took me a long time to learn, but it's true:~~ Sometimes saying no *is* the experience." It was exactly what I needed to hear. And a lesson I appear to be continually relearning since.

I didn't regret not sleeping with that "mentor" twice my age. Not when he planted one on me with a performatively adolescent tongue after a dinner out anyway, and not when he wouldn't stop calling me during freshman year of college against my requests, and I had to block his number. And I don't regret saying no to pegging Liam that night. Saying no is what finally allowed me to see him for who he was. Not a bad person, no. More like my self-loathing, personified. An expenditure of valuable energy I could elect to place elsewhere.

That Moment of Awakening

---

*"When patriarchal men are not cruel, the women in their lives
can cling to the seductive myth that they are lucky to have a real man,
a benevolent patriarch who provides and protects. When that real man is
repeatedly cruel . . . she may begin to interrogate her own allegiance to
patriarchal thinking. She may wake up and recognize that she is
wedded to abuse, that she is not loved. That moment of awakening
is the moment of heartbreak."*

—BELL HOOKS, *THE WILL TO CHANGE: MEN, MASCULINITY, AND LOVE*

Fall 2018

OAKLAND

I was up in Oakland full-time now. It was temporary, to help my uncle
and mom. Adam and I had just convinced my mom to put her house
on the market (she couldn't afford the payments anymore, even with
renters) when my uncle Willie was diagnosed with cancer (and
promptly lost his job and housing). The resulting storm proved a com-
plicated mess, and I decided to stay and clean. Adam remained in LA,
but made it clear we weren't on any sort of break. "You're my woman,"
he said softly, hurt I'd even ask. I told him I didn't need to know what
he was up to unless he thought it was becoming a new relationship. We
spoke every day about everything but who he might have been with the
night before. I rationalized it didn't matter to me that my partner wasn't
there to help in person. He was supportive remotely, for sure.

Perhaps, I began to fantasize, I'd even find someone new in the Bay

Area. Then I'd have different lovers in different cities. It sounded cosmopolitan to never be rooted in one place or dedicated to just one partner. *Or perhaps you'll find a way to leave him,* another smaller voice whispered. I wanted a distraction from what my life looked like in Oakland—work during the day, surrounded by doctors' visits for my uncle, packing boxes, doomed co-loan and home-aide applications. I didn't have much free time or energy, but dating had become another compulsive workout; I felt compelled to exercise those muscles lest they weaken, no matter my psychological condition. I also missed being held. So I logged on to OkCupid. I was up front in my profile about my situation—partner in LA, a temporary relocation.

When I first saw Asa's photo, I had a feeling, too. A blond doppelganger for Coach Taylor in *Friday Night Lights.* A humble smile that seemed almost embarrassed to be admired. He asked if he could take me to the fanciest vegan restaurant in Oakland for our first date, a gesture as refreshingly old-fashioned as the rest of him. He didn't drink or do drugs. I liked the idea that I might be attracting someone sober. I'd noticed I didn't feel a need to smoke every day since I'd come up north. My family's problems were quite stressful, but apparently still prompted fewer addictive behaviors than my seemingly chill life with Adam in LA. I tried not to overthink what that meant, especially since I already knew.

Asa spoke softly. His eyes were hooded and amused in a completely sincere way, squinting at me like I was the sun he'd burn in. He told me, in much less direct words, that he was open to dating someone in my situation because he was still in love with his ex. She'd moved across the country for a tenured job. They spoke daily but were technically no longer together. They didn't talk about what the other person was doing, either. When he kissed me it was slow and soft and nibbling, exploratory. An entirely new language. A light hand around the waist, a soft sigh indicating he too might be starved for affection. His gentleness felt so innocent it was . . . kinky. His body was strong and chiseled—and yet sometimes, if I closed my eyes, he reminded me of a woman. Was it the glutastic results of his epic bike trips? Yes, but it was also his energy, a blend of masculine and feminine I was pleased I could be so attracted to.

"I don't feel particularly attached to being a man," Asa told me when I asked if he felt at home in his assigned gender. "But I don't feel like a woman, either. I'm happy with my body, my pronouns, and all that. I just don't identify with a lot of the things people seem to expect being a man means." He shaved his legs for swimming and "because it felt nicer," which added to the effect. I found myself wordlessly topping him as he moaned beneath me, massaging his smooth tonality in a slow worship. Then we'd switch. Sex was a big deal for him. I'd be only the fifth person he'd slept with in his forty-one years. He'd only had long monogamous relationships; I was new and uncharted, potentially risky territory. When he was ready, it felt all the more rewarding, filled with feeling and trust. *This is certainly different.*

"*I want to fuck you,*" he'd say into my ear, softly. Like he was giving in to something that scared him every time. As he massaged my back, I realized I was hungry for tenderness. Asa accepted and admired me so fully and gently it felt as if he were kissing a still-open wound. As I had flashes of harsher moments with Adam, I realized my body now stored physical trauma. *Don't throw around that word,* I immediately scolded myself. *You aren't abused, so don't call yourself traumatized.* But another voice was getting stronger, too: *Listen to your body. It isn't a betrayal to notice you feel safer with someone else. And not only just as aroused, maybe more so. But maybe you really are polyamorous, because you definitely still love Adam, too . . .*

———————

To my own pleasant surprise, away from Adam, I wasn't pining or projecting onto Asa the way I normally would—nor was I losing interest. I was slowly and unusually sanely falling in love. We saw each other once a week, at most, and I felt no need to rank or label our relationship. I suppose I was practicing relationship anarchy. I wasn't trying to make my dynamic with Asa into something other than whatever it evolved into. Emotional intimacy and partnered commitment were not the same thing, and I could parse out the difference with a newfound clarity. It was exciting, realizing I loved two people at once.

Yes, being with Asa reveals the ways I no longer feel relaxed with Adam. But maybe the problem is Adam and I trying to act like husband and wife in the first place, pantomiming something neither of us really want, but think we should. Maybe he's been right about me, and I just needed to be away long enough to figure out how polyamory might work for me.

I'd tried calling Adam one morning, to tell him the first good news we'd gotten about my uncle's treatment—the first PET scan that suggested chemo might be working. Adam didn't pick up, which was unusual. He didn't answer my texts all day in fact; also very unusual. When I asked if he was okay that evening because I was starting to really worry, he finally texted back that he was busy and loved me, and would call me tomorrow. *So he's with someone else.* "Someone new, you don't know her," he answered when I asked. He told me he had to go and that he loved me again.

Okay, well, I did say I didn't need to know what he's up to unless it's becoming a new relationship . . . but . . . he can't even bother to reply to my text about my uncle's big news at any point today? Like, while he's in the bathroom even? How can he say I'm his life partner and shouldn't worry about primacy if he doesn't even respond to me because he's on a date all day and night? When he "needed" to talk to me about buying a goddamn condo when I was at Liam's I immediately excused myself to prioritize him! And I'm not even asking him to be up here with me to help because I know he doesn't want to be. Like, what the fuck is the point of this commitment shit if not to be there for things like this? Okay, maybe I'm just overreacting and being jealous . . . I can sit with this feeling.

But then I did something unusual, something I hadn't done in many months—I looked at Adam's OkCupid profile. And there, next to the black-and-white portrait I'd taken of him, I saw it: He'd changed his relationship status from "seeing someone" to "single." He'd taken out the line in his profile stating that he had a long-term live-in partner who "with all the future certainty of human plans" he planned to share his life with. One section was exactly the same as when I'd met him, though. Under the prompt "six things I could never live without," he'd written only one thing: "fiction. none of us does without it."

KATHY/RACHEL COUNSELING SESSION TRANSCRIPT

11/3/18
Recorded Phone Call

RACHEL:

[Through tears]
The only thing he had about non-monogamy in his profile is the same way he sold it to me in the beginning of, "I don't believe in restricting people."

. . . [When I confronted him] he's like, "I just wanted to see as an experiment how it changed anything." I was like, "That's not ethical." And he's like, "I didn't know that it said 'single.' I just took off 'seeing someone.'" But I know you have to physically change it to single, it's not the default. . . . It's like, he's always asking other people to take responsibility for themselves but when he has an opportunity . . .

KATHY:

[Aghast]

Well, it's so dishonest [for him to say he's single] when you and him are still officially living together. You just happen to be up in the Bay Area. You're living together as committed partners. But you happen to be here [temporarily] helping your mom and uncle. I mean, it's sort of convenient he's suddenly erasing you.

RACHEL:

. . . There's another thing, too, I didn't tell anyone about because I was too embarrassed. [Mira] basically said she needed space from him and cut it off because they saw each other and it was after the [Supreme Court nominee Brett] Kavanaugh hearings and he said the same thing to her he said to me, which was like, basically that he thinks "Kavanaugh is an asshole but he has a point because there's no evidence against him and we can't just incriminate people without evidence."

KATHY:

Wow.

RACHEL:

Yeah. [Mira]'s an assault survivor and so she was like, "I can't do this."
I feel embarrassed that when he said that to me, I tried to argue back with him . . . But that doesn't change the fact that I'm with someone who—that's their reaction to this? *That's their main takeaway?*

KATHY:

. . . At least four women say [Kavanaugh] sexually assaulted them. Probably at least one of them is telling the truth, you know? Probably at least one of those women, if not all four, are telling the truth. Just the idea that someone could say, "Well, maybe it's all made up. Maybe it's just character assassination." Wow. That's kind of shocking.

[Helping Rachel draw the connection]

. . . You don't have to *prove* that [Adam]'s abusive, you don't have to *prove* he's manipulative, you don't have to *prove* he's doing anything wrong. All you have to prove to yourself is that you're unhappy in this relationship.

RACHEL:

[Dreading managing family crises entirely alone]

[He's saying] "You don't know how to handle all the real estate stuff . . . Please let me help. If you don't handle this right, you could lose a lot more [of your mom's money]."

KATHY:

[Firmly]

. . . It's an overt lie to say you're single when you've been living with your primary partner for three and a half years . . . The more you allow him any contact with you, the more it undermines your own sense of reality.

There's sometimes a certain relief when the thing you've been so afraid of happens. You can finally surrender to the grief without struggling to stave it off. Though your body hollows, there is a sort of rest there, an absence of struggle. All there is to do is cry and cry. I knew not to call Asa, not yet. To stay with my grief as best I could, as long as I could. To call on the skills I developed while sitting with jealousy. And so I wept and wept and screamed into my pillow and wept and read and emotionally ate and wept and sat with my discomfort some more.

Less than twenty-four hours after I cut off all communication with Adam—before I stabilized my family or living situation or weight or grief in any way—my body knew. After many, many months in hiding, my period returned. In the months that followed, though nothing in my life felt steady beyond my new meditation practice, I was more regular than I'd been in my entire reproductive life.

Whatever Brings Less Suffering

11/27/18

FAIRFAX, CA & LOS ANGELES

I hadn't spoken to Adam in three weeks, except to tell him I'd be moving out the day after the meditation retreat. I also hadn't gotten high once. Not that I didn't crave it, but I had something to prove now. I sobbed frequently and ached and other clichés that exist for good reason. And yet this week at the meditation retreat I felt more at peace than I had . . . maybe ever.

Monk Tashi Nyima was leading the retreat, sponsored for people working in the animal rights movement. In his late sixties, Tashi has full tattoo sleeves and speaks in a comforting baritone. He's Puerto Rican, outspokenly vegan, and worked as a doctor with some of the world's most vulnerable populations for decades before and after he became a monk.

I told him a short version of my story during our one-on-one session in the zendo. I had a lot of questions. "But if you can theoretically control your emotions with mindfulness," I asked on Adam's behalf, "shouldn't I have been able to handle whatever was arising in my relationship? The jealousy?"

"Well, when the emotion is yours, it's your responsibility. But when somebody is misbehaving and blaming your emotions for it, if you go along with it, you are enabling it," Tashi answered. "I don't have to tolerate ill treatment. No. I'll deal with my emotions, but very kindly and very gently, I will pack my bags and leave the situation. Because I have to deal with their *behavior,* too, not just with my emotions."

"But a lot of ill treatment is not necessarily intended as such by the other person," I defended Adam reflexively.

"Are you going to put up with what you experience as ill treatment, and make excuses for it? Because if you do, you're not really helping the other person. If they are nasty to you, they're probably nasty to other people as well. They're accumulating nasty points everywhere they go," Tashi answered. "If there is something that is troubling you, that is agitating you, that is making your life unnecessarily difficult, it's probably something you should eliminate."

I nodded, let this sink in. "But as a relationship model, isn't non-monogamy more Buddhist, or more enlightened? Less attached by definition?"

"Buddhism doesn't have a problem with non-monogamy, but tends to recommend monogamy or celibacy. But that's simply because they are less complex." Tashi smiled. "It's like, *You want two problems? Three problems? Or just one problem? Or how about no problem?*"

"So then less complex is more important than less rooted in attachment?" I asked skeptically.

"Ideally, not-attached, either. Attachment produces the contrary of what you want. Attachment produces resentment, and resentment is a surefire way to push somebody away," Tashi answered.

"Right, exactly! So if you're approaching non-monogamy with an attitude of not-grasping, it's not causing more suffering in your life, and there's more net love overall, wouldn't polyamory be a less attached way to be in a relationship? To say, 'I don't demand your monogamy'?"

"It depends on the individuals. If it works out in a particular situation, it works out." Tashi shrugged. "What matters is the *intention,* and how that meets the *result.* You should go with whatever brings less suffering in your life, monogamy or non-monogamy. I mean, I've seen a lot of open relationships end very badly. I've also seen a lot of closed

relationships end very badly. *Most* relationships don't end so well."
Tashi laughed kindly.

"But if I could just practice non-attachment, I'd feel less jealous and
there wouldn't be so much suffering . . ." I mumbled, trying to reconcile Adam's years of programming with what Tashi was saying.

"I think it's important to remember that non-attachment is not
indifference. Non-attachment doesn't mean that it doesn't matter to you
if you eat poison or healthy food. That you make your life any more
difficult than it needs to be. That you associate with harmful people
indiscriminately," Tashi said firmly. "No. Actually, non-attachment allows you to leave a relationship. Non-attachment means that you are
not fixated on a particular outcome. That you're actually allowing for
the fact that everything changes."

———

I drove straight from the retreat with my friend Gwenna* to move
out. When we arrived, Adam was playing our songs, one of my favorite
meals warm on the stove.

As I packed with Gwenna, Adam hovered. "Hey, those are mine!"
he joked when I took my tampons. I laughed. I was trying not to be
cold, since he'd already accused me of acting unfeeling as I was maintaining some distance. He grinned at my response and spanked me. I
looked up in a confused shock, realizing this once-cherished gesture
already felt like a violation of personal space. *My ass is no longer his. But
he still doesn't believe it.*

Gwenna went to her car to pack some things I was giving her and
he cornered me, tears in his eyes. He got up close to my face. I took a
step back.

———

* A shout-out to my dear friend Gwenna Hunter, founder of Vegans of LA and Vegans for Black
Lives Matter. Check out her Patreon and support her work if you're inspired.

"It doesn't have to be like this. I know you're leaving, but after all this time, you're not even going to hang out? You're not even upset? Don't you love me? Don't you want to do justice to what we've had?" It was the reverse of our normal. He was demanding I be *more* emotional.

"I am upset, trust me," I said. "But I just got back from meditating for a week, and I feel pretty even. I'm trying to stay calm and just get through this."

"*Talk* to me. Come on. Look at me. You can't even look at me?" I looked. His eyes welled an inch from my face. The scared little boy was so exposed now. What he feared most deep down—being left, out of control—it was happening. And he felt so powerless. I wanted to comfort the person I loved in this painful moment. But to give myself over to that urge might be to lose myself in his reality again.

Gwenna came back into the room. She looked back and forth between us and broke the silence. "Okay, Rach, what's next?" He retreated to the other room. "I didn't realize till now what you were dealing with," she murmured to me. "That is some *strong* energy. So thick even I can feel the pull. I won't leave you alone again."

Does she know what a mitzvah* she's performing? "I swear, I'll never forget you being here, Gwenna. Thank you so much."

"Girl, I got you," she said and smiled. "And we got *this.*"

After we'd finished packing, Adam stood outside my car while Gwenna watched from a respectable but protective distance. "This isn't what I want. But it's what you want. So I'm not going to try to stop you," he said, eyes full but mostly held back.

"Okay, thanks."

"Give me a hug." I gave him a hug. "No, not some bullshit hug," he said, squeezing me so hard I felt my back crack. He whispered in my ear. "I'll always love you and be here for you. *You know you'll always be my girl.*" It felt like a curse intended as a blessing, an inescapable truth.

---

* Hebrew/Yiddish for a sacred good deed.

The same sensation from when he held me down washed over me. The instinct to say whatever he needed to hear to release me. Only this time, I felt so sorry for us both.

"I love you, too," I said.

"What?" I knew he could hear me. He just wanted me to say it with more conviction.

"I love you, too," I repeated louder, knowing it was the truth but also already different. That admitting I still loved him was now the way to set myself free. And with that, he let me go. I glided tearfully down the hill in my possibly dying uncle's definitely dying car. I was so fucking sad and scared. But another part of me already felt anything but.

Yes, Rachel, perhaps this is liberation.

———————

Gwenna told me that only after I left did Adam really sob, heaving into her shoulder when she gave him a hug goodbye. "He was trying to be strong, but he was *hurting*," she remembered. "He was really hurting. I remember my shirt was *soaked*." Gwenna told me this in 2020, a couple of months before this book's manuscript was due. *My little boy. What have I done? What am I about to do? How could I do this to him?*

Beloved early readers of this book have written comments in the margins like, "I hate Adam!" or "I want to kick him in the balls!" They say it in solidarity, but it distresses me. That's the opposite of the feeling I seek to elicit: a non-dualistic compassion beyond boxes and blame. I've taken every precaution to protect Adam's identity—I seek no revenge, no public or professional fallout (though I'm not saying the latter is inappropriate in many other people's situations). This certainly doesn't mean I absolve Adam of responsibility for his actions, or that I don't hope this book spurs dramatic internal changes, as it has for me. But I still feel an immense compassion for the confusion and suffering that fuels harmful behavioral cycles.

"Hurt people hurt people," Tashi later told me. "How much suffering must a person be feeling to want to control another person's mind? People who are content do not do such things. We tend to love those who are good and dislike those who are caught up in ignorance. But those caught in suffering need our love, too—in some ways even more." Often, Tashi added, our love must be from afar, filled with protective boundaries. Having compassion starts with oneself; you shouldn't stay in a situation that causes you unnecessary suffering, or passively accept injustice and mistreatment. Quite the opposite—indulging others' harmful behavior is what many Buddhist teachers call "idiot compassion." If anything, true, not-idiot compassion should afford you more energy to make the necessary boundaries and changes. And make changes I did. I do.

PART 5
Age 31

Into the Innermost Cave

January–May 2019

OAKLAND

1/3/19

Journal Entry

*Uncle Willie cried in parking lot of grocery outlet . . .
[he said, out of breath,] 'sometimes i wonder if
[chemo's] worth it. I didn't think i'd end up like this.'*
   *. . . Held his hand and looked at the birds outside
the window . . .*
   *[I said] 'I was with someone who told me i wasn't
capable and couldn't take care of myself, and you're
helping me prove i can' . . . he seemed to hear this,
and gave me an extra hug on the way out.*

1/4/19

Journal Entry

   *Next day [Uncle Willie]'s in the hospital for
possible heart attack. . . . Dried blood on his iv. We've
been here so many times before.*
   . . . i have to be strong and am, but also get tired.

The deep desire for someone to walk in the door and take care of me.

Besides helping family, I now almost never broke my silence or solitude. Something instinctual knew this was what I needed to do. I burrowed deeper and deeper into myself, but it didn't feel like depression or avoidance. It felt like a natural conservation of energy, a caterpillar in a cocoon crossed with a hibernating bear. I continued to weep at least once a day, but I wasn't bitter. After years of anticipatory anxiety, sadness was softer. That my uncle was fighting for his life certainly also helped keep things in perspective.

Appropriately enough, I'd found myself a cave. A downstairs in-law studio, literally next door to the motel-style apartment on Fruitvale Avenue I'd grown up in with my dad. I tried to walk a short woodsy trail in Dimond Park most days, resolved not to stay indoors for more than forty-eight hours straight, as was my new preference.* I wore earplugs everywhere. I wanted life to be quiet enough to hear my own thoughts again. Adam's voice followed me, but some days it was almost rather faint. I still had to keep my remote job, and trying to fix my mom's and uncle's considerable housing, financial, and health crises was indeed stressful. But I was realizing I *could* figure things out without Adam after all.

I lived in an oversized blanket robe called a Comfy, heating pad on my tummy as I read voraciously during any spare hours. For the first time in my life, I felt allergic to anything written by a man or about men. I downloaded my first book about gaslighting, Dr. Robin Stern's aforementioned *The Gaslight Effect*. My friends and Kathy were saying

---

*   "A life-threatening illness or accident, the loss of self-confidence or livelihood, a geographical move . . . a confrontation with the grasp of an addiction, or a broken heart can open the space for dismemberment and descent. The mud and the trees become her companions. She enters a period of voluntary isolation. . . . Many women describe the need to remove themselves from the 'male realm' during this period." Murdock, *The Heroine's Journey.*

that that's what had been going on, so I figured I should finally make myself learn about it. As soon as I read the words "abuser" and "victim," I felt Adam's eyes roll inside my own. But as Dr. Stern listed the signs that you're in this kind of situation, I experienced them as nails in a coffin I blamed myself for climbing into:

> You are constantly second-guessing yourself. You ask yourself, "Am I too sensitive?" a dozen times a day. . . . You buy clothes for yourself, furnishings for your apartment, or other personal purchases with your partner in mind, thinking about what he would like instead of what would make you feel great. You frequently make excuses for your partner's behavior to friends and family. You find yourself withholding information from friends and family so you don't have to explain or make excuses. . . . You have the sense that you used to be a very different person—more confident, more fun-loving, more relaxed. . . . You feel as though you can't do anything.

I would add: You hear his voice in your head even now equating this to pop psychology written to make everyone feel like a special abused snowflake. You'd like to clarify that he never used those words. You still don't want anyone to think he's doing any of this on purpose or that he's a bad person.

Yet the diagnostic checklist went on and on: The gaslighter accuses you of using your fear to manipulate them; they make open or veiled threats against you; they tell you not to incriminate them against your family or friends by sharing your doubts about the relationship; you become increasingly anxious, self-isolating, and self-medicating with drugs and compulsive behaviors in order to cope; when presented with evidence of their lies, they fail to take responsibility and claim their words were taken out of context; they portray you as irrationally

ous or oversensitive or like your mother for feeling hurt or angry; they say or imply they're the only one who will love you enough to deal with your flaws and take care of you; you come to believe them and question your own character, self-sufficiency, sanity, lovability, and good intentions . . .

My heart was in my ears now—I was having a panic attack. I did not force myself to keep going. I shut the book and sat with my hand over my heart and belly, trying to breathe deeply. I splayed my hand across my chest the way Adam used to, though this made me cry anew. I tried to nurture myself.* *I'll always love you, Rachel. I think you are so strong. You are a resilient person. You don't have to be perfect. You are doing so good. I promise I will take care of you. You can learn to trust your own judgment again.*

When a baby cried upstairs, I heard the father singing through the floorboards, a rocking chair creaking. Miranda had just miscarried, and I sent her love telepathically. I knew I was really raw when I'd crave a baby of my own to hold. *Everything would be so much harder if I had one, of course. But I would at least know what I had to do, maybe.* I thought of a book I'd read called *Motherhood,* by Sheila Heti.† "There can be sadness at not living out a more universal story—the supposed life cycle—how out of one life cycle another cycle is supposed to come. But when out of your life, no new cycle comes, what does that feel like?" Now I was also disenchanted (in the spell-breaking, not cynical sense of the word) of the other "most important thing" I'd been socialized to want: a soul mate. With Adam, I'd finally let myself lean into

---

*   I practiced RAIN, which I'd learned about from meditation teacher Tara Brach. First, you
     (R)ecognize a sensation or feeling, and simply name it, see it ("This is sadness, grief, rejection,
) ı (A)llow it. ("This sadness is part of the weather system, too. I accept you
                     Then you (I)nvestigate it. ("I feel this in my throat, in my hunched shoul-
                     nd then, and this is perhaps most important, you learn to (N)urture it.
                     this place inside you would most benefit from hearing—what your future
                     her, or an ideal parent might say. Brach calls this "spiritual reparenting."
                     od (New York: Henry Holt & Company, 2018).

the fairy tale so vulnerably. Now that it had eroded and imploded, far from feeling cornered, I sensed more expansive possibilities.

Above my head, I heard the constant work that was having a family and knew being a mother was not my task at hand. My mission was to learn, at thirty-one, how to properly mother myself. And I didn't need to worry this was selfish. If I could become clear and strong again, I vowed I would pay forward what these many writers were giving me. I would strive to give birth to a book that might also empower someone curled up in this very same ball.

———

Heartbreak and Tashi's teachings seemed to help motivate a calm discipline. I meditated for at least ten minutes every morning when I woke up, and each night before bed. The effects, for me, were swift and profound. They say that when you meditate, you can expect to feel better—and it's true. That is, you feel your sadness and neuroses better . . . *and* your joy and peacefulness better, too. You feel all of it better. The feelings become clearer and more fluid at once; grief bleeds into gratitude, joy into welled eyes. I was beginning to learn that seeking more equanimity in my life didn't mean giving up feeling deeply. In some ways, the subtler "highs" and "lows" might be even more poignant in their increasing clarity and obvious transience.

I also kept a journal logging five good things about each day.* I continued not to smoke weed, just to know it was possible. I craved it sometimes, but the more I meditated and the farther I got from Adam's

———

* Research measuring the impact of writing down just three good things a day found that after only one week, people reported being happier than before. Many participants kept the practice going after the study was over. In follow-up tests, those people's happiness kept increasing for months after that. M. E. P. Seligman, T. A. Steen, N. Park, and C. Peterson, "Positive Psychology Progress: Empirical Validation of Interventions," *American Psychologist* 60, no. 5 (2005): 410–21. https://doi.org/10.1037/0003-066X.60.5.410.

voice, the less it felt like a compulsion.* I learned to cook again. I tried
not to be at war with food, but knew this would be ongoing work.
Sometimes I managed to eat simply by candlelight with no distrac-
tions, though that was the hardest practice of all. Mostly, I ate in the
company of Tara Brach. Someone on the retreat had recommended
Brach, and I worked my way through years of podcast archives. She
spoke in a soothing voice, with all the wisdom of her decades as a
meditation teacher, clinical psychologist, and author. She blended the
spiritual with the utterly practical, giving me cognitive-behavioral
mindfulness strategies to regain a trust in reality. She taught me to really linger on the beauty of trees or a bird, to commit at least one act of
kindness a day. She was my bridge to respecting my inner mother
again.

Appropriate to my monastic life, I'd also entered a period of delib-
erate celibacy. Asa had found an ingrown hair by his pubes in January,
and believed it was HSV-2. I didn't have the virus and was only dating
him now, but even though the doctor reassured him it was a pimple, he
became afraid of having sex. I recognized his OCD-stuckness from my
own prior bug phobias and had compassion for it. But I found I had
actual boundaries now, so clear they felt reflexive as a knee when jerked.
I told him I couldn't be with someone who wouldn't have sex with me,
not now anyway. My interest in a romantic dynamic that left me pining appeared to have (at least temporarily) vanished. Asa understood,
and told me he loved me. Adding another cherry atop my breakup
sundae was of course not ideal.† But it also felt appropriate to be alone,

---

*   These days, when I feel a pull toward addictive or numbing behaviors, I try to redirect my dis-
     sociative tendencies. This tip from Brach helped me, so I'll share it in case it will help you, too:
     I first examine my desire to escape as an observer. I try to ask myself before getting high—*What
     are you unwilling to feel right now? And can you be with it first, even for a minute?* Sometimes, this
     simple pause helps the craving dissipate. Meditating daily and not being in a gaslit relationship
     has certainly helped, too.

†   For more on the particular challenges of non-monogamous breakups, I recommend Kathy's
     guide, *The Polyamory Breakup Book.*

to stop relying on other bodies for comfort. It would help solidify my growing realization that the only person who could really promise to always take care of me was . . . *me.**

3/2/19

Stream of Consciousness

Keep meditating and go[i]ng deeper yes rachel yes
You can do this yes rachel yes
I believe in you even though no one is fucking you right now yes rachel yes . . .
If you tell yourself this is garbage it will be
Yes rachel yes
If you tell yourself it's the beginning of art it will be
Yes rachel yes
. . . And i am going to eat now
Yes rachel yes

---

*   Interestingly, researchers have found that when people addicted to drugs go through a period of abstention, they regain gray matter where they'd previously eroded it. And not only that, but they gain new gray matter in an area of the brain associated with compassion and mindfulness. Perhaps all this was at work as I began temporarily abstaining from my two main addictions: romance and weed. Xuyi Wang, Baojuan Li, Xuhui Zhou, et al., "Changes in Brain Gray Matter in Abstinent Heroin Addicts," *Drug and Alcohol Dependence* 126 (2012). https://www.doi.org/10.1016/j.drugalcdep.2012.05.030.

The Initiator,
the Author, the Action Hero!

May–July 2019

OAKLAND

"With the practice of mindfulness, we have new eyes, and we can learn many things from the past. If you are really grounded in the present moment and the future becomes the object of your mindfulness, you can look deeply at the future to see what you can do in the present moment for such a future to become possible."
—Thich Nhat Hanh, *How to Connect*

Even though he was very sick and had little savings, my uncle had remembered to get me something for my birthday in December: a gift certificate for a massage. By the time spring came, I still hadn't used it, or been touched, in months. So I decided to treat my uncle to the same gift at the same spa. We would celebrate his last round of chemo together this way.

As I sat with my uncle in the waiting room, I saw a very compelling man. It wasn't just that he was unusually handsome; it was an energy he was radiating. Like a wide, streaming river. Strong, tattooed arms displayed what he'd built out of untying other's knots. His ears stuck out a little, and I had a flash of holding on to them while I rode on his lap. His big brown eyes locked with mine. *Holy shit. Who is that? And why do I feel like I know him from the future?* Sure, I'd eye-fucked strangers before. But this was something unusual. Like a small crack in the space-time continuum had opened up, daring me to walk through. Not fate, no. More like an invitation not to be passive. When he called another woman forward for her massage, I could tell she was pleasantly flustered. I was happy for her and stuck my neck back into my shell.

———

A month later, with my uncle officially in remission and my mom's housing finally stabilized, I decided to treat myself to a massage with that mystery guy I'd seen the month before. I described him to the front desk—"Um, my friend said she got a really good massage from someone in his thirties maybe, with a lot of tattoos on his arms? She couldn't remember his name . . ."—and booked a session with the massage therapist the receptionist suggested. I figured I could maybe give him my card after, if we had a decent rapport. At the very least, I was ready to be touched kindly and safely by someone I found so crushworthy. But when I arrived, another tattooed massage therapist called me forward instead. *So much for that. Oh well.*

Grabbing the doorknob to leave afterward, something in me again whispered not to give up. *You don't get this kind of intuition about a stranger often . . . why ignore it? You won goddamn national awards for investigative reporting when you were twenty-two. I think you can handle this, Rachel.* I turned around and described him, again, to another receptionist. When she gave me another name—Teo—I easily found his website and confessed the whole plot via text, and asked him out cold. I figured as a very attractive massage therapist (*with dimples, too!*), he must have this kind of thing happen all the time and he would be like, *great, another stalker.* But although a few men had made passes at him, he later told me no woman had so much as left her number in the tip envelope. Now, *plenty* had flirted heavily and returned as regulars; a few even lay naked on the table without a sheet on, contrary to his instructions. But they all seemed to expect him to make the first direct move.

And Teo was not about to risk his license or abuse his position's power. He believed in sticking to the moral boundaries he'd promised to uphold. He told me up front he wouldn't go on a date with me *and* book a massage. And that after googling me, he'd prefer the former option.

I was pleased, but also rather offended on his behalf. *No other woman asked him out? In ten years of being a hot massage therapist?!* But mostly it made me sad for women and our conditioning, how we've been placed in the position of *waiting* rather than *doing. What a different way men are taught to go through life—to trust you are supposed to be the initiator, the author, the action hero! To expect no rescue other than the one you set in motion!* Before my adventures in non-monogamy, I knew I probably wouldn't have had the guts to ask Teo out. But now that I'd faced jealousy *and* heartbreak *and* rescuing myself and, well, all of it? I genuinely didn't fear that kind of low-key rejection anymore. This new sense of empowerment, an ability to sit with discomfort, and a clear sense of my boundaries? The benefits of the last few years were already rolling in.

———

As it turned out, Teo was more romantic than my still-recovering heart had budgeted for. Before I even decided to break my celibacy with him, he'd come over with his table, massaging me for hours, studying and examining my body with expert dedication. He was profoundly kind, humble, and smart. He'd immigrated from Lima fifteen years before and appeared to be a lifelong student. Human anatomy, craniosacral therapy, psychology, Peruvian shamanism—whatever might help heal, he was curious to learn and apply.

I was game for him to try any and all of it on me. It turned out this had long been his fantasy, too. A test subject who needed his expert care . . . that very slowly and consensually resulted in revelations like "pelvic unwinding." *Literal "happy endings"—what is happening? What is my life?* I would laugh to myself over and over as he brought me back into my body.

Having now deliberately ended my period of celibacy in spectacular fashion, I also reconnected with Asa. Though I hadn't planned it that way, I once saw them both in the same night. Asa worked me up to a fever pitch; I switched the sheets quickly before Teo came to finish the job. That I didn't change my lingerie between them made me feel dirty in a wonderful way, my own hotwife, unashamedly myself. They knew of each other, and both consented to the situation. To my surprise, I also began having frequent fantasies of seeing Teo massage and fuck other women. I felt Amalia-level turned on by his touching other people in any way. *Is it because I have more power than I'm used to? Maybe, but it's also just because I actually trust Teo and Asa and feel safe with them. Safe to be polyamorous. Safe, I guess, to be myself.*

I was in many ways still haunted (Teo later admitted he too felt Adam's ghost in the room). But Teo made himself uncomplicatedly, completely available to me anyway—no demands, no games—just a clear intention to let me be myself, while also giving me his best shot. I felt courted and seen as special, but certainly not lovebombed or pressured. My identity and boundaries remained firmly, protectively intact.

Wait, am I the unattainable Liam now? No . . . I'm being honest and intimate. I just don't want to be someone's committed partner again anytime soon. And I'm communicating with Teo and Asa kindly and clearly. I realized I might always want to date at least somewhat non-monogamously from now on—and that figuring out how to do it my way rather than Adam's would be its own new adventure.

———

That summer, I saw Adam for the first time since I'd moved out, at a conference we were both attending. He told me with a smile that he'd recently gotten married to the woman he'd met right before we broke up; the one he was with the day he didn't reply to my uncle's good news. He added that it was "pretty asexual"; a marriage of convenience for her to obtain certain legal benefits. "I wanted to help a friend out," he said, shrugging. He was dating other people, mostly. In fact, one was here, did I want to meet her? I was shocked. He seemed to be enjoying dropping this bombshell. First Lady Michelle Obama whispered in my ear, *When they go low . . .*

"Thanks for letting me know. I'm happy to see you seem happier." I realized only as I said it that it was true. *So I still love him. But I'm already no longer _in_ love with him, maybe. Now, the _idea_ of him, his voice in my head, I might never fully shake. But the real man before me now? He's lost much of his pull on me already.* He seemed so much smaller than I remembered. Just another scared animal yearning to be free, like me.

...And She Lived Openly Ever After

"Yeah, I'm my own soulmate
I know how to love me"

—LIZZO, "SOULMATE," LISTENED TO 118 TIMES ON SPOTIFY
(JANUARY 2019—SEPTEMBER 2020)

6/21/19

PHONE SESSION

I caught Kathy up about Teo, and my worries that I was the Adam in our dynamic. I reminded Teo periodically that I didn't want to be monogamous. I continued to be very turned on by the idea of him being with other people and reminded him he was "allowed" to date. He tried for a few weeks, but decided he wasn't interested in pursuing anyone else on his own for the time being (dating someone together would be another story). He didn't expect me to feel the same—just for me to be safe and honest. Teo was nine years my senior; his choices were clear and mature. But I still worried I was luring a person with no experience into an open relationship that might one day break their heart.

"Well, I'm just so impressed you're still open to non-monogamy after your experience. It would have been easy to write it off after what you went through!" Kathy exclaimed. "But your worries sound mostly like projection to me. That you'll hurt Teo the way Adam hurt you, even though you're an entirely different person. You're just being honest that you're not ready for a serious partnership right now, and that if you are later, you still want to be non-monogamous. And who knows how things will unfold? Maybe you just feel trapped sometimes because the traditional, couple relationship has so many fences around it. I know couples who've given each other huge amounts of freedom, but they're still monogamous. One person might travel, or work a totally opposite schedule. You don't have to be a polyam relationship anarchist to have more freedom in a relationship."

"And someone non-monogamous doesn't automatically have more freedom, either," I added. "Adam kept telling me, 'You're totally free with me. You can do whatever you want.' And I saw how in some ways I was becoming more open and sexually liberated. And yet I also felt like my supposed 'freedom' with him gradually became its own cage, a way I felt even more trapped, because he told me no one else would let me be as free."

"Well, ultimately, it comes down to power, and how power is shared in the relationship," Kathy said. "If a man is using some kind of leverage or power to coerce a woman into being monogamous or non-monogamous, it's not right either way. It's not always gendered that way, but because women have less power in society and less economic power in most relationships with men, the men often exercise more power—and women are often more afraid of losing it. Women are more likely to think, *This is what I have to do to make the relationship work.*"

"I felt like, *If I really love Adam, I should want him to experience whatever he wants to in life, the way he loves me.* I still find that a compelling argument. It feels true, that real love is not about possessing someone or restricting them . . ."

"—Oh, I hear men say that all the time. And it's not really true," Kathy said. "There's no such thing as being in a relationship and being totally free. It's just a delusion to think that you could be in a long-term, committed relationship and never have to give up any control. It doesn't mean you can't have any freedom. It just means you're agreeing that whatever you're getting out of the relationship is worth making some compromises for. I just think it's a false dichotomy to say, 'Well, if I don't let my partner do anything and everything that they want, then I'm a bad person or I'm too controlling.' But that's what society expects of women. We're supposed to be masochists and sacrifice everything we want to make the husband happy, whether that's giving up our career in order to raise children or moving all over the country with them as they move up the corporate ladder. Why should men get to use non-monogamy as an excuse to continue the pattern we're trying to reject?

"At the same time, I see how some women *have* experienced non-monogamy as a path to some form of liberation," Kathy continued. "They realize, *I own my sexuality, I own my body, I am not dependent on any one person.* And that in itself is extremely liberating to feel. Especially for women with men. Many women are not getting enough attention and affection and romance. They're starving, but they're accepting it. So I think it can be extremely freeing to realize they have other avenues to get their needs met."

"We're so used to dualistic thinking in our culture," I thought aloud. "Like, either non-monogamy is being used by men to manipulate women or it's the pathway to feminist liberation and maybe never being dependent on a man again. But it could sometimes be both. And there's certainly nothing inherently abusive—or enlightened—about non-monogamy. The individuals' behavior determines that."

"Yes. And I've certainly seen some women who've told me, 'Kathy, once I started being polyam, all these other expectations I had placed on myself crumbled. I realized I don't have to get married. I don't have to live with a guy. I can live by myself, or with a group of women. I don't even have to have children!'"

"That's exactly how I feel!" I said. "I know now that I wasn't so free

with Adam. But also, being in an open relationship was a gateway drug
to realizing I don't have to do any of those things I thought I did to
'arrive' at my adult life. Non-monogamy was sort of a . . ."

"—A gateway drug to liberation?" Kathy offered.

"Perhaps, yes." I paused. "That makes me think of the day after I
moved out of Adam's place last year, my shroom trip. Did I tell you that
story?"

"No, I don't think so . . . tell me!"

"Well, I was offered a comped night last-minute at this hotel in Palm
Springs, in exchange for writing a review. I figured it would be a good
way to mark the transition. To remind myself I was my own sugar daddy,
I guess. And when I got inside the room, I saw that right outside the
big picture window, a wedding was being set up, like thirty feet away."

"Oh no!" Kathy laughed.

"No, but it ended up being great! I decided I'd take the shrooms I'd
packed and make a trip of it." I proceeded to tell her what happened
that day.

It had seemed like hours until all the white folding chairs filled with
strange light green creatures, half human, half amorphous dragon. As I
watched the wedding unfold, it looked like a scene on a medieval tap-
estry. The couple stood under a grand arch, flanked on each side by
family, enmeshed in a seemingly circular ceremony. I crouched in the
plush hotel bathrobe on the floor and turned the heat all the way up,
riveted by the free theater before me. I sent the couple my love, and was
glad to see it was not laced with any envy. It was easy to want them to
be happy. Like Tashi had told me, what you wish for others, you really
do wish for yourself. "Get out of the way of their love," I kept mumbling to the priest and family, their constant penetrations into the couple's glowing bubble *so clearly energetically disruptive.* "Get out of the

way of their love!" I laughed and loved these interlopers, too. I saw how the traditional wedding ceremony was more about the merging of families than the couple's bond. I understood the proprietary and tribal origins of it all, and felt like an anthropologist watching aliens. I savored being hidden. Holding a secret in child's pose, hands gripping the sides of my face in glee, the way I'd loved spending my days as a little girl. Playing a game alone, perfectly content writing a story in my mind.

I knew shrooms tend to reveal what feels like "my innermost truth": *So I really don't wish it was me up there with Adam instead. And I only moved out yesterday?!* Maybe someday I'd marry (though the idea felt newly unappealing). But I saw my deepest dream was actually much closer to what I was, in this moment . . . *already living.* I was a writer on drugs who'd travel-reviewed her way into another free luxury hotel room, rapt and laughing and odd, marveling at the accidental poetry of everyday life. This was more than enough. I realized that perhaps I really would be content with this being my happy ending instead. *In fact, might I even prefer it?*

"You're a fucking genius," I mumbled to myself over and over as I cried tears of relief and grief. I knew it wasn't true in any literal sense, but I repeated the phrase nonetheless. Something in me told me these words would help stabilize the pendulum that had swung too far the other way. *Adam was wrong: I do know what's good for me. I am brave and capable. I can take care of myself.*

When I drove back to Oakland the next day, I passed an Adopt-a-Highway sign sponsored by "Adam Go-Go." I laughed and winked back, humming with all the giddiness of someone who'd pulled off a heist. But when one of our many songs came on shuffle, I'd skip it quickly, tears immediately rising, humbling me. I'd packed "Roombi," as we called him. Our AI-dog periodically turned on and made a sad nineties-video-game-loss-sound from the trunk: *"Error. Error. Please reconnect Roomba."* I laughed. Adam was right. The symbolism and meaning we ascribe to objects and events is our choice. Though my past blared "*error, error, please reconnect,*" I could decide to trust I'd committed anything but an error, and guide myself home.

―――――

"Well, there's your perfect happy ending for the book!" Kathy exclaimed when I finished telling her the story.

"If I even write it one day," I said, laughing. I was still unsure I had what it took, but increasingly remembering I was strong enough to find out. "You know, I keep looking for some perfect stop anyway? Some solid ending to this chapter of my life. But then I think . . . maybe endings are just another construct I don't need to believe in anymore."

―――――

As I "complete" this book, I bear a different magic word. It would be even funnier as a tattoo, but alas, it's another engraved ring. I bought it three months before the pandemic hit, to remind myself of reality. Above me now, the clouds are (and are not) passing Rorschach tests. Have you ever noticed how you can put on a song, any song, and the birds will appear to fly perfectly in tune with it? I think it is one of my favorite things about being alive. I look down at this perishable hand. The inscription on the silver band is outward facing, no secret now: "Impermanent."

Acknowledgments

Perhaps the greatest gift of writing my first book (and there were so many) was that I learned to ask for help. And wow, did I receive a lot of it. I don't have room to do you all justice here, not even close. Expect additional gratitude coming your way. That said, a brief immense thank you (appropriately, in no clear hierarchical order) to . . .

Donna Loffredo, for encouraging me from the very beginning to write the book I wanted to write. For knowing, maybe before I did, that I was capable. For your patience and attuned editor's eye. For appreciating my voice and never trying to censor me.

"Ayesha"—without your exacting intellect, loyal friendship, and most-trusted advice, this book and my life would be so diminished. Someone get this human a book deal/podcast! Contact me if you want a shot at interacting with their brilliant mind.

Eric Rayman, Quinn Heraty, Nakia D. Hansen, and the Harmony legal team. Diana Baroni, Katherine Leak (thank you for your patience with my emails!), Tammy Blake, Lindsey Kennedy, Christina Foxley, Odette Fleming, Serena Wang, and the rest of the Harmony Books team. Margaret Sutherland Brown, for watering those initial seeds. Iris Blasi, for helping me harvest.

My core writer support group, my chosen sisters: Yulia Greyman, Laura Bridgeman, and Shannon McLeod—all brilliant writers to watch, with the kindest of hearts. Mady Schutzman, for her mentorship and expert early read. My other beloved early readers, for their detailed notes, time, encouragement, friendship, and sensitivity: "Robin" (for helping me figure out the ending, and so much else), Dr. Kyle Livie (hearing your socio-political reading of my book was a highlight of my life), Lux Alptraum, Imran Siddiquee, Liv Stratman, Kenny, Gabe (you know what you did), Alejandra, Lauren, Jamie, Jane, Kelly, Erik, and Alex Kapitan ("The Radical Copyeditor").

My pseudonym-ed lovers and friends: Leah, for your continued generosity and solidarity. Miranda, for letting me worship The Divine Feminine. Rich and Pam, for giving me a place to stay and heal. Amalia, Rory, Liv, and Nate; for your friendship and being game to shatter stigma. Liam, for being such a good sport/muse. Asa, for showing me another way to love. Mo, for all the big hugs. Adam, with enduring love, compassion, and gratitude. It is my deep wish this ultimately helps more than it hurts.

Monk Tashi Nyima, for his ethical guidance throughout this project, and in general. You once told me "I will always be there for you, Rachel," and isn't that the unexaggerated truth. Kathy, for listening with so much compassion, and collaborating. Knowing you're always a phone call away is like wearing a parachute. My gratitude for you is the air.

All the many other experts I interviewed/consulted for this book. I'm sorry that I couldn't fit everyone in, but each conversation informed this project and work to come: Special thanks to Dr. Ryan Witherspoon, for his many hours of interviews, research, and commentary; Amy Marlow-Macoy, LCSW; Dr. David Ley; Dedeker Winston; Dr. Justin Lehmiller; Jonathan Foust; Dr. Tara Brach; Dr. Wednesday Martin; Katherine Angel; Emily Anne; Dr. Christopher Ryan; Kevin A. Patterson; Evette Dionne; Dr. Baruti Kopano; Michael & Holli; Avi Klein, LCSW; Kaira Jewel Lingo; Ruth King; Annie Chen, LCSW; Dr. Lisa Hamilton; Dr. Nicole Prause; Jonathan D. Lane; Dr. Margaret Brinig; Dr. Curt Stager; Ann Friedman; Emma Kaywin; Courtney Maum; Matthew Salesses; Qian Julie Wang; and Daniel Bergner.

My dear imaginary reader made real. My debut author and memoirist support groups. Every author and musician mentioned in this book. Greenery Press and Shambhala Publications, for granting permissions to reprint from *Love in Abundance* and *The Heroine's Journey.* Spotify, for helping me access some of my listening data. Hedonism and Desire resorts, for putting me up and giving me a safe place to be naked. Mercy For Animals, the Pollination Project, YR Media, and GirlVentures—all wonderful non-profit organizations I owe so much to.

My Girls Write Now mentee Kiara, for teaching me so much over all these years. Gwenna, Jasmin, Brian, Lauren, Kyle, and the many other aforementioned friends who especially helped me through the roughest time. My sangha and teachers, especially Mr. Grodin. Anne, Mark, and Sophie, for the love and shelter from the storm. Victor, Magali, Arturo, Susan, and the rest of Teo's beautiful family. My three father figures—Dad, Uncle Willie, Pedro—for each of their unique forms of love and support. My mom, for being a gracious subject, and loving the free woman she raised.

Finally, "Teo," for having my back in all ways literal and figurative throughout this process, this pandemic, and beyond. You've never once failed to come through for me, yet when it comes to expressing the depth of my gratitude, words appear to fail me now. They can only point at the moon.

ABOUT THE AUTHOR

Rachel Krantz is a journalist and one of the founding editors of Bustle, where she served as senior features editor for three years. Her work has been featured on NPR, the *Guardian, Vox, Vice,* and many other outlets. She's the recipient of the Robert F. Kennedy Journalism Award, the Investigative Reporters and Editors Radio Award, the Edward R. Murrow Award, and the Peabody Award for her work as an investigative reporter with YR Media.